SEEKING GOD'S KINGDOM

SEEKING GOD'S KINGDOM

The Nonconformist Social Gospel in Wales, 1906–1939

ROBERT POPE

UNIVERSITY OF WALES PRESS
CARDIFF
1999

© Robert Pope, 1999

British Library Cataloguing-in-Publication Data.
A catalogue record for this book is available from the British Library.

ISBN 0–7083–1568–2

Typeset by Action Publishing Technology, Gloucester.
Printed in Great Britain by Dinefwr Press, Llandybïe.

And did those feet in ancient time
Walk upon England's mountains green?
And was the holy Lamb of God
On England's pleasant pastures seen?
And did the countenance divine
Shine forth upon our clouded hills?
And was Jerusalem builded here
Among those dark, Satanic mills?

Bring me my bow of burning gold!
Bring me my arrows of desire!
Bring me my spear; O clouds unfold!
Bring me my chariot of fire!
I will not cease from mental fight,
Nor shall my sword sleep in my hand,
Till we have built Jerusalem
In England's green and pleasant land.

William Blake (1757–1827),
Preface from *Milton*

A fu ei draed mewn amser gynt
Yn rhodio bryniau teg ein gwlad?
A welwyd santaidd Oen ein Duw
Ar ddolydd gwyrddlas Cymru fad?
A fu Ei wyneb dwyfol Ef
Gynt yn goleuo'r tywyll fro?
A welwyd unwaith Ddinas Duw
Yng ngwlad y mwg a'r pyllau glo?

Rhowch im fy mwa o aur llosg
A saethau fy nymuniad glân!
Fy mhicell rhowch; gymylau hollt,
Dygwch i mi fy ngherbyd tân!
Ni chwsg fy nghleddyf yn fy llaw,
Ni ddianc f'enaid rhag y gad,
Nes codir muriau Dinas Duw
Ar feysydd gwyrddlas Cymru fad.

tr. D. Miall Edwards (1873–1941),
'Gweledigaeth a brwydr',
Yr Efrydydd, III/1 (October 1922), 28.

I

Philip a Winifred Thomas,
Tadcu a Mamgu

Contents

Editor's Foreword

When the Centre for the Advanced Study of Religion in Wales was established within the School of Theology and Religious Studies at Bangor in January 1998, it was intended that it should not only encourage scholarly research but also ensure its publication, and thus contribute towards a better and wider understanding of the history of religion among the Welsh people.

As Christianity has been the dominant tradition in Wales for over thirteen centuries, it was anticipated that much of the work undertaken by scholars would be studies of diverse aspects of its growth and decline over the centuries. However, it is recognized that by the end of the twentieth century other traditions and faiths have made inroads into Wales, and it is hoped that future studies will also encompass them.

Robert Pope's study of theology in Wales between 1906 and 1939 not only places the developments during that period against a wider backdrop but also sheds new light on an important era in the evolution of Christian thinking in Wales.

Geraint Tudur
Centre for the Advanced Study of Religion in Wales
University of Wales, Bangor

Preface

The period between the two world wars was a golden age in Welsh intellectual and literary life, and yet very little has been published exploring the issues involved in the debates of the time. As far as theology is concerned, there can have been few comparable periods in Welsh history when religious thought flourished and was recognized to have a vital contribution to make in solving the multifarious problems of society. This book sets out to say something about theology in Wales as it developed from the end of the last great religious awakening in 1906 to the outbreak of war in 1939.

Chapter 1 sets the Welsh scene in its wider context of theological developments in Europe during the eighteenth and nineteenth centuries. It concentrates on identifying the main issues involved in theological formulation generally by the beginning of the twentieth century and identifies some of the theologians involved in appropriating those developments to the Welsh context. Chapter 2 offers a detailed look at the thought of the most important Welsh Nonconformist theologians of the period. These men attempted to work out a theology which would speak directly to the prevailing problems of their contemporary society. Their work is compared to that of English Nonconformist theologians and to the protagonists of the American social gospel. Chapter 3 takes up the story from the mid-1920s when the prevailing liberal understanding of theology was challenged forcefully by new developments on the continent. It explores how the same theologians reacted to neo-orthodoxy as it was expounded at the time. Chapter 4 primarily contains some general, concluding remarks concerning the theological developments in Wales, highlighting their strengths and weaknesses. It focuses on the importance of the contemporary context for the development of a socially orientated theology. The chapter contends that while liberal theologians argued for the importance of context in theological formulation, in fact they neglected the challenge to their thought thrown up by the tempests of the 1930s.

Although primarily concerned with the attempt to express a social gospel, this book also tries to demonstrate the more general theological standpoints of the protagonists of liberalism in this important period in Welsh religious history. As well as that, it offers an insight into the reasons why the younger generation of theologians could not hold to the same axioms and consequently suggested a different exposition of theological truth from their mentors and tutors. But more than anything the theologians of this period, both the liberal and the neo-orthodox, recognized that society would never work upon principles of justice and righteousness unless there was a spiritual element to life. Their major contribution was to argue that an adequate expression of the Christian faith was required in order to feed that spiritual life. As such, theirs is an abiding legacy for succeeding generations. Their story also demonstrates effectively the danger which accompanies offering spiritual guidance, namely the controversy which almost always follows attempts to express the Christian faith in modern terms. Yet the vision and commitment of this generation of Nonconformists in speaking about God and how God relates to men and women as individuals and in society is as potent today as ever, even if the issues, now as then, are ultimately difficult to resolve.

This book grew from a chapter on 'Wales and the Social Gospel' in my doctoral thesis entitled 'Nonconformity, labour and the social question in Wales 1906–1939' submitted to the School of Theology and Religious Studies, University of Wales, Bangor, in 1995. An expanded version of that chapter is contained here as chapter 2. The other chapters were written specifically for publication here, while the rest of the thesis was published by the University of Wales Press as *Building Jerusalem: Nonconformity, Labour and the Social Question in Wales, 1906–1939* (Cardiff, 1998).

Mention should be made of the language issue. Theology, like all other disciplines during the period here studied, was written exclusively in masculine terms. Welsh Nonconformists spoke about 'man' and 'men' when they meant 'men and women'. Although this is easily dealt with when discussing the meaning behind their theological statements, and the adoption of 'humankind' as opposed to 'mankind' is relatively straightforward, the terms 'Fatherhood of God' and 'brotherhood of man' which found favour at that time are not easily replaced, for theological, stylistic and historical reasons. It has therefore been my policy to avoid exclusively male terms as far as is possible in discussing the work of these Nonconformists, but to retain them when the argument revolves around fatherhood/brotherhood and consequently requires a retention of the original terminology.

It is appropriate here to record my thanks to those who have helped with the research and publication of this book. My colleague, Dr D. Densil Morgan, read the manuscript and offered many suggestions to improve the style of the work, and the Revd Principal W. Eifion Powell of the United Independent College, Aberystwyth, was kind enough to grant an early interview on the subject of D. Miall Edwards and his work. It is with sadness that I must record thanks to two men who have died while the project was being prepared for the press. Dr Gwilym Arthur Jones, Bangor, readily responded to my request for information about W. D. Davies and I was grateful to have an interesting and illuminating conversation with him about that most brilliant and yet enigmatic of men. Dr R. Tudur Jones read the manuscript and, with his usual eye for detail, saved me from a number of inaccuracies. Those of us who work in the field of Welsh theology and religious history owe him an enormous debt. Dr Geraint Tudur, director of the Centre for the Advanced Study of Religion in Wales, has been a source of encouragement for this book and offered valuable editorial support. It is with much satisfaction that I see this volume published as part of that Centre's activities. It is right, also, to record my thanks to Mrs Beti Llewellyn for her help in preparing the index. Finally, I am grateful to the staff of the University of Wales Press, especially its director, Susan Jenkins, and editorial manager, Ceinwen Jones, for their work on this book and for their support of the project. I am grateful to these people for helping to make the book what it is, but I, and I alone, am responsible for what is presented here.

I have been fortunate in my life to have had the support of family and friends in all that I have done. In some measure of gratitude for their love and support over the years, in happy and hard times, I dedicate this book to my grandparents.

1

Discovering Jerusalem

*And in the Spirit he carried me away to a great, high mountain and
showed me the holy city Jerusalem coming down out of heaven from
God. (Rev. 21.10 NRSV)*

It has been claimed with a considerable degree of justification
that, even at the end of the nineteenth century, Wales was a
Christian country.[1] General religiosity, enhanced by periodic
outbursts of revival, pervaded the land, though it had developed
for social as well as spiritual reasons. The religious census that
took place on a single Sunday in 1851 recorded 976,490 attend-
ances at religious services throughout the country, 80 per cent at
Nonconformist chapels and 20 per cent at the parish church. Of
course, the significance of such a figure is difficult to assess: some
people must have been counted more than once. But conservative
estimates put 40 per cent of the population in touch with one or
other of the religious denominations[2] and such a significant
number of religious communicants would inevitably have far-
ranging consequences for society at large, affecting in some ways
even those who kept far away from religious portals. Those who
attended Nonconformist worship were usually presented with a
Calvinistic interpretation of the Christian faith. The prospective
convert was expected to be convinced of the depravity and
desperation of the human condition and then to experience
personally the power of redeeming love mediated through the
vicarious suffering of Jesus Christ, thus convincing the individual
of his or her salvation not by merit but by God's grace alone.

When the twentieth century was merely four years old there
occurred a national religious revival that gave fresh impetus to
evangelical thought and practice and ensured that the Christian
faith remained an important aspect of Welsh identity, at least for
a time. Congregations swelled in towns and villages throughout

1

the nation and churches coped with the influx only by the erection of additional galleries or balconies and, occasionally, larger premises. It is important to note that the proliferation of chapel buildings in Wales was largely due to the population movement of the nineteenth century. As people moved from the country to take up residence and employment in the developing industrial districts, so they took their religion, and constructed chapels as social and cultural as well as strictly spiritual centres for their locality. When it came in 1904, revival primarily added to the number of adherents and posed the problem for a number of churches of insufficient space for their congregations. Of course, it led some into missionary movements and evangelistic campaigns, but the new churches established during the revival period were largely located in recently developed residential areas and were seen more as a natural expansion than as the product of revivalist enthusiasm.

The revival of 1904 was marked by an intensity of spiritual experience on a national scale. Gifts of the Spirit (see 1 Cor. 12.8–10) were in evidence during some meetings, while worship services were often ardent and filled with passion, the result of men and women of every age group having perceived their escape from eternal torment and having found the joy of entry into God's Kingdom. Scenes of extreme emotion were not uncommon as men and women experienced for the first time the reality of divine acceptance and forgiveness; for the vast majority of them life would never be quite the same again. Tears, laughter, the beating of breasts and intense prayer for mercy followed by spontaneous and joyful expressions of thanksgiving marked revival meetings where social mores and human inhibitions were cast aside as those present perceived higher values and principles, not to mention their own eternal destiny, to be at stake. Others responded in a quieter fashion but were equally convinced that they had met their Saviour and were consequently inheritors of the Kingdom of God. Such experiences led indirectly to the subsequent foundation of Pentecostalist denominations. George Jeffreys, who helped found the Elim Four Square Pentecostalist movement, and Daniel Powell Williams, who founded the Apostolic Church at Penygroes, Carmarthenshire, were both converted during the revival.

Nonconformist religion at that time was largely individualistic, stressing each person's need to seek Christ's forgiveness. It was

2

rigorously moralistic, recognizing the need for the believer to strive after holiness which was particularly expressed by the late nineteenth and early twentieth centuries through temperance movements. And it was other-worldly. The believer's eyes were to be firmly fixed on the next life having discovered that Christian citizenship was in heaven and, though still abiding *on* the earth, the Christian no longer belonged to the transitory corruption *of* the earth (cf. e.g. Col. 3.20; Phil. 3.20). Thus, following conversion, Christian men and women often considered their earthly situation to be an ethical and spiritual endurance test for the world to come. They interpreted life on this earth as a passing phase which they could neither affect nor change. The convert was encouraged, whether explicitly or by implication, to ignore the condition of this earthly existence. Eternal salvation was to be the primary concern of the Christian heart. When the treasures of heaven awaited the convert, the things of the earth did indeed pale into insignificance.

Much space was given in denominational journals and in secular newspapers to the extraordinary events of 1904–5 and the need to exploit the religious revival to the full by instructing the new converts in the faith. And before the revival fires had died down, a new element was introduced, though not in any developed sense. As thousands had discovered a purpose to their lives through evangelical conversion, so the world at large could be conformed more adequately to God's plan for creation. The conversion experience led to hundreds discovering a new dignity and purpose for their lives and the corollary that this belonged by right to all men and women made, as the creation narrative of Genesis affirms, in the image of God. The need, then, was for mass-conversion. When religion was effective in individual lives it would automatically make a difference to the prevailing principles which governed social and economic attitudes and practices. Thus the chapels and churches of the land were being challenged to lead men and women from an initial evangelical conversion into a life of obedient discipleship that would transform society by individual dedication to the higher, spiritual life and to the establishment in the world of its values and principles. The result was not a social gospel *per se* but a recognition that individual conversion, particularly on a large scale, could not leave the world untouched. Despite the mass-conversion effected

3

during the revival, or perhaps because of it, the opening decade of the twentieth century presented many challenges to prevailing religious practice and ideology. This period saw the preparation for a transition in theology which would install social improvement and reconstruction as if not the necessary goal then certainly the inevitable effect of religious belief. The fact was, then, that the promulgation of a socially orientated gospel grew either naturally from, or as a reaction to, the experience of widespread individual salvation during the revival. And individual salvation would remain a central characteristic of Nonconformist theology in Wales throughout the years of liberal ascendancy (1906–39), albeit in a modified form.

Alongside the strictly religious developments which occurred as the revival spread and social issues began to emerge on the agenda of the church, there were also other forces which had a great effect on religious thought and practice. There had been a small but vocal group of Welsh Nonconformists that had been conscious of their social and political responsibility certainly from the middle of the nineteenth century. Men such as William Rees ('Gwilym Hiraethog', 1802–83), Samuel Roberts ('S.R.', 1800–85) and Henry Richard (1812–88) had all sought to work out their Christian faith in a way that would affect Welsh society for the better. They contributed to the debate about society and politics in Wales while also agitating for peace, the repeal of the Corn Laws and education reform. Alongside this, Welsh Nonconformists, like their English counterparts, became increasingly associated with Liberal and radical politics, an association which reached its peak in the landslide Liberal victory of 1906 when all but one Welsh constituency returned a Liberal MP. Yet it was forces generally located beyond the obvious orbit of the chapel which would engender the claim that the revivalism popularized in the 1904–5 period by the remarkable and mystical figure of Evan Roberts was an insufficient revelation of Christian truth.

Certainly the most populist challenge came from the Independent Labour Party (ILP) and its supporters. Founded in 1893 by Keir Hardie, the ILP propounded a 'religion of Socialism', a peculiarly ethical and social interpretation of Jesus' teaching which prompted many working men to question the exigencies of traditional chapel teaching with its stress on

4

individual salvation from sin and eternal punishment. The ILP provided a strong challenge to Nonconformity's traditional allegiance with radical Liberal politics by claiming that industrial society had created a sub-class consisting of working men whose cause was not represented in Parliament. Its claims, though not always geared towards specifically political goals, were argued with a profoundly religious zeal and drew much strength from the use of popular religious imagery. Its message emphasized the value of human brotherhood and the need to adopt ethical principles such as co-operation and economic collectivism which would ensure that provision was made for everyone's need conditional upon their contribution to the common weal. Many of the ILP stalwarts and leaders had been raised within evangelical Christianity, so it is hardly surprising that they reinforced their political message with common biblical motifs, particularly those of God's Fatherhood and the Kingdom of God. One of the most popular verses of scripture amongst those agitating for social reform was 'Seek ye first the Kingdom of God and his righteousness' (Mt. 6.33). For Christian ministers attracted to social reform, this verse required a personal and ethical commitment to the establishment of justice and righteousness within the economic system. The result was a message that encompassed a challenge to the other-worldly piety of much contemporary Christian practice and belief. This precipitated the transformation in Nonconformist teaching from an individualistic religion to a social and ethical redemption, but it was not social and political factors alone which accounted for this change. Philosophical developments during the eighteenth and nineteenth centuries had affected theological formulation and by the turn of the twentieth century they were beginning to filter through to Welsh pastors and Welsh churches.

Theology during the nineteenth century was profoundly affected by two movements of thought. One was the German philosophy which stemmed from the Enlightenment, particularly the work of Immanuel Kant (1724–1804) and Georg Wilhelm Friedrich Hegel (1770–1831). The other was the development of 'liberal theology' with Friedrich Daniel Ernst Schleiermacher (1768–1834) as its founding father.[3] These three men all made considerable contributions to the world of philosophical and theological reflection, and their influence on subsequent generations has been immense. Indeed, it can be said that all theological reflection since their day has had to take account in one way or another of their various claims and systems of thought. Their work is often illuminating and subtle, but frequently it is complicated, if not at times obscure. It is not necessary for us to understand all the intricacies of their thought and method, but here we look at those parts of their teaching which would later become important for Welsh theology particularly in the development of social thinking amongst Nonconformists in Wales.

Kant had emphasized that religion's moral imperative alone could give it any value and meaning. Empirical factors did not regulate the truth or otherwise of moral arguments. Instead, moral arguments were to be regarded as maxims from which Kant developed his theological statements. According to Kant, human beings possess an innate moral sense by which they are naturally persuaded to aim for the highest good and to believe that fulfilment of such goodness is possible. However, as the highest good is not always attainable in this life, Kant was led logically to assert the fact of humankind's fundamental immortality. Ethical achievement initially depended on human orientation. For Kant the category was that of 'good will', implying that men and women will accept their duty *qua* duty and for no other reason. Individual duty, the recognition and then practice of good will, meant that each person would live according to the dictates of impartial and universal reason rather than to the whims of personal preference and self-concern. Reason would lead towards a recognition of universal principles and then to inspire a life in which what ought to be done is done. Reason imbued with moral considerations offers a glimpse of the noumenal world, the divine or spiritual realm in which 'God' exists, which is ordinarily hidden from the phenomenal realm of human existence. The second requirement on which Kant insisted as necessary for ethical achievement was the recognition that, because men and women are also the victims or beneficiaries of factors beyond their control, the natural realm must consequently be ordered in such a way as to work for the moral life rather than against it. God therefore exists *a priori* as the moral force which has so ordered the universe. In this way moral arguments, despite their axiomatic nature, could be used to verify the existence of God. Religion, then, is to be interpreted in moral terms its value being to encourage the living of a moral life. Thus, for Kant, it was the ethical awareness inherent in humankind that made knowledge and talk about God both possible and necessary.[4]

Hegel's Idealist philosophy had held to the primacy of ideas and to the immanence of Absolute Spirit (*Geist*) within the universe. The presence of Absolute Spirit bestowed both spiritual and moral authority leading to a perception of the real which would eventually, through the historical process, become an empirical reality. For Hegel, the universe was essentially Reason which is known through its virtual incarnation in the natural realm and the historical process as well as in the human mind. It was Hegel's emphasis on reason and his philosophy of history that were most important for the development of Welsh theology. In the latter, he had averred that there was a linear development within time leading to the ultimate unity of the creation. Thus, progress and ultimate perfection were the inevitable results of the historical process. This process was dialectic where a starting-point (thesis) provokes initially an alternative and opposite proposition (antithesis) and then a combination of the two (synthesis). Synthesis was the final goal and consummation of all things. When it was achieved, then perfection too had been reached. Although Hegel considered this historical perfection to have been attained in the political developments of his homeland, his philosophy of history offered the potential for further development within the historical process. In other words, any synthesis becomes a new thesis and the process begins again. In this way, the dynamic within history, already perceived within Christian thought as leading to a final apocalyptic consummation, was seen to lead in each generation to a higher good, provided that the inherent goodness of humankind, by virtue of the immanence of Absolute Spirit, was emphasized and realized. Hegel's thought, dependent as it was on the presence within creation of the moral and developmental force of the universe, prompted the view that God and humanity (and ultimately all things) are one. This monism would become important for those who sought a religious justification for social improvement. It meant that everyone had a moral duty to act according to the regulation of Absolute Spirit while also insisting that the dynamic for development and improvement already existed within creation and within humankind. All that was needed to allow Absolute Spirit to work in and through individual lives was

7

a self-abnegating openness.[5] During the late nineteenth and early twentieth centuries, Idealism became the dominant philosophy in Britain and, differences in emphasis notwithstanding, was expounded by such teachers as F. H. Bradley, T. H. Green, the brothers Edward and John Caird, and the Welshman Henry Jones. Although an appreciation of the divine or spiritual (or perhaps moral) realm was inherent in the work of both Kant and Hegel, their basis was in philosophy rather than theology *per se*. Though they eschewed the old metaphysics which argued God's existence from nature, they were metaphysicians whose concern was with questions of reality. The spiritual and the divine entered their work only in so far as they could legitimately be perceived in reality. It was Schleiermacher who offered a more comprehensively theological system of thought, partly in reaction against the rationalism of Kant. Schleiermacher recognized that the scientific and philosophical advances of his age had left the traditional validations for holding religious faith void of any meaning. He believed that educated people no longer looked to religion to provide an explanation of the why and wherefore of the universe, while Kant had shown them that morality existed independently of religious inspiration or conviction. Finding himself more attracted to the romanticism of the period and to the pietistic tradition of his youth than to the rationalistic tendencies in philosophy, Schleiermacher's response was to ground religion in human experience and 'feeling' rather than in the reason or the will. No longer being concerned with issues of epistemology or ethics, he ensured that religion claimed its own sphere of authority. He rooted human awareness of God within personal experience, that, in the depth of being, men and women recognize their own 'feeling of absolute dependence'; that is, at the depths of personality the individual realizes that he or she does not cause him or herself to exist. This feeling, which is universal in the human condition and not necessarily void of cognitive content, convinces its subject of the existence of the divine.[6]

The implications of Schleiermacher's theological system are profound. All human beings were now in contact with God whether they affirmed, denied or chose to ignore God's existence. But this God was the immanent God present in all creation and known as the cause of all things. Gone was the objective, personal

and present, yet transcendent deity of traditional Christian interpretation, the Creator who redeems and sustains the creation,
perceived or revealed as Father, Son and Holy Spirit. In fact,
Schleiermacher tended to avoid any reference to God as a
personal being. The theological task was simply to give expression to individual experience. The traditional categories of heresy
and orthodoxy were rendered redundant as there could no longer
be an objective standard for religious truth against which theological claims based on personal experience could be measured.
With the grounding of all religious reality in each individual's
experience of the immanence of God, all claims to religious truth
were deemed valid. Human beings, as they experienced themselves and the world around them, became all-important. In this
way, these three thinkers paved the way for an increasingly
anthropocentric theology, one which emphasized individual
human experience and ethical duty above all else and saw God as
real to the extent that he was to be found within human experience and in the quest for the moral life. René Descartes
(1596–1650) had already affirmed that the key to understanding
reality was the recognition of the thinking self. It is the human
subject, this thinking self, which becomes the centre not so much
of God's creative and redemptive purposes as of reality itself. In
other words, reality is meaningful only through the individual's
perception of it. It was this, together with Kant's ethical imperative, which ensured that inter-personal relationships, on social,
industrial, economic as well as personal levels, would become
vitally important in theological and philosophical discourse. The
danger, of course, was that as human beings assumed the central
role in creation and in the universe on both theoretical and pragmatic levels such theology would finally cease to be *theo*logy, the
knowledge of *God*.

There are two further developments which should be
mentioned here in order to understand both the theological
context and the social concern of the age. First, there was the
development in liberal theology culminating in the thought of
Albrecht Ritschl (1822–89) and his school. Ritschl rejected metaphysics and in its place presented a system of 'value judgements'.
It is likely that Ritschl intended the 'value judgement' to corre-
spond to empirical reality. But there was still the possibility that
a distinction was to be made between what something is *in se* and

the value that thing has *pro nobis*. Jesus is God in so far as he has the value of God for us. Provided the latter clause can be affirmed, any ontological conception of the former becomes superfluous. Ritschl affirmed that the absolute value of humankind was demonstrated by the individual's inherent ability to know what is good and therefore to know God through the goodness of God's active, redeeming will. As love was the key to relationships within the justified community, Christian faith, for Ritschl, led naturally to ethical and quasi-socialistic considerations.[7] Ritschl's work was continued after his death by his many pupils and followers, the most important of whom were Adolf Harnack (1851–1930) and Wilhelm Herrmann (1846–1922).

The second development occurred within the field of defining religious experience. Experience of the divine had been recognized as encompassing the perception of ultimate moral values, those of truth, goodness and beauty. Rudolf Otto (1869–1937) posited that such an experience was that of the holy, the *mysterium tremendum et fascinans*: the eternal mystery which fills one at once with both dread and fascination.[8] God was wholly other than humankind yet human beings could experience the divine by their innate capacity to feel and perceive the *numinous*. Otto's description inevitably renders dogmatic definition unnecessary. While it could accurately describe the divine, experience of the numinous required no adherence to complex trinitarian and soteriological creeds. They could be believed if desired, but they could not be posited as definitions of unique authority. Indeed it was through the study of comparative religion rather than reflection on Christian doctrine that Otto had discovered this common experience amongst other religious peoples of the world. More critically, simply because this was an experience of the eternal values of beauty, truth and goodness, which were in turn revelations of divine holiness, it led theologians naturally into a critique of social injustice. If experience was the vital component for faith, how could people ever experience the divine in the context of a dreary, unjust social system which condemned many to a life of poverty and thraldom, to existence in poor housing, to labour in dangerous industries and left to the mercy of rapacious bosses? As one Welsh liberal theologian, D. Miall Edwards, commented, 'a man's soul can hardly grow to its utmost possibility in a slum, any more than a geranium can grow to its full beauty in a cellar.'[9]

Despite the emphasis placed on the value of the individual, this all meant that the religious life could not be interpreted merely as a matter of personal piety. This should not have been a new discovery. As the New Testament reveals, there was a sense in the days of the apostles that faith affects life and brings all moral requirements and interpersonal relationships under a critical spotlight. There was in Jesus' teaching the claim that love of God required the love of fellow human beings (Mt. 22.37–39; Mk. 12.30–31; Lk. 10.27). The early church shared all in common so that each received according to need (Acts 4.32). At its most basic level there was a need always to be truthful in dealing with others as the fate of Ananias and Sapphira clearly demonstrated (Acts 5.1–11). But by the late nineteenth and early twentieth centuries it was apparent that the industrial context of Western society required an unprecedented response from the church because the situation in which it found itself was unique. The effects of the environment and the wider concerns of socio-economic practice were seen as stumbling-blocks to religious commitment and the corollary to this was that improved social conditions would facilitate personal faith. Thus social reform became the concern of theology and the church not because of a direct, religiously inspired condemnation of injustice, but because environmental conditions were perceived as hindering its spiritual mission.

New Theology

All these developments were somewhat theoretical. They may have filtered down to congregations if ministers had undergone a rigorous theological training and adopted the claims of contemporary philosophy and theology. They would probably have remained totally beyond most chapel people, and even beyond the interests of many of the leaders and pastors of Welsh Nonconformity, if it were not for a remarkable popular movement in which the theological and philosophical developments of the previous hundred years came to a head. Though it had been developing for a number of years, the 'New Theology', as it was called, burst into the nation's view on 11 January 1907 following a provocative article published in the *Daily Mail*. It was basically an attempt to demonstrate the intellectual and moral strength of

Christianity, on the one hand by interpreting the faith in the terms of modern knowledge and on the other by rendering obsolete any Christian teaching found to be incompatible with a contemporary, ethical understanding of the world. At the same time, it was intended as a means to make the gospel real for a populace which showed signs of being progressively alienated from traditional and Calvinistic expressions of the faith. It undoubtedly went too far, and in emphasizing the maxims of Kantian and Hegelian philosophy lost the particular salvific dynamic of traditional Christianity. There were 'New Theologians' in all denominations who had been charmed by the recent philosophical ideologies and doctrinal developments, but the movement's figurehead was the Revd R. J. Campbell, the pastor at the City Temple in London, a Congregational church which, under his predecessor, the celebrated Dr Joseph Parker, had become a virtual epicentre for radical Nonconformity. Campbell had received no formal theological training but had read widely in philosophy while minister of Union Church in Brighton. His popularity in Brighton was remarkable and during this period his fame spread rapidly. As new leaders were sought to take Nonconformity into the new century, he became a natural successor to Dr Parker. After his arrival in London in 1903, *Y Dysgedydd*, organ of the Welsh Independents, hailed him as being 'old without being "old fashioned"' and 'new without being revolutionary' (January 1904, p. 6). In the light of later events these words appear ironic to say the least. By 1907, he had adopted a largely humanistic theology which recognized the divine potential of all human beings and which, allied to the nascent Socialist and labour movements, offered the prospect of social renewal. Campbell had clearly been influenced by the work of both Kant and Hegel. He was a monist, one who recognized the fundamental unity of all things. The result was a philosophical world-view in which God and humanity, the created order and the spiritual realm, and ultimate reality itself were all one. There could consequently be no dualism between good and evil, or sin and righteousness. This was, of course, too much for many more evangelically minded Nonconformists. They criticized Campbell for preaching such heresies while drawing a stipend from an evangelical church. They criticized the officers of the City Temple for not acting to preserve the apostolic faith 'once given to the saints'. Very soon what had been at least initially a genuine attempt to make the Christian faith more compatible with modern life had degenerated into something of a slanging-match. The debate simply highlighted the emerging gap between representatives of different theological positions.

What perhaps is most interesting about the New Theology controversy is the way in which it was associated almost exclusively with R. J. Campbell. It was he more than any other protagonist of the new teaching who suffered hostility and criticism for his opinions. This may have been simply the inevitable fate of any popular leader whose success generated jealousy, particularly those who are courted by the media as indeed Campbell was. Campbell himself had been truculent in his criticism of the old orthodoxy. It is therefore hardly surprising that he in turn was vilified by more traditional Nonconformists. There was considerable distaste expressed for the personality cult which grew up around Campbell, particularly as he appeared to enjoy, if not encourage, adulation from (often female) admirers. He was by all accounts a striking, if not handsome, figure in the pulpit, a factor which added both to his popularity and to his effect as a preacher. But Campbell felt isolated within Nonconformity, a situation fuelled by the vitriolic response to his book. His mentor at Oxford had been Charles Gore whose far more conciliatory response persuaded Campbell that God was transcendent as well as immanent and that in Protestant theology transcendence had been transmuted into deism. As a result, Gore convinced Campbell that his home was not in the rationalistic tradition of Congregationalism but in the more sacramental, even mystical, traditions of Anglo-Catholicism. He resigned as pastor of the City Temple in 1915 and entered the Anglican Church soon afterwards.[10] By this time, the 'New Theology' controversy had already abated. Yet many of the ministers involved in the movement continued to propagate the same ideas for the next twenty years or so without being subjected to the same level of vilification. This is in part symptomatic of the way in which the heresies of one age become the orthodoxies of another. But it also demonstrates the hostility aimed at one individual who revelled in his status as the *enfant terrible* within contemporary Nonconformity. He died in virtual obscurity in 1956 as a minor canon of Chichester Cathedral. His 'New Theology', which had caused such a stir less than half a century previously, was all but forgotten.

Almost all Welsh denominational periodicals at this time published articles discussing Campbell's ideas. They imply that Nonconformists were unanimously opposed to the New Theology. Campbell had denied God's objective personhood, recognizing his presence at the depths of humankind's inner struggle where the individual comes into contact with his or her own being and therefore with Being itself, that place where men and women discover their 'feeling of absolute dependence'. The all-pervasive presence of the immanent God within the world prevented Jesus from being claimed as unique and divine. Any claim of divinity had to be ethically engendered and based on moral living. It was in living the perfect life of service and self-denial that Jesus had reached the heights of human personality and had thus revealed the divine life in himself. This meant that any human being could emulate Christ's efforts and achieve divinity, for the truly human was also the truly divine. This was not a rediscovery of the Greek patristic doctrine of *theōsis*, that Christ became human that we might become divine, for Athanasius and his fellow theologians were not exalting the fleshly human existence or, more specifically, the ideal of a moral and self-abnegating life. Athanasius was offering an explanation of the Pauline teaching that the baptized believer was a new creation *in Christ* rather than positing inherent divinity within physical human life. Through Christ the Christian partook of the nature of the divine, because Christ was truly God and truly man. For the liberal theologians, on the other hand, divinity was associated with a moral idea that could be practised by human beings in this world and as a result tended to offer itself as a system of 'works righteousness'.

Even when affirming the positive aspects of the New Theology, Welsh Nonconformists could only admit that the immanence of God, axiomatic as it was to Campbell's understanding, had been neglected rather than rejected in orthodox theology, preaching and worship. According to Hugh Jones, a Wesleyan divine, everybody already believed in the immanence of God.[11] On the other hand, it cannot be denied that Campbell influenced certain individuals substantially. The Revd Herbert Morgan, a young Baptist minister who was also a member of the ILP, certainly appeared to support his interpretation. It is said that he discussed the New Theology with his minister at Porth, the Revd R. B. Jones, while the latter was searching for a deeper relevance of religion and a further experience of God after the revival of 1904.[12] Jones, who gained considerable recognition as Wales's leading fundamentalist in the next few years, rejected Campbell's modernism and emphasized instead the gospel's call to personal repentance and holiness rather than the relevance of its reforming dynamic to economic and social structures. He was sorely disappointed with Herbert Morgan's theological development and, as a result, refused to attend his ordination service at Castle Street Welsh Baptist Church, London.[13] Both James Griffiths (later MP for Llanelli and first Secretary of State for Wales) and S. O. Davies (later successor to Keir Hardie as MP for Merthyr) professed Christian faith only according to the edicts of the New Theology. By emphasizing God's immanence and the life of self-denial and service, Campbell had shown these men a vision of hope for this world, but they had to look to a political movement in order for it to be achieved.

The implications of such a stance are clear. Nothing should be allowed to prevent the full development of human character and personality for they were the abode of the immanent God, where men and women perceived the deepest things of life. If social conditions prevented such a development, then society would have to be reformed. Thus the church had to look to encourage individual morality and also to rid society of all immoral aspects that hindered spiritual growth. Questions of politics and economics had to be faced and answered if the church's salvific work was to be effective. Such an approach would inevitably provoke condemnation amongst Nonconformists who had stressed both God's transcendent holiness, and the natural (original) sin of humankind and its consequent need of redemption. But these changes in religious thought were beginning to be perceived in Wales as early as 1891, and in some circles, they received a warm reception. In that year a correspondent to the *South Wales Daily News* claimed that 'everywhere the conviction is growing that the preaching of the present age has hitherto savoured too much of the skies and too much of the hereafter'. This religion was becoming increasingly irrelevant and far-removed from ordinary people faced with the difficulties of everyday life. In concentrating on 'setting up brilliant prospects' for the hereafter, Nonconformist religion had become 'too intangible for people who are going deeper and deeper into the too real and tangible miseries and privations of life'. Instead, religion should gear itself towards the more practical concerns of softening 'the heart of the hard taskmaster' and making 'the dishonest and slothful servant faithful'. Men and women had 'bodies to be fed as well as souls to be saved'. They were, of course, the inheritors of 'mansions in the skies which are undergoing preparation for them', but they currently lived in denuded dwellings in dire need of 'many substantial improvements'. Sincere religion, if it was to stand any chance of being taken seriously by the masses, needed to speak directly to their current predicament and offer the means to change it rather than provide hope for a better life after death. According to this author, only a religion which took account of the practicalities of temporal life *as well as* offering eternal life in paradise could be acceptable to all people regardless of social standing and class.[14]

Welsh New Theologians

There were some Welsh Congregational ministers such as Thomas Rhondda Williams (1860–1945), David Adams (1845–1923), Ebenezer Griffith-Jones (1860–1942) and John Morgan Jones (1873–1946) who were attracted to these new ideas, and their names came to be associated with the New Theology and its emerging social concern. This does not mean that R. J. Campbell's thought influenced them directly, and the latter three at least confessed at different times to having doubts about Campbell's exposition of the New Theology. John Morgan Jones admitted that he preferred the work of the London Congregationalist and former Unitarian Dr Joseph Warschauer, whose stress was on God's immanence rather than on the unity of all reality, while David Adams's penchant for blending the discoveries of modern science with the Idealist philosophy of Hegel had been known and had gained him notoriety years before the controversy of the New Theology had burst into public attention. In his criticism of Campbell, Griffith-Jones revealed an inherent conservatism which always modified any sympathy he had with new movements in philosophy and theology. Although he believed that the content of theology needed to be reviewed in the light of scientific discovery, in his view Campbell had gone too far. The 'New Theology' as preached by the London Congregationalist was not an obvious development from the theology of the previous age nor did it take the 'central and essential doctrines and truths' of the Christian faith sufficiently seriously. It was for these reasons that Griffith-Jones predicted that Campbell's theology would soon be abandoned and even forgotten.[15] Rhondda Williams, on the other hand, was a definite Campbell-phile. Williams's rhetoric in support of the quasi-mystical figure of Campbell gives an idea of the mesmerizing effect that the London-based Congregationalist had on his public. 'He [Campbell] must have been let down from the sky', Williams later wrote. 'He gave me the feeling before he said a word that he had arrived from some other world.'[16] None of these men shared the same fate as R. J. Campbell. Although they all met opposition from more traditional Nonconformists, they neither forsook Congregationalism nor did they end their days in obscurity. On the contrary, each achieved a position of respectability and honour within their denomination. Griffith-Jones and John Morgan Jones became principals of theological colleges, Griffith-Jones at Bradford and John Morgan Jones at Bangor. Griffith-Jones and Rhondda Williams would later become chairman of the Congregational Union of England and Wales in 1918–19 and 1929 respectively, while David Adams and John Morgan Jones would receive the corresponding honour in the Union of Welsh Independents in 1913 and 1939 respectively. They all remained denominational men and lived long enough to receive recognition from institutions which once would have offered them only vilification and rebuke.

Adams and Griffith-Jones shared first prize at the National Eisteddfod of 1893 for essays on Darwinian evolution, and it was Adams who would first publicize the 'new' movements through the medium of the Welsh language in his three books *Datblygiad yn ei Ddylanwad ar Foeseg a Duwinyddiaeth* ('Evolution and its Influence on Ethics and Theology', Wrexham, n.d.), *Datblygiad yn ei Berthynas â'r Cwymp, yr Ymgnawdoliad a'r Adgyfodiad* ('Evolution and its Relationship with the Fall, the Incarnation and the Resurrection', Caernarfon, 1893) and *Personoliaeth Dynol*

17

a'r Ymgnawdoliad ('Human Personality and the Incarnation', Dolgellau, n.d.).

Adams's importance is principally as an expositor of Idealism. His intention was to synthesize Christianity with modern philosophical and scientific ideas, particularly the theory of evolution and the philosophy of Hegel. In his books, Adams presented to the Welsh public the view that the natural and unstoppable progression of history was towards the ultimate harmony of the whole universe; his interest was not in a specifically social interpretation of Christian doctrine. His fascination with Hegelian philosophy had led him to concentrate on God's immanence in creation,[17] and also, with some debt to Kant, to the fundamentally moral nature and requirements of the gospel.[18] As a result, Adams offered an ethical critique of the human condition which emphasized that rights, whether they be in individual lives or in commercial situations, incur responsibilities. 'Capital' thus had responsibilities to the workforce and to society at large.[19] Although he recognized that the church should always support social justice, he insisted that it should never take sides in industrial disputes.[20] This was impractical advice and far-removed from the idea of the 'preferential option' popularized by late-twentieth-century Latin American liberation theology in which God is seen specifically and without embarrassment as 'on the side of the poor'. Even while eschewing the confidence of South American theologians, it is still possible that the cry for justice for the victims of industrial society required on occasion that one side (i.e. society's victims) be supported against the other (i.e. the perpetrators of injustice, which in Adams's context may very well have been the capitalists and bosses). Furthermore, Adams's was hardly the most expedient policy at a time when the labour movement was growing in strength almost daily, a growth largely due to the effectiveness of its message which was gradually convincing the working classes that they had justice on their side. None the less Adams's attitude proved to be pioneering, as the next generation of Nonconformist theologians believed that they, too, could somehow represent an ethic which rose above sectarian debates and which never required the support of any specific political grouping. In his work, Adams demonstrated that Hegelian and neo-Kantian ideas had important implications for a social interpretation of Christianity. It may not have been rigorously defined, or for that matter a vital part of Adams's thinking, but it was there and others were later able to build on this early foundation.

The crux of the matter for Adams was the inherent value of humankind.[21] This meant that the 'specific need of current Christian civilization is to restore the idea that honest labour in order to provide temporal welfare is a true "service" for God'.[22] The notion of individual responsibility in the physical sphere corresponded to humankind's spiritual responsibility to discern the implications of the truth of God as taught by Jesus.[23] Jesus did not supply a detailed blueprint for all situations, it was up to his followers to put his teachings into practice as they saw fit. Thus, the moral status of a human being would be preserved when human value was calculated according to the effort made in fulfilling personal responsibilities. Men and women had a physical responsibility to work, in whatever sphere, as a service to God, and a spiritual responsibility to work out the implications of Jesus' teaching to ensure that society developed along the lines ordained by God.

All these ideas had profound implications for any specifically Christian contribution to solving the problems facing industrial society in the early twentieth century. Indeed, it was generally accepted that any theological construction needed to take account of these issues in order to be relevant to contemporary society and the lives of ordinary men and women perceived to have been left untouched by traditional religion. As a result, for the next forty years or so, similar ideas were repeated by Nonconformists involved in the call for social reform. Adams himself remained quite conservative, however, in the sense that he worked to induce a recognition of the true gospel as he himself had perceived it rather than the creation of a new society. Although he helped to spread liberal theology in Wales, it was left to others to apply it more specifically to social issues.

Ebenezer Griffith-Jones had trained for the Congregational ministry at the theologically suspect and decidedly liberal Presbyterian College in Carmarthen. While there he shared lodgings with fellow student Rhondda Williams. Williams remembered 'kicking' Griffith-Jones out of bed one night as a punishment for swaying from the Calvinist faith. The irony of this adolescent response is that, while Griffith-Jones may have been attracted to modern thought some years before Williams, it was the latter who would become far more heterodox in the years ahead. The difference between the two men would become clear as they expounded their personal systems of religious thought. But at its root, this difference was little more than one of emphasis. Griffith-Jones was committed to an Idealist and scientific interpretation of Christianity through which the faith should learn to speak in contemporary terms. Williams, like R. J. Campbell, was a monist and consequently far more interested in seeing modern movements either as being explicitly religious or as requiring religious language and imagery to describe the common and vitalizing experience of the Divine. Idealist philosophy, Socialism and psychology all came in for such treatment at his hands.

It is true, on the one hand, that in many respects Griffith-Jones was not particularly representative of Welsh theology and church life. He published very little through the medium of Welsh and was never pastor of a Welsh-speaking congregation. Apart from a pastorate at Park English Congregational Church, Llanelli, between 1887 and 1890 and his oversight of Llandeilo English Congregational Church after his retirement, he had ministered all his life in England. When his expanded Eisteddfod essay was finally published as *The Ascent through Christ* (London, 1899) he was ministering at Balham, London, and would remain there until his appointment as principal of the Yorkshire United Theological College at Bradford in 1907. It is also true, however, that his book is of considerable significance if we are to understand fully the concerns of the time. It demonstrates clearly the main issues facing the church at the turn of the twentieth century, including the difficulties of the modern learning of which biblical criticism was a part, the advance of science and the advent of the labour movement with its corresponding cry for social reform.

If anything, Griffith-Jones demonstrated his concurrence with a Hegelian philosophy of history together with a neo-Kantian ethic. History was progressing, or ascending, towards its perfect consummation which was fundamentally moral and spiritual. This final consummation primarily concerned individual character (p. 7), but man was also a social being. Because man's social character and function stemmed from his commitment to an idea, a moral cause rather than purely instinctive, mechanical action, he was evidently superior to the rest of creation. This idea originated 'above' him, and through this 'Man [rises] into the lofty heights of unselfishness and gives his life for others – the strong for the weak, the wise for the erring, the good for the vicious' (p. 54). Man's fundamentally moral character was the result of years of evolution, a journey along the path of history which had moved upwards as well as onwards. It was a journey of gradual perfection, with each new age surpassing the previous one for moral, intellectual and social advance as humankind stamped its authority and presence on the created order. Thus 'in Man physical Evolution has reached its limits', and this leads on to the far more startling proposition that 'all future development is in his own hands and under his own control' (p. 56). This was in many respects the result of God having ordained the evolutionary process, but it also pointed to a kind of 'man come of age' who no longer needed a personal divinity as a source of comfort and support, as a source of inspiration and direction or, for that matter, as the one who brings creation to its consummation through effecting the salvation of sinful, fallen, finite humankind. The path to social reform was clearly mapped. It was down to human choice and effort to get on with it.

For Griffith-Jones, it was humankind collectively that held this supreme status and not any one individual either in the past or in the present. As a result, Christ's incarnation was merely a demonstration of the ability of even sinful, fallen flesh to bear the image of God. In Christ the possibilities of moral nature are supremely fulfilled and through his perfect example, men and women are inspired and led to recognize the 'possibilities of human nature when voluntarily and perfectly delivered into the hands of God' (p. 235). 'Men must be taught to honour their own nature,' he wrote, 'to believe in its high possibilities, ere they can make adequate efforts after reformation' (p. 236). Christ then was the inspiration for a moral life and the ideal to which man should conform (p. 274) and thus the means for humankind's 'ascent'. Jesus Christ is 'Man as God meant Man to be' (p. 312). Unlike Campbell, Griffith-Jones emphasized the difference between human beings and God at least in their moral function, but in so doing no difference could be maintained between Christ and the rest of humanity, apart from the fact that Jesus succeeded where all others have failed. Redemption restores human beings to their primary place in creation, to their God-appointed position of honour, but also enables them to achieve their spiritual potential in the creation of perfect society (p. 282) which is in fact the Kingdom of God.

Griffith-Jones's emphasis on the moral idea at the heart of the gospel message would inevitably have had to consider human actions and thus also to consider society at large. In agreement with contemporary biblical scholarship he perceived the Kingdom of God to be the central aspect of Jesus' teaching. Because he spoke of a Kingdom, Christ's purpose was 'by no means fully accomplished in the salvation of individual souls' but required the embodiment of 'the principle of the Divine life' in a new society (p. 280). The salvation of the individual and of society as a whole were intimately connected, as could be seen from one important saying of Jesus (Lk. 17.21) where '"The Kingdom of Heaven is *within you*" may with equal correctness be read "The Kingdom of Heaven is *among you*," i.e. it is either within the heart of the individual as an unawakened possibility of character, or latent among the community as a social order' (p. 281). In this, Griffith-Jones was a precursor for later Nonconformist theology which emphasized the need for individual salvation, where one was saved from immorality and sinful choices into the moral life lived in service of others, and such a life would lead inevitably to a transformed social life, even if it did not lead automatically to definite policies for social reform. This was the order. Salvation of the individual was the priority, but this would inevitably lead to a vitally important corollary, namely the salvation of society and, as a result, the establishment of God's Kingdom on earth. Jerusalem, the apocalyptic promise that the City of God would one day be established, had been rediscovered. Though the New Testament image in the Book of Revelation stresses that the principal significance of the holy city was the achievement of harmony between human beings and God, it was perceived at this juncture as an ideal society where the principles of 'brotherly' love and self-sacrifice on behalf of the other were *de rigueur*. But most significantly, the image and vision of Jerusalem, the holy city, was a call to human beings to respond to God's call to establish the Kingdom on earth, and ground it in the reality of social and national institutions. Thus, the Kingdom of God was transferred from the realm of speculative eschatology to the realm of empirical history, from the apocalyptic activity of God to the moral activity of humankind.

22

Religion and Politics

While it is true that Nonconformist theologians at this time had discovered a dynamic for social reform inherent in the Christian gospel, they were more often than not united also in the belief that it would not be through political methods that a new society would be established. Despite a general recognition of the need to address what was after all the overtly political issue of the social problem, it was also averred with increasing certainty during this period that Nonconformity had been over-political in its interests by becoming virtually synonymous with the political aims and policies of the Liberal Party.

Although not immediately apparent, these two factors, the need to address the social problem and the need to remain *apolitical*, became evident in the life and work of the Revd John Morgan Jones, who was ordained as pastor of Tabernacle English Congregational Church, Aberdare, in 1900 and would later become professor of Church History and subsequently principal of the Bala-Bangor Congregational seminary. A progressive in theological terms, he was at that stage a member of the Liberal Party and would sit as a Liberal member of the town council from 1904 to 1907. Two years into his pastorate, he addressed the Aberdare Free Church Federation giving his justification for ministerial involvement in politics.

The address is interesting because it delineates his theological beliefs while also outlining his political convictions. In so doing he offered the church a conception of its role both specifically in politics and more generally in civic life. Jones's thought and career marks the transition in Welsh Nonconformity which was about to occur. A young man in his late twenties, he still retained a link with the past in being a politically active Liberal. Even he would ultimately break with that past and join the Labour Party and, more significantly, abandon overtly party political activity in favour of a theology and churchmanship that looked directly to the gospel to influence society. He would eventually adopt the idea that God (the divine, the spiritual element inherent in life) would do this automatically providing that men and women, through a process of enlightened education, allowed their spiritual side to dictate all empirical activity. This, in his mind, would render the church redundant except as an educational institution.

But in 1902, and without discerning a definitive alternative, he represented the frustrations of other young Nonconformists by acknowledging the inadequacy of contemporary ecclesiastical practice:

> The old Protestantism was incomplete in its application of the Gospel and the religious spirit to social affairs, because it still retained the Romish idea that to look after the social condition of the world was secular work. Will our Free Church Councils help to show us that municipal government and imperial interests are sacred and religious affairs, and can we not through our councils make an attempt at least to apply our Christianity to our politics? Is it not the work of the Church to hold up even higher ideals for municipal activity – to keep our councillors reminded of the fact that the manufacture of men is the aim and end of all institutions: and that men of strong fibre can only be bred in clean, well-lighted streets and healthy homes, and sound moral and social conditions.[24]

The emphasis on 'ideals' along with the refusal to differentiate between the sacred and the secular is most significant. They mark Jones out as a convinced liberal in theology from the very beginning of his public ministry. Later, though dissatisfied with many of Campbell's ideas, he would align himself with the New Theology movement. His name became synonymous with liberal thinking particularly after he contributed articles to the *Christian Commonwealth*, the journal which more than any other became the platform for the New Theology.

Possibly because of Jones's later eminence as principal of a denominational seminary, it is difficult today to realize how radical his views were at the turn of the twentieth century. R. G. Owen recalled that following meetings of the local ministerial fraternal, such orthodox Calvinist divines as the Revds H. A. Davies, Cwmaman, and D. Silyn Evans, Aberdare, were often left concerned that the gospel had been completely dissipated. Stopping short of actually naming Jones, Welsh Congregationalism's Calvinistic patriarchs prayed, even from the platform during meetings of the Union of Welsh Independents, that the new theologians would be saved from their heretical ways.[25] But the intellectual climate was rapidly going against more traditional formulations of belief. Throughout his life, Jones would hold firm theological and political views and was not averse to expressing them. But in the years to come he would eschew direct political involvement in favour of Christian ethical influence on social matters. And it was in the most recent biblical scholarship that he gained inspiration for his interpretation of Christian faith. Although Jones had not yet worked out the full implications of Christianity's teaching as far as social and political matters were concerned, his attitude, at least in 1902, appears to have been pioneering. He had concluded that sociality was unavoidable for human beings and that every part of life, whether the religious or the political, the individual or the social, was not a distinct unit but a piece of the jigsaw which was to be fitted together in order to see the whole picture. Political conviction and religious adherence could not be kept apart nor could personal morality and public action be put asunder. For this reason he reminded municipal officers that the successful exercise of their duties was vital, for 'the Town Government is to a large extent responsible for the kind of men bred in the town.' This stance also had important implications for the church. The church was not primarily a political organization but a religious and spiritual one. Although, for Jones, religious and spiritual considerations led inevitably to political influence, the church ought still to be loyal to its particular commission, which he recognized at this time to be its prior concern over social matters:

> But amidst all our activities we must ever and always remember that we are Churches of Christ in the first place, and that in whatever direction we may carry on our work, it must be in the interests of the Religion of Jesus. All our ends and all our methods must be touched by the spirit of our Master. It is by rousing and awakening the hearts and souls of men that we must do our work and it is to make men nobler and purer that we exist. All else we do must be subordinate to that mission.[26]

Once it did this, its influence on all aspects of humanity, personal and social, was assured. It is how Welsh Nonconformist theologians tried to work this out in the years ahead, how exactly they perceived that 'the interests of the religion of Jesus' were best served, that will concern us in this book.

25

Till We Have Built Jerusalem...

During the religious revival of 1904–5 men and women had
sought, and discovered, a religion dedicated to eternal life in the
hereafter. In the following ten years a variety of factors transformed this into an expectancy that religion, to be of any value at
all, had to create a better environment and establish justice and
righteousness in this life and in this world. Much space has been
given to the way in which the labour movement came to offer just
such a 'religion', or at least came to fill the gap once filled by religion in the life of ordinary working folk. (There are many possible
definitions of the term 'religion'. The one used here would be that
of 'family-resemblance' – after Wittgenstein – that both
Nonconformity and the labour movement held certain common
characteristics such as the offer of salvation, a purpose and cause
given for human life and the absolute loyalty demanded of their
adherents.)[27] However, little has been written on the dedication of
at least a caucus of Welsh Nonconformist ministers and theologians to offer a specifically Christian theology which was
explained in contemporary philosophical terms and was compatible with scientific discoveries but also attempted to answer the
burning issues of the day. Such a response was forthcoming,
certainly by the outbreak of the Great War, amongst some
younger Nonconformists. The Revd Herbert Morgan wrote to the
Welsh Outlook in 1914 confessing that 'the modern emphasis of
social service' was 'the prime need of our time, and a first function
of a genuine Christianity'. Few would have disagreed with his
interpretation of contemporary needs, though the latter claim,
that Christianity had a primary duty to meet those needs, would
not have engendered universal approval. He continued:

> The social problem is uppermost today in the minds of all serious and
> thoughtful people and organized religion can only commend itself to
> them by helping effectively towards a solution. Practical and social
> issues have come to take the place of the old theological speculations.
> 'What must I do to be saved?' is a question still on men's lips, but salva-
> tion is conceived of socially and collectively. Real salvation must be
> achieved by the establishment of a social order which shall embody the
> greatest possible spiritual good in the widest and fullest distribution.
> Religion must be shown to be relevant, really relevant, to the actual

needs of our contemporary life in all its forms. This is why it must face, and must lead in solving, the social problem, the widely prevalent disorders of our common life.[28]

Interestingly, Herbert Morgan's article, entitled 'The religious outlook in Wales', lacked any reference to Christian doctrine or belief, or their application to an industrialized, scientific society. Instead, he maintained the classic liberal emphasis on the fundamental authority of experience and moral effort. Christian living required the imitation of Jesus 'who at the prompting of love, forgets himself in an absolute devotion to the widest service'. Salvation, then, is inextricably bound to moral decision. Ethical practice, not theological opinion, is what makes salvation real in people's lives. Given this ethical emphasis, it is hardly surprising that Morgan saw 'social service' as the primary work of the church, though he added (somewhat vaguely) that this must not be an appendage, but 'an inevitable expression of ... [Christianity] ... its very life and essence' supplying 'the motive that shall nerve us into action'.

Herbert Morgan had eagerly adopted both the current trends in theology and the new labour politics and social teaching of the ILP. New theological claims had led him, along with John 'Gwili' Jenkins, another liberal theologian, into publishing a commentary on part of the book of Isaiah, for which both men were censured by their fellow Baptists. Developments in labour politics had led him to vocal support for Keir Hardie and working-class parliamentary representation. He would later, in 1918, stand unsuccessfully for Parliament as an ILP candidate, and ultimately leave the ministry in order to follow a career in adult continuing education.

During the ten years between the religious revival of 1904–5 and the outbreak of war in 1914, Welsh Nonconformity had faced the onslaught of new and often hostile forces. The labour movement, with its militant unionism and Socialist threat to the Radical Liberal dominance in Welsh political life, the arrival of the union lodge and workingman's club to challenge the social supremacy of the chapel in the industrial communities of the south, and the gradual filtering through to Welsh ministers of the most recent discoveries of biblical criticism and philosophy all appeared to be replacing the old Calvinist orthodoxy and Nonconformist hegemony in Welsh life. Yet through all this, in the period before 1914, religionists, in the churches and in the labour movement, discovered Jerusalem. Labour agitators had preached the new Socialist message with a specifically religious ideal and imagery. Biblical criticism and theology were leading Nonconformist ministers and church members to consider that Jesus' purpose was to announce the arrival of a social utopia known as the Kingdom of God. Many labour stalwarts, including Keir Hardie, had offered the vision of a Socialist state as the fulfilment of Jesus' teaching. For them, Jesus' message exclusively concerned the establishment of this social state and had nothing to do with the Christian message, as traditionally understood, of individual redemption. But the Kingdom had also been reclaimed by Christian theologians. After the Great War other biblical images were used, particularly that of the (new) Jerusalem. Although this is associated in the New Testament with apocalyptic literature, it was not this aspect which was emphasized by Welsh theologians and labour leaders. Rather, such imagery was used to promote the necessity of human effort geared towards social amelioration, and in some sense it inspired a dedication to that end. It was this that prompted the widespread use of William Blake's poem quoted as a frontispiece to this book. Such was the importance of this poem that D. Miall Edwards translated the words into Welsh, later revising them so that they could be sung as a hymn to Hubert Parry's tune, 'Jerusalem'.

Edwards's translation was careful to adapt the poem to the Welsh situation. Rather than refer to 'dark Satanic mills' he spoke of the 'smoke and coal pits' (*gwlad y mwg a'r pyllau glo*), leaving his readers in no doubt that it was the industrial revolution, which had scarred the Welsh landscape with countless coal mines, slag heaps, and iron- and steelworks, and bringing with them slum housing and economic misery, that had set the task of solving the social problem. Industrial society was to be seen as the antithesis of Jerusalem, the city of God. In order to see a transformation each man and woman had to take up what arms they could find in order to bring about a better society. This required a love of fellow men and a dedication to their service, but it also needed to stem from a correct attitude to society and homeland. Thus, he replaced the references to England with Wales, linking the need for social reform with the need for a degree of patriotism and the recognition of national heritage.

By the 1920s, the poem had been adopted by the Student Christian Movement (SCM) specifically because it reflected the Christian social idealism of the period. Virtually all organizations with an interest in social and political reform recognized the unprecedented opportunity not only to build a truly just social organization, but a new world on the ruins of a society that had been deservedly swept aside by the European War. The poem also appeared to support the ideals and principles of the liberal theological establishment, particularly in its social and political concern and policy. Whatever meaning Blake had intended to convey, his words came to represent an inspirational vision which led men and women into the realm of ethical and political perfection, with the added bonus of religious imagery which, despite all evidence to the contrary, convinced its hearers (and singers) that God was surely going to establish the Kingdom. The basic premise of theology at the time was that of unavoidable progress, and Blake's poem seemed to suggest the inevitability of the Kingdom, or the city of God, being established certainly on this earth, if not within the lifetime of that generation.

The poem also encouraged the liberal theologians of the day that the precepts of their theology were vital to the quest for a better society. Jesus had become a great ethical teacher, his divinity measured only by the extent to which he displayed the eternal moral truths. His teaching centred on the Fatherhood of God and the natural brotherhood of the human race which this implied. But it was not his teaching alone that made an impression. Jesus' character and personality reflected his innate filial consciousness. He lived his life in communion with the Father and opened the way for others to enter into that communion. When other men and women were brought, through him, into a relationship with God, this would establish certain rights such as the inherent and eternal value of humankind. But it also involved moral responsibilities on the part of the individual; namely the embodiment of brotherly love, justice, fairness and equality within the sphere of all his (or her) activities. This would enable the establishment of the Kingdom of God which was most definitely perceived as a human function rather than a divine gift. This is fundamental in understanding the theology of the period. Nonconformist theologians basically attempted to apply a characteristically Christian doctrine of individual salvation to the need for social reform.

Society was to be transformed by large-scale individual effort. Thus the vital work of the church was to ensure that souls were saved with the hope that they would then sanctify themselves to service of the wider community, dedicated to establishing Christian principles in public life, particularly in political and industrial spheres. 'Salvation' was seen as a moral reorientation. It replaced the 'self' with society or 'the other' as the primary concern of the individual. It required that people look not to the 'things that are above' (cf. Col. 3.1–3), but to the surrounding environment, with the responsibility to make all possible attempts to improve the lot of others. Love of God was seen to be impossible without first opting to love one's neighbour (cf. 1 Jn. 4.20), and demonstrating that love by abolishing economic and social injustice. Simply because it was a moral reorientation, and because the philosophical context of the time had affirmed humankind's natural progression to higher and more advanced forms, education was considered to be the most vital element to the scheme. Moral values could be taught to succeeding generations. Once men and women had grasped the principles of the higher life, then progress in social terms was inevitable. As a result of this there was a danger, or at least a tendency, on occasion to recognize the education system as a far more convenient and expedient method of salvation than the churches themselves. On the other hand, men like Ebenezer Griffith-Jones recognized the importance of Christianity itself as a 'great educative influence' which would organize and inspire human potential to greater things and the achievement of the highest good.[29]

The fundamental issue for Nonconformists during the period between 1910 and 1939 was that of theology, recognizing this to mean both an adequate theoretical base as well as an inspiration and guide to Christian praxis. As they faced increasing demands for a social application of Christianity to meet the needs of modern society, they needed to discover and articulate a theology which geared itself towards those needs. Without an adequate ideological basis the Nonconformists would be doomed to inaction and, as a result, face relegation to the sideline in the social debate. Dedication to the establishment of a Socialist state, which some ministers enthusiastically adopted, was an insufficient response to the social crisis on the part of the church. Nonconformists could recognize the social problem as a manifestation of injustice, condemn it unequivocally and give cautious and tacit support to any organization seeking improvement. But, before commending any involvement in the new social movements as compatible with Christian faith and practice, Nonconformists needed to articulate the inherent dynamism of the Christian gospel as a more uniquely Christian response to social injustice. As a result, fundamental questions had to be asked concerning their message, the life and teaching of Jesus and ecclesiological practice as it had evolved to the present day. This implied a wholesale change in outlook, including the transference of emphasis from the future spiritual and eternal existence to the present, material and transient world. Perhaps even more vital was the need to recognize the interaction of circumstance, environment and character within the social system which left the individual at best only partly responsible for his situation and at worst the victim of forces beyond his control. That this largely occurred during a period of gradual but constant decline in chapel attendance and religious commitment (though not in actual membership figures) is undeniable. But it is not the intended aim of this book to explain why Welsh Nonconformity lost its status and influence among the working class; the answers in fact appear to be as numerous as the number of individuals who left the chapels. Instead, the purpose is to show that working-class withdrawal from the chapel could hardly have been due to a lack of social concern or a socially orientated theology on the part of Welsh Nonconformists. This in itself is a point which needs to be made. Welsh Nonconformity, certainly up to the Second World War, was distinctly social in its practical concern and in its theology. It is to the question of a Welsh social gospel, as it was worked out by the Nonconformist theologians of the period, that we must now turn.

2

Wales and the Social Gospel

All who believed were together and had all things in common; they would sell their possessions and goods and distribute the proceeds to all, as any had need. (Acts 2.44–5 NRSV)

Now the whole group of those who believed were of one heart and soul, and no one claimed private ownership of any possessions, but everything they owned was held in common. (Acts 4.32 NRSV)

The early years of the twentieth century were characterized by social and industrial unrest throughout Britain. South Wales appeared to be a hotbed of radical influences which were threatening the Liberal and Nonconformist *status quo* as well as highlighting the injustices of the industrial system itself. The Independent Labour Party (ILP), various Socialist organizations and the trade unions all attempted to give legitimate expression to the general aspirations of the working class, which occasionally spilled over into illegal and seditious activities. The temperature rose steadily during the first decade as the ILP increased in popularity and the most powerful local trade union, the South Wales Miners' Federation (the 'Fed'), increased in influence. The labour movement's message of social and political transformation came at a time when considerable attention was being paid to the housing and working conditions endured by so many ordinary people, and the transformation in social thinking which occurred during this period. According to Edward Foulkes, writing to *Y Geninen* in 1908, to live in Wales was the equivalent of living in a social utopia in which peace and harmony reigned and all people were content with their lot:

Blessed is Wales that there is very little of the urban poverty and wretchedness here. Even if the miners' work is miserable and dangerous, the towns are not so big as to imprison them. The fields and the groves are nearby, and the chapel and the church, and the choir and the eisteddfod keep their spirits up. Who can look at the choirs of the coalfields in the National Eisteddfod without seeing that they, both men and women, enjoy life?[1]

In 1909, a year after Foulkes's article, Dr Richards, the medical officer responsible for the Swansea Valley, recorded a completely different picture of working-class life in Wales:

> The overcrowding, consequent upon the scarcity of houses, in addition to having a detrimental effect upon health, has a demoralising influence upon the inhabitants, the lack of home comforts leads to the occupiers and lodgers seeking comfort and pleasures elsewhere and, while no other provision exists, the public-house with its attendant drinking is the chief attraction.[2]

Housing conditions in parts of the Swansea Valley had been recognized to be insanitary and unfit for habitation as early as 1902. But following the appointment of one Dr Lewis as local health inspector in the period 1910 to 1912, the issue was rarely out of the news. Lewis constantly drew attention to the local council's failure to act to provide better housing for the working class and he also drew attention to the fact that such an environment was sure to result in wide-scale immorality. His report for 1910 stated that 'these are conditions which are inimical to all forms of life except the lowest: fatal to moral growth and social uplifting'.[3] Overcrowding, the sharing of single dwellings by more than one family and the sharing of rooms by people of the opposite sex, were the particular concerns of the time.

The year 1910 supplied social reformers with statistics which enabled them to claim that Wales suffered housing conditions which were far worse than in any district in the rest of Britain. The death rate that year for England was 13.46 per thousand while in Wales it was 15.32 with Carmarthenshire recording the worst death rate for Britain as a whole (an interesting statistic if only because it was a rural, not an industrial, area which recorded the worst death rate). In an address given during the Carmarthen Eisteddfod in August 1911, D. L. Thomas concluded that 'over 4,200 persons died last year in Wales who would have survived under English conditions'. He compared Welsh districts with

Stepney in the heart of London's East End. Deaths in Stepney had numbered 13.5 per thousand, while the figure for Rhondda and Pontypridd was 15, for Merthyr and Llanelli it was 16, for Aberdare it was 16.5, and for Swansea it was 17.6. In Stepney 113 per thousand infants under one year of age had died, while the figures for Welsh districts were far higher: Swansea 123, Merthyr 134, Rhondda 136, Aberdare 149 and Llanelli 160. Swansea recorded 15 per cent more principal epidemic diseases than Stepney, while Merthyr and Aberdare recorded 33 per cent and Rhondda a massive 100 per cent.[4] As far as Thomas was concerned, society's ills were caused by poor housing and, consequently, slum housing posed the most urgent social problem. In solving that problem, the death rate, the infant mortality rate and the rate of epidemic disease would all decrease accordingly. But until that time the slum conditions endured by many in Wales would continue to affect adversely both the health and the morals of the population. Edward Foulkes had displayed a romanticism that was blind to the reality of the situation. Social problems had not emerged overnight but were the direct result of the rapid industrialization of south Wales as the coalfield was developed during the nineteenth century. The fact was that Welsh society had been like this for decades.

The interesting thing is that the medical officer's reports were not simply concerned with the disastrous effect of bad housing on people's health but also upon their morals. In demonstrating the moral effects of bad housing, the officers for health were implicitly accusing the church of failing in its duty, while at the same time encouraging church leaders to become involved in the social debate. The church, after all, was meant to be the guardian of all that was good and pure. If conditions external to the human heart could be shown to have an adverse effect on character, then the case for church involvement in political and social debates would be won. Alongside this, a class consciousness was emerging among the *gwerin*. Far from seeking 'fields and groves' to get away from the squalor, the working man was on the verge of revolt. Boiling point came during 1910–11 with the Cambrian Combine dispute, the Tonypandy Riots and the national railway strike, which saw in turn Metropolitan police officers and battalions of troops stationed in south Wales, and the death of two workers in Llanelli after the soldiers opened fire on protesters.

Law and order was threatened, even if only briefly. If solutions were not provided for social problems the situation could deteriorate from civil unrest into full-scale revolution.

In 1911, the churches took the initiative by convening special meetings to discuss the mounting social crisis and formulate a practical but fundamentally religious response. In September the annual Welsh School of Social Service was inaugurated at Llandrindod Wells, while a one-day conference to discuss the problem of working-class abandonment of the chapels was held in Cardiff in December that year.[5] All religious believers involved in the social debate, the Nonconformists particularly, now required a theology to undergird and provide justification for their social pronouncements. It was in the claims of nineteenth-century liberal theology that a basis for a distinctly social interpretation of Christianity was found. Such claims had developed in some degree as a response to the mounting social and religious crisis. Christianity began to be perceived as offering a social dynamic rather than providing exclusively for the salvation of individual souls. The teaching of the 'historical Jesus' was used to support such a view. Jesus came to be interpreted much more as an ethical teacher than as the Son of God, crucified for the redemption of the world. His teaching demanded complete personal dedication to the highest ethical standard. As a result, individual effort was perceived to be the key to all social renewal and thus Christianity's function became the 'preservation and enrichment of life', with the ultimate value of humankind being its fundamental theological assertion.[6] Henceforth, the church's task would be to proclaim the ethically superior life and establish a society – the Kingdom of God – which would be 'rooted and grounded in love'. With the emphasis having been put squarely on the responsibilities of each person, the idea of human partnership with God in the creation and evolution of a more just and fairer world developed rapidly.[7] By the 1920s, this interpretation of Christianity was being presented as 'positive religion', something real, and part of human experience. It stressed a practical and social view of religion over the theological and speculative, and placed the emphasis on ethical relationships rather than doctrinal accuracy. Such a religion was collective, retaining the value of each individual as he or she contributed to the construction of a perfect society. As a result, it would not only actively oppose the degrading and oppressive forces in society, but also offer a positive programme as an alternative to current social life.[8]

This was not the social gospel *per se*. It was presented as a reinterpretation of Christianity which restored its original values, principles and objectives. The claim was made that current Christianity, if true to its original aim of constructing a Kingdom, would *ipso facto* meet all social needs. Such an understanding of the nature of Christianity depended on the most recent developments in both Idealist philosophy and liberal theology, particularly that of the Ritschlian school. The seminal principles were the importance of experience, the eternal value of human beings which was clearly demonstrated in God's fatherly love and humankind's consequent 'brotherhood', and the ethical task of constructing God's Kingdom on earth.

During the late 1890s the theology of Albrecht Ritschl achieved a measure of popularity amongst the students of Mansfield College, the Congregational seminary and centre of Nonconformist thought in Oxford (though not at that time part of the University).[9] This popularity reached its height in 1899 when Andrew Fairbairn, the College principal, invited Alfred Garvie to lecture on Ritschl's thought. Even in 1899 the social question was 'one of the most characteristic features' of the age and Garvie referred specifically to social involvement as a gauge to the usefulness of the Ritschlian theology.[10] Yet the churches were not responding with any 'organizing principle' or 'Christian motives' which could then be employed to promote social change. They had merely offered the traditional view that individual salvation would automatically lead to social salvation. For Garvie, this preconception had to change:

> The task which the prominence of the social question sets to theology in the present day seems to be this, Christianity must be shown to be, not only in its truth but also in its life, a social community under God as well as an individual communion with God.[11]

Though not completely at ease with Ritschl's anti-metaphysical approach, Garvie believed that his emphasis on the Kingdom of God as a basic doctrinal category would enable the church to meet the social demands of the age.[12]

The popularity of Ritschl's theology at Mansfield College is of considerable significance for the development of Nonconformist social thought. Almost all the men who would lead the quest for a social interpretation of the Christian gospel, as well as many of the men who were responsible for the theological training of generations of ministers, had been students at some point of their academic career at Mansfield. The Revd Will Reason, secretary of the Social Service Committee of the Congregational Union of England and Wales and the author of several books discussing the church's social responsibility, the Revd Malcolm Spencer, Reason's successor, and Garvie himself had all been students there. But the link with Mansfield College was all the more significant for Welsh theology in the period between the two world wars. Fairbairn was the chosen consultant for the curriculum in theology when the University of Wales began to offer its own degrees in the subject, while in the main it was former Mansfield students who were appointed to the professorial chairs at the two Welsh Congregational colleges for most of the twentieth century, particularly in the years before the Second World War. Both Thomas Rees (1869–1926) and John Morgan Jones (1873–1946) became principal of the Bala-Bangor College, while David Miall Edwards (1873–1941), Joseph Jones (1877–1950) and John Daniel 'Vernon' Lewis (1879–1970) became professors at the Memorial College, Brecon. They all studied at Mansfield either in the last years of the nineteenth century or in the early years of the twentieth. The most important protagonists of a social Christianity, Thomas Rees, D. Miall Edwards and John Morgan Jones, were all present when Garvie delivered his lectures. Indeed, Edwards later confessed that the lectures on Ritschl had convinced him of the value of theological study.[13] The fourth member of this group was Herbert Morgan who, despite being a Baptist, also attended Mansfield in the years 1902–5. Undoubtedly their study and acceptance of Ritschl's theology while students at Oxford influenced the development of their social conscience. This is one reason why it was men from the Older Dissenting Congregational and Baptist traditions who became leaders in the social debate. A further important factor was that the Older Dissent had a far more pronounced political tradition than that of the Methodists. The Independents and Baptists also enjoyed at least theoretical freedom from confessions of faith, which enabled them to explore ideological areas officially declared off-limits for those of other traditions. If these Dissenters had a weakness it was the lack of denominational direction, a policy which had proved to be impossible to uphold within religious traditions that emphasized the importance of the local, gathered congregation. As a result they tended to contribute strong personalities and cogent theologians to the social debate. The Calvinistic Methodists, on the other hand, took a lead in facing the issues as a denomination, particularly after the Great War. They instigated the five-year 'Campaign for Morals and Religion' (*Ymgyrch Moes a Chrefydd*) in 1921 and adopted a report of their Reconstruction Commission on the Church and Social Issues in the same year. Their contribution was connexional and denominational rather than individual. While it is true that the Welsh Independents also published a report, *Cenadwri Gymdeithasol yr Efengyl* ('The Social Mission of the Gospel') in 1923, it could not be considered as a denominational statement of policy and, as a result, it remained no more than a discussion document. More important than the document itself were its authors, particularly Thomas Rees and D. Miall Edwards. The intention of this chapter will be to trace the development of the main themes of liberal theology in the thought of the principal Welsh Nonconformist theologians of the period. We must ask whether or not they offered a tenable 'social gospel' in reality.

David Miall Edwards

D. Miall Edwards[14] was the most productive Welsh theologian of his generation. He gained an international reputation as a philosopher following the publication of his book, *The Philosophy of Religion* (London, 1924) for which the University of London awarded him the degree of Doctor of Philosophy in 1925. Such was the scholarship and erudition displayed in the book that it gained an international readership and was even translated into Japanese. In the same year that the University of London honoured his work, the University of Wales conferred on Edwards the degree of Doctor of Divinity (*honoris causa*). Most of his work attempted a synthesis of two needs, namely that social reform should be supported by the gospel, and that theology should respond to the intellectual needs of the day. He was appointed successor to Thomas Rees as professor of Christian Doctrine and the Philosophy of Religion at the Memorial College, Brecon, in 1909 and although his duties there were principally didactic and theoretical, it is also true that the practical concerns of the age were never far from his mind.

Edwards believed that organized religion was vital to the life of society, but in order to meet the needs of the time religion would have to include three major aspects: worship, theological expression and social service. Only when it provided all three would religion be able to make a constructive contribution to solving the social problem. Worship pointed men and women away from themselves and towards God with no thought of personal or social gain.[15] The task of theology was to commend religion to the rational mind, but its value, he claimed, 'is tested by its capacity to generate a healthy social consciousness and a high sense of social responsibility'.[16] Thus, vital as worship and theology were, the ultimate guarantor of the value of religion would be the moral effect it had on its practitioners. Worship, and theology in particular, would have to be geared towards promoting a particular ethical response in the congregation. For Edwards, this was where the religion of the day was deficient and, throughout his years as a minister and theological tutor, he was at the forefront of movements intended to give practical guidance to ordinary Christians concerning the application of their faith. His own regard for Christian social service resulted in a commitment to the Welsh School of Social Service, and in fact Edwards had helped organize its first gathering in 1911. But he was aware of the danger of overemphasizing one of the three aspects of religion. Nonconformist failure in the past had been to consider worship, theology and social service as distinct units and not part of the one single religious endeavour. Edwards attempted to address all three aspects in his work. He first turned to theological expression, convinced that theology had not fulfilled its proper function of providing a clear declaration of the social and economic principles implicit in the teaching of Jesus. The principle of the cross, namely self-sacrificial love, offered direction and inspiration for the social movement.[17] But gospel principles had to be drawn out, emphasized and clarified, as well as given validity and authority, by the provision of an adequate and systematic theology.

As a liberal theologian convinced of the importance of doctrine,

Edwards emphasized the need for the rational expression of Christian faith and experience. Important as practical measures were in the pursuit of a better and more just social system, they would never be sufficient in themselves. There would always be a need to express fundamental principles in order to inspire social improvement; this was the doctrinal task facing the church. Admittedly, theology's need to speak directly to the problems of the age required a reinterpretation of the traditional dogmas of the church in the light of the most recent biblical criticism, of philosophical and scientific advance, and an appreciation of the needs of the modern world. But it required that theological reflection be given a vital, and even seminal, place.

For Edwards, theology was crucial for an understanding of both the gospel and the social needs of the day. It is unlikely that his interest in social problems and his conviction that it was the Christian experience alone which could ultimately solve them, arose from the wretched and unjust conditions endured by the majority in the wake of industrialization. Llanfyllin, Llandderfel and Bala, all small Welsh-speaking rural communities, were the towns of his youth, and his upbringing had been grounded in the traditions of Nonconformity in religion and the Liberal Party in politics. Following an apprenticeship as a gardener, he attended universities at Bangor and Oxford before being ordained in 1900 at Blaenau Ffestiniog in the heart of the slate-quarrying district. He moved to Brecon, another small rural town, in 1904 where he spent the rest of his life. Even when he was most involved in the social debate, he was actually still quite detached from the areas that suffered the despoiling effects of rapid industrialization most. He had little or no direct experience of the living and working conditions of the south Wales Valleys or of the revolutionary politics of the time. This is a vitally significant point. Rather than being awakened by the direct experience of living in economic hardship, his social conscience had been stirred and sustained by more theoretical considerations; by an understanding of the gospel in the terms of philosophical Idealism, the doctrine of God's immanence, and the social implications of the Ritschlian interpretation of the Kingdom of God.

As one schooled in Idealistic philosophy, it was the Hegelian dialectic, the vision of a world as it should be, or the Kingdom of God, which lay behind both his recognition of society as it was and his longing for a better world. His vision and his critique were made possible because of his acceptance that the fulfilment of the moral, eternal values at the heart of the Divine was the purpose for which human beings were created. The world was that in which 'gradually and increasingly those ideals and intentions which have their eternal home in the mind of God are realized'.[18] The influence of Ritschlian theology is evident in Edwards's use of the term 'value'. He continued to propagate the idea that 'moral values' provided the key to understand both God and humankind. Each human being needed to be understood as a 'moral personality',[19] thus enhancing individual status and emphasizing the importance of moral over economic, industrial or commercial considerations. The centrality of value in his thought, both the implicit value of the individual human personality and the requirement that all people recognize the eternal values as vital to the religious spirit, meant that slum life could not be tolerated. Liberal theology's greatest contribution at the time was that it recognized this, and used it as its fundamental axiom in a search for a possible social gospel.

Doctrinal formulae were called into question as a result of the ascendancy of moral considerations. Although Edwards was prepared to reinterpret traditional doctrine radically, he was not willing to discard the doctrines themselves. This resulted in virtually unrecognizable expressions of traditional doctrines such as the Person of Christ.[20] The basic inspiration for this reinterpretation was his conviction that the creeds spoke in a language which was completely alien to the modern mind. Furthermore, the traditional doctrinal expressions of the church were far from offering any kind of solution to the demands of the modern age. Chief amongst contemporary problems was that of the social question. Consequently, doctrine had to be delineated in such a way that it provided an answer to this question, even if this meant that its content would have to be radically transformed. This was clearly demonstrated in an address given by Edwards to the Welsh School of Social Service at Llandrindod in 1913.

In this address, Edwards attempted to demonstrate the social implications of certain key Christian doctrines. The doctrine of immortality gave a greater value to present life through linking it to the life of eternity.[21] Providence had encouraged men and women to leave this world a better place than when they had entered it.[22] The Trinity pointed to the existence of a fellowship within the Godhead, and thus constituted a pattern on 'which human society should be constituted'. He later modified his position over the doctrine of the Trinity. His earlier comments arose from a virtually ontological preconception, centring on the actual relationships thought to exist within the Godhead. Later, he stated that the Trinity's significance lay in a conception of religious experience. The Christian experienced God as creator, as the one who sacrifices, and as the one who enlightens and leads humankind towards the formulation of a society, namely the church.[23] Although the nature of his explanation had changed, he still saw the relevance of the Trinity for a doctrine of human society, even if such a doctrine was not forthcoming. Having said that, it should be noted that Edwards's position on the Trinity poses certain theological difficulties. Saying three things about God's activity, or three things about how human beings and God relate to each other, is not necessarily an affirmation of the Trinity. It is in fact true that a unitary God can be *experienced* as a creator, as one who sacrifices and as one who enlightens. Furthermore, it is the case that Christian theology has tended to affirm that these attributes rightly belong to the triune God whom we know as Father, Son and Spirit. Appropriation of divine actions to the persons of the Trinity has usually been held to be an inadequate interpretation of the Christian doctrine of God. Neither is it without significance that, in his mature exposition of the doctrine of the Trinity in 1932, Edwards chose not to affirm the human experience of God as that of a heavenly Father. Certainly during the Llandrindod address, and in most of his work, Edwards had posited that God's Fatherhood provided the basis for human value and a paradigm for the interpretation of religious experience. As such it was the seminal theological component in a social gospel. However, it seems that as he reflected on the doctrine of the Trinity later in life, God's Fatherhood lost something of its appeal. The reason for this was never made apparent.

Continuing his Llandrindod address, Edwards claimed that the Fatherhood of God, carrying as it did the corollary of the Brotherhood of Man, posited an infinite value upon all humankind and had inspired much social action.[24] The doctrine of the person of Christ, or the incarnation, demonstrated 'the sanctity of human life in all its interests and relations, the sacredness of that human nature which was found competent to be the abode of God'.[25] The Holy Spirit was the 'doctrine of the immanence of God in human life' which is present in the 'labour of all those who strive for the realisation of his Kingdom on earth'.[26] The Atonement demonstrated the infinite nature of the divine love and the value of human beings in God's sight, as well as the existence of sin as the root of all social problems. However, he did not explain whether it was personal sin or structural sin or both which caused social evil. He emphasized the act of atonement rather than the reason why atonement was necessary. It did mean that an important question in the social debate, namely what caused society's problems, was left unanswered and this inevitably meant that direct solutions were more difficult to discover. Although Edwards held fast to the traditional doctrinal expression of Christian truth, it should be clear that his interpretation of the faith and his consequent exposition of doctrine differed considerably from classical orthodoxy. Nevertheless, the meaning which Edwards attributed to traditional doctrines succeeded in doing one vitally significant thing. It transferred the centrepoint of theology from God to humankind. Even God's Fatherhood and the person of Christ remained meaningful only because of the wider implications for men and women which Edwards interpreted to be inherent in the traditional formulations. This was a fine attempt at expressing the basis for a theological anthropology, or perhaps even an anthropocentric theology.

For Edwards, the starting-point in theological construction was not the traditional interpretation of dogmatic formulae but the application of theological ideas represented by the doctrines to the modern crisis. All doctrine was to be reinterpreted according to Edwards's acceptance of the tenets of liberal theology and philosophical Idealism. Following Schleiermacher, the theological task was to interpret religious, moral and spiritual experience. The significance of the doctrine of the Person of Christ was that in Jesus of Nazareth religious experience had reached an unprecedented height.[27] This, of course, entailed considerable reinterpretation of the classical doctrine:

Our formula [for the doctrine of the person of Christ] would be something like this: 'One nature of the man Jesus Christ filled in all his

43

being with the quality of God.' We confess that this is a somewhat radical change. It is the change from the theocentric to the anthropocentric Christology, but with the important qualification that the *anthrōpos* is not the antithesis of *Theos*, but is in Christ the abode of God.[28]

Thus, in his reconstruction Edwards attempted to retain the uniqueness of Jesus' person by stressing his value as a man whose experience came closer to the Divine than any other in human history. The implication was that Jesus revealed the divine potential of all humankind, for there is no *logical* reason why all *anthrōpoi* should not in some measure also be 'the abode of God'. Jesus became the example to be imitated, the corollary being that human beings possessed the necessary means to succeed in so doing. Unfortunately, Edwards never acknowledged, and therefore never applied himself to, the inherent problem in such a Christological understanding. If other people *could* reach such heights, did they too become divine and, as a result of this, was there the possibility that all men and women could be Christs? The ethically superior Christ becomes solely the precursor to an ethically reformed human race. Once the latter is achieved, the former *ipso facto* loses his uniqueness. This is nowhere near the credal orthodoxy which sees the sinner redeemed through Christ's sacrificial death and through unmerited grace, and invited with him to experience the benefits which are his alone. Such a radical reconstruction of the 'value' of Jesus' person was obviously the result of Edwards's theological understanding, rather than any kind of response to the need of society. But it naturally lent itself to social reform by insisting that the means for reform were inherent in humankind. According to this interpretation, it was the moral rather than the metaphysical which was important in theology. This was reflected and supported by Edwards's interpretation and development of the concept of 'value', both the inherent value of men and women, which was supported by the doctrine of the Fatherhood of God and the doctrine of Atonement, and also in the ethical interpretation of the Kingdom, which became the moral task and responsibility of all Jesus' followers. According to Edwards, Christians existed for the sole purpose of realizing the Kingdom of God on earth, an all the more vital point 'while unrighteous conditions prevail among

men'.[29] In this he satisfied himself that he had done justice both
to the traditional Nonconformist view that each man and woman
stood before God as a responsible individual, and to the need for
a better society which was met in Jesus' teaching by the concept
of the Kingdom of God.

To Edwards, the Kingdom involved both individual and social
aspects and so met all the world's needs. The personal aspect
required that all people deepen their spiritual life through repentance and the recognition of the lordship of Christ over their lives;
this would enable men and women to judge everything according
to Christ's standards.[30] The social aspect would be the inevitable
result of the spread of religious influence until all things would be
brought under Christ's authority.[31] Edwards continually stated
that a correct translation of the Greek *basileia tou theou* would
render not the 'Kingdom of God' but the 'reign of God'.[32] With
Ritschl, Edwards posited that the Kingdom represented God's
reign over *humankind* and, following the recognition of his reign,
the formulation of a perfect society would become inevitable.[33]
His interpretation of even the apocalyptic view of the Kingdom
included its orientation towards a social ideal established within
the realm of space and time. The apocalyptic interpretation
proved that 'the Christian experience contains the immovable
belief in the fact that the powers which will save the world from
the grip of the forces of darkness and save the believers, come
"from above"'.[34] But the Kingdom was also 'in your midst' and
required that all of life be so orientated to realize the 'gracious
purposes of God'.[35] It was 'the organised community of those
who recognise and obey God's sovereign will. It is the realisation
of God's will in all the relationship of men to each other; it is the
answer to the prayer "Thy Kingdom come, thy will be done on
earth as it is in Heaven."'[36] Because Edwards could claim that
'the individual can only attain fulness of life in so far as he
partakes of and contributes to the life of the community',[37] he
had to insist that it was through the development of moral character, whose primary function was sacrificial service, that the
Kingdom would finally be established. As a result, both the
church and all movements and societies which sought social
reform, had to concentrate on the moral regeneration of the individual. Such regeneration would be achieved by the appeal to
higher moral values, particularly the principles of love and service

for the benefit of the community. These principles alone justified all social activity in the personal, economic and industrial spheres and the first aim of social reform would be to establish moral values as the governing principle of trade, commerce and all occupations.[38]

Edwards believed that producing men and women of good character through encouraging the adoption of the moral principles of love and self-sacrifice would naturally create a perfect society, but that it was also crucial to recognize that social conditions could impinge upon such character development. That alone was the inspiration for, and validation of, social reform as well as the justification of the church's role in the social debate:[39]

> If it is true that our present civilization is so destitute of the Spirit of Christ that it creates pagans more rapidly than the churches create Christians, then it is obvious that the responsibility of the church is to Christianize civilization, and create an atmosphere that will bring about social regeneration.[40]

The church, according to Edwards, had forgotten 'that a converted man cannot fully and permanently function in an unconverted system'.[41] While the church had concentrated on individual conversion, social conditions themselves had forced ordinary people to concentrate on the struggle to live, to the total exclusion of spiritual considerations. It was therefore true that the conditions of working-class life were actually an obstacle to effective witness by the church. As a result, claimed Edwards, the church should raise its voice against such conditions.[42] However, because even the most perfect of social systems would be weakened by the individual sins of the people contained within them, Edwards insisted that a new world would only be achieved by the development of personality and moral character. He sought to avoid a polarizing of the social and the individual which would lead to an over-concentration on the one to the detriment of the other. Environment and character interacted in such a complex way that reform of both needed to be pursued simultaneously.[43]

To the extent that the contemporary social and labour movement drew attention towards the need for social and moral reform, Edwards was happy to welcome it. As such, it was a practical revelation of the eternal, moral values of truth and goodness.

He did not, however, offer unqualified support for the social movement. He criticized social reformers for overemphasizing the influence of environment and thereby neglecting the true path to social reform, namely the development of character. This stemmed from his belief that moral and therefore personal values, rather than material ones, formed the root of reality and thus the basis of any true reform. Despite the genuine need for social improvements, it was the church's task to emphasize the moral importance of personality. The fundamental basis to the new society that was to be established was that all things exist in order to promote and develop human character:

> The social problem is at bottom an ethical and spiritual problem. It is the question of the right of personality to have adequate room in the world to expand and grow to the measure of the stature of its possibilities. And what right have we to expect a human soul to blossom as the rose in the slum? Every child born into the world has an intrinsic right to have a reasonable opportunity for self-expression.[44]

It was religion alone which possessed the dynamic to transform character, which meant that the social movement, in order to be effective, needed to be allied with the forces of religion.[45] Religion was necessary in order to give strength and depth to the new society and rescue it from superficial materialism.[46] Moral and spiritual values were to govern all aspects of life. Thus if industry were to be justified at all, it had to be shown to contribute to the improvement of human life. Its purpose was to serve the employer, the employee and the community at large. No other purpose could be justified. On that basis, industry as it had developed during the nineteenth century, could no longer be tolerated. Its orientation was 'thoroughly pagan' because it had caused class suspicion instead of promoting fellowship and brotherhood.[47] Industry needed to be reformed along the principles of partnership and social service, and the governing principle of self-interest overthrown. In this, and in the practical measures he advised, Edwards demonstrated that on occasion the moral principles which guided his thinking did enable him to take sides over particular issues. For Edwards, there were five aspects involved in a truly moral approach to social reform. First was the need to raise the standard of the worker's life by establishing a living wage; second was the provision of adequate leisure time and facilities; the third involved giving the worker responsibility in the running of his industry; the fourth concerned security for working men through ensuring continuity of employment; and fifth was the establishment of a better living environment for the working class.[48] An industrial system needed to be developed which embodied the principle of social service and the moral responsibility of each worker in the control of industry.[49] In recognizing himself as a 'partner' in the control of industry, Edwards believed that each worker would be provided with the moral status both to improve his own life and to contribute to the social good. Such a 'recognition of the personality of the worker would enhance his self respect and feeling of personal responsibility and pride in his work'. Edwards believed that the church had lost the loyalty of the working class through its failure to express its mission clearly, in stark contrast to the clarity of purpose and ideal found in the labour movement.[50] He sought to correct this by emphasizing a Christianity which demonstrated its wholeness, that the social problem could be included in an overarching philosophy based on the principles of value and service. The church, he claimed, had not hitherto worked out a Christian theory of society or applied its principles to all aspects of life. It was, then, theology which was at fault and what was particularly lacking was an adequate apprehension of the 'foundation of the whole superstructure'.[51] Here Edwards betrayed his unwavering allegiance to philosophical Idealism. All reality formed an ultimate unity. Such an ideal prevented Edwards from viewing individual issues in isolation but also dictated his belief that the right principles would answer those problems and affect the whole of existence. As a result, Edwards insisted that the prerequisite for correct human relationships was a right relationship with God. Unfortunately, this dependence on Idealist philosophy also prevented him from being pragmatic about social questions and ultimately prevented him from offering any specific answers. Edwards claimed that the church's purpose in entering the social debate was not to answer any particular social question but to demonstrate the principles of a fulfilled life. That was possible only through the gospel of Jesus Christ. Life had to be 'elevated' towards 'an atmosphere of idealism' which would demonstrate the 'high dignity and destiny' of life and would be 'practical and constructive'. The fundamental need was to view life in its relation to the Divine and to apply the divine principles of love, truth, beauty and sacrificial service to matters of everyday life:[52]

> It [Christianity] must insist that economics and politics are not self-contained and independent departments of life but are within the control of the spiritual life. It should aim at humanising and spiritualising even the industrial system by relating it to the central purpose of man's life and to the Kingdom of God.[53]

Although he regarded organized religion as important, Edwards's adoption of liberal theology and monistic philosophy forced him to believe that the essence of religion, namely brotherly love and service, existed outside the church. Because of his belief in the immanence of God, he saw a basic relationship between religion and the social movement. God, being immanent, could be found wherever the higher morality and the eternal values of truth, goodness and beauty were revealed, in the world and in the church. There was, then, an inherent connection between ideas about God and ideas about social reform, and it was in the nature of reconciliation to God that human relationships, too, would ultimately be reconciled.[54] This was achieved partly as the result of the inevitable moral transformation which followed fellowship with the Divine, and partly as an automatic consequence of God's immanence within the creation: 'Behind all our efforts for social reorganization, if the effort is to possess strength and effectiveness, we must possess deep convictions which are based on the character of God and in the order and moral purpose of the creation.'[55]

The Socialist and labour movements, he claimed, were truly religious when they encouraged selflessness and humanitarian concern; the desire for social amelioration and justice 'is born of religious faith'. Where such philanthropic work existed, where the eternal moral values were given an opportunity to grow and flourish, there the religious spirit was also incarnate, and true religion was to be found:[56] 'And truly the battle to win for the worker better facilities to develop his personality is an essentially religious thing, and part of the work of the Kingdom of God in the world.'[57] But Edwards also warned that those groups which sought social amelioration alone were in danger of losing sight of the higher moral concerns and descending into selfishness and materialism. The major cause of the social problem was, according to him, that industry was materialistic and encroached on the moral and spiritual purposes of life to which it should have been subservient.[58] The existence of industry could only be justified at all according to a philanthropic purpose. The Christian principles should reign supreme there too.[59] It was for the labour movement to ensure that moral values were not obscured through concentration on material gain.

In Edwards's view, the question of nationalism was related to that of social reform. As the establishment of basic principles was essential for reform, so a national ideal was required to inspire men to recognize their social status and responsibilities. He discussed the topic at length in a philosophical and detached, if not wholly abstract, manner.[60] However undeveloped his ideas were, he nevertheless believed that Welsh civilization could only be reformed by means of the Welsh Nationalist spirit. In post-Versailles Europe it is no surprise that he came to believe that Wales should be granted self-determination.[61] But he was never a member of the élitist, and somewhat peripheral, Nationalist Party, nor did he support a narrow and exclusivist nationalism. In fact, as a keen supporter of the League of Nations, and as one who deeply believed in the brotherhood of man, Edwards desired international rapprochement, and eventually even a world-state.[62] This did not imply a hegemonous, monolithic state that stifled and ultimately obliterated national characteristics. Instead, it represented the logical conclusion of practising a doctrine of brotherhood. All people were united as brothers and sisters, and a world-state would ensure that this resulted in justice and equality for all. On the personal level, it would require that all people contribute to the well-being of the whole, world-wide community and, under the influence of Hegel's philosophy, Edwards therefore looked to Welsh nationalism to contribute something unique, something of the Welsh spirit, to such a world-state. His nationalism called on Wales and the Welsh to take their place on the world stage:

The true nationalist is a world citizen; the windows of his mind face the four corners of the world, and the doors of his sympathy are open towards all the families of the earth (*y mae ffenestri ei feddwl yn wynebu pedwar ban y byd, a drysau ei gydymdeimlad yn agored tuag at holl dylwythau'r ddaear*). But he is anxious also for his own nation to take her rightful place within the partnership of the nations and fulfil her mission within the human fellowship. And he believes that it would be through preserving the Welsh language and other national characteristics and sanctifying them on the altar of mankind that she would make her best contribution to the life of the world.[63]

It was his desire to promote a philosophy which expressed the essentials of Welsh national life,[64] but in order to 'take our part with dignity in the work of promoting international peace and justice', Wales needed its own Parliament. Once self-determination had been granted, then Wales could apply for a seat in the League of Nations. Edwards never really explained this idea as clearly as he might. If he had, then the forces of liberal theology, already linked to the need for social reform, would have been linked also to a specifically Welsh, though not necessarily partisan, religious nationalism. Instead culture, nationalism and the language issue remained abstract concepts in much of his writing.

Through arguments such as these, Edwards believed he had made a contribution to the social debate that was not governed by party-political motives but instead arose directly from his understanding of the gospel. His emphasis on individual personality also maintained the link with traditional, evangelical Christianity's aim of personal salvation. His scheme left open the possibility for political action but kept party politics at arm's length. None of this was presented under the specific title of a social gospel. When Edwards finally attempted a systematization of his thought in 1929 it was obvious that he had identified his own theological scheme as a means to social reform. Individual 'persons' would save society through the recognition of the lordship of Christ and the commitment to work out the principles of his teaching in practical forms.[65] Edwards averred that the gospel, when understood correctly, was essentially social.[66] As a result, the actual title 'social gospel' was unimportant.

Edwards's aim was to be a catalyst, attempting to cause others to discover the theological needs of modern society. His scheme concentrated on Christian principles which dealt initially with the relationship betweeen human beings and God possible through Jesus Christ. The natural by-product of this was the reform of human relationships. Such a view was based on the doctrine of God's Fatherhood which implied the brotherhood of the human race. It meant championing the spiritual over the material and the sanctity of human personality as an implication of its spiritual value and its relationship with the Divine. Although humankind possessed an inherent value, and that value was appropriated individually, the resulting status achieved also invoked responsibility, namely the stewardship in all aspects of life and self-sacrifice for the good of the community. Thus would the Kingdom of God be established wherever God's reign was recognized in all aspects of human life.[67]

Although Miall Edwards occasionally demonstrated misplaced optimism, he was generally able to read clearly the contemporary social situation. In the 1920s he recognized that despite the church's zeal for social matters, the new interpretation of Christianity had not permeated through to actual church members. Edwards was horrified that ordinary people had been more attracted to the religion of discontent and revolt as represented by the Socialist movement than to the idealism and contentment of the religion of Jesus. There were two reasons for this. In the first place, the labour movement was a highly organized propaganda machine. It was getting its message across to its public in an attractive and an effective way. But alongside this, men took more interest in labour problems than church polity, for it was these which were felt to touch them more directly.[68] The labour movement had managed to convince the masses that its message was relevant, and that in his everyday struggle for existence, the working man found labour agitators to be speaking the truth. And in this Edwards touched upon the greatest weakness within Nonconformist social concern. It was not reaching the people who needed to hear it, neither the working class who suffered the injustices of industrial society and regarded the church as champion of the status quo, nor the government to which they looked to change the situation. Moreover, this failure was shared by Edwards himself. Despite his insistence on the need for understanding, and his efforts to disseminate knowledge amongst ordinary people in university extension classes, public meetings, lectures and sermons, the message seemed largely to fall on deaf ears.

Despite the lack of response, it was Edwards more than anyone who attempted to bring social Christianity to the attention of ordinary chapel-goers. He did this in sermons and in poetry, particularly in poems which he intended to use as hymns during worship. He was not an accomplished poet, but during the last twelve years or so of his life as he tried to cope with a debilitating illness, he found personal solace and intellectual stimulation in the writing of strict metre verses (*englynion*). A series of his *englynion* entitled 'My Heroes' (*Fy Arwyr*) appeared in the *Western Mail* and included tributes to David Lloyd George and Sir Henry Jones, indicating even during the late 1920s and early 1930s where Edwards's political and philosophical sympathies truly lay. Similarly, his contribution to the hymnary is not the greatest in Welsh literature, but it demonstrates the importance that Edwards attached to both social issues and the primary need for worship. Thus, he fulfilled his responsibility as a professional, church-based theologian not only by writing essays and expounding the teaching of Christianity but also through providing doxological material which encompassed a theological position sympathetic to the social needs of the age. And he did this through the medium of the Welsh language. His translation, and subsequent modification, of part of William Blake's poem *Milton* has already been mentioned. He also published his 'Prayer for Students' in *Yr Efrydydd* and his 'Social Hymns' in *Y Dysgedydd*.[69]

The publication of Edwards's 'Social Hymns' was symbolic of the importance which the social problem and Christianity's response to it had accrued within Welsh Nonconformity. The Revd J. Griffiths, a Baptist minister at Ammanford who had written on social issues for *Y Darian* from a Christian standpoint, had written a circular to several ministers bewailing the lack of hymns concerning the social side of religion in Welsh:

> If a series of meetings were held to clarify the Bible's social message, we would not have any appropriate hymns despite searching all the books. Why is this? Is it not because of the simple fact that we have only just realized the value and meaning of the social gospel. The majority of our hymns were born in the period of individualism before we clearly saw the meaning of our prayer to do God's will '*on earth* as it is in heaven'.

Edwards confessed that these words 'touched his heart' and he offered two hymns as an encouragement to others with greater poetic skill to make more appropriate offerings. This showed Edwards's readiness to attempt to meet what he perceived to be the needs of the day. Even hymnology should be geared towards meeting those needs, and in his 'Prayer for the World' (*Gweddi dros y Byd*) and 'Social Hymn' (*Emyn Gymdeithasol*) Edwards attempted to do just that, and to make provision for the primary aspect of religious life, namely worship. He also suggested possible hymn-tunes to which these poems could be sung.

Both hymns follow a similar pattern, composed in the traditional form of an eight-lined verse and both followed similar ideological development which reflected Edwards's theological views. 'Prayer for the World' had three verses which called on God to act to bring his Kingdom to the earth, which would 'transform the desert into a fair paradise for God' (v.1). God's will was to be done on earth through 'the dawn of the light of his love' which would naturally encourage the practice of justice by earthly governments (v.2). The third verse was a prayer for Jesus to rule on earth and to 'burn away all violence and treachery' by his heavenly fire. The final verse was an invocation of divine power for the singer to recognize his or her responsibility as a citizen of the world and then to act upon that responsibility:

> Arglwydd Iôr, sancteiddier D'enw
> Ar y Ddaear lle 'rwy'n byw.
> A sancteiddia finnau hefyd
> I wasanaeth dynol ryw;
> Ennyn ynnof fflam Dy gariad
> Yn aberthol nefol dân,
> Fel y gallwyf lwyr ymdrechu
> Troi wylofain byd yn gân.[70]

Similarly the 'Social Hymn' called on God to 'support the weak and the poor' and to 'subdue all oppressors' (v.1), and then, by his love, to 'reconcile ... all the kingdoms of man' and to establish peace on earth (v.2). Then the hymn turned towards the individual by invoking personal responsibility once again:

O Dduw, fy Ngheidwad innau,
Rho'th Ysbryd imi'n awr,
Yn ysbryd o wasanaeth
Yn rhwymau'th gariad mawr;
Ti feddyg clwyfau dynion
Rho imi ddwyn y groes
A llwyr gysegru 'mywyd
I leddfu dynol loes.[71]

It was God's transforming power, then, which the hymns initially celebrated. God could turn men and women from sin to life, and from selfish acts to acts of incredible valour and self-sacrifice. This was the purpose of redemption, that human beings sanctify themselves to the service of the higher good and thus establish the kingdom of human brotherhood on earth where all physical and spiritual needs are met. This, for Edwards, would be the revelation of God's Kingdom.

Edwards was a theological humanist. He never denied the existence of God, or his importance to the well-being of the universe, but God tended to take a subordinate place to humankind in his system. 'Man' had been endowed with ultimate 'value' and possessed the means for improvement through the immanent deity. Everything which existed did so for his benefit. Through dedicated service, he possessed the ability to work out his own salvation and that of his fellows. Despite his theological language, in a scale of values man appeared to become more important than God in Edwards's thought.

Edwards was sympathetic to the claims of the oppressed and came closer than any Welshman of his generation to offering a social understanding of the gospel rather than merely emphasizing the moral imperatives of Christianity. But he was ultimately too much of a Protestant to lay responsibility anywhere but squarely upon the individual, and too much of a philosophical Idealist not to see this as the beginning of a true social reform. He died on 29 January 1941 and D. J. Williams (Bethesda), wrote of him, 'he was the greatest light of our theological forms (*ffurfiau diwinyddol*), and in his death, Wales lost her principal theologian.'[72]

Thomas Rees

Thomas Rees[73] in some ways personifies the withdrawal of
Nonconformity from overtly political activity. He was appointed
to the chair of Christian Doctrine and Philosophy of Religion at
the Memorial College, Brecon, while still a student at Mansfield
College, Oxford. During his years in the town, he played an active
role in local politics as a fervent Liberal, taking particular interest
in matters relating to education.[74] When he was elected principal
of the Bala-Bangor College in 1909, however, all party political
activity ceased. Rees's political interest had always been dictated
by principle, but before 1909 these principles had been virtually
synonymous with Liberal policy. From then onwards, it was the
overt connection with the Liberal Party which diminished, though
he continued to voice his opinion whenever he perceived that a
moral principle was at stake. Rees's argument identified the task
of the minister of religion as bringing the 'light of Christ' to bear
upon all aspects of human life. This would involve the application
of Christian 'principles' to laws and social conditions as well as
individual lives 'so as to transform them into an environment
where the soul can grow'. Inasmuch as this required political
intervention, the minister was required to be a politician.[75] This
formed the basis for his enthusiastic support of disestablishment
of the Anglican Church in Wales, conscientious objection to the
Great War and also his tacit support for the Labour Party during
his later years. Although he would never again become as highly
involved in the political scene as he had been previously, his
support for the Labour Party was such that he was invited to
stand for Parliament on its behalf,[76] a request which he declined.
His support for 'labour' was never uncritical, however. Like Miall
Edwards, Rees believed that the labour movement would never
succeed completely in its quest for social justice because, in its
concerns and aims, it was exclusively materialistic.[77] As a good
Idealist, Rees claimed that the labour movement needed to base
its claims on spiritual and moral ideals.

Rees's withdrawal from party-political activity was indicative
of two particular changes in his thought. The first was a rediscovery of a more all-encompassing and overtly Christian
philosophy of life which was less sectarian than the politics of the
day. This resulted in a more concerted attempt to make the

Christian gospel relevant to modern needs, both intellectual and social. The second was his general disillusionment with party politics, particularly the activity of the Liberal Party.[78] Certainly after 1918, Rees was scathing in his criticism of politics generally and Liberalism in particular, a situation largely prompted by the advent of war. The Great War had not affected his espousal of philosophical Idealism or liberal theology. Instead, it had opened his eyes to the hypocrisy which was deeply embedded in the policy of the Liberal Party. For him the Liberal Party had betrayed all its principles in order to win a war that was in itself evil and should never have been fought:

> And however many diseased elements there were in our Liberalism before, it was the part which it played in the war that killed it. It was so contrary to all its previous professions and in the end it was driven to betray its basic principles. When Liberalism fails to protect personal freedom and the rights of every man's conscience, it loses the purpose of its existence.[79]

During the war, the Liberals had disregarded the fundamental principle of personality, namely the right of every individual to act according to the dictates of conscience. This was made especially clear following the introduction of conscription. He would hardly have been satisfied with the policies of the Labour Party unless it made primary provision for the development of individual personality. To the extent that the Labour Party could be accused of neglecting this, Rees's support was not assured. For him, the political parties of the period had not adopted the most important principles to promote the right life and to establish the perfect society. It is, therefore, hardly surprising that Rees left the political arena in order to perfect a more manifestly Christian response. His Christian response to the social and political needs of the post-war world was based on the moral status of individuals before God and their consequent responsibility to the moral personalities which formed the human race. In other words, because God as Father had given all human beings a moral status, each individual had a responsibility to his or her neighbour. In the language of the period, God's Fatherhood implied the brotherhood of men.

By 1920, Rees was conscious of a grave crisis which was facing

Welsh Nonconformity. It had failed to face the implications of issues such as disestablishment, education, theological change, the problems of the aftermath of war, and the breach with the working class. The way forward, he argued, was mutual comprehension between the labour movement and the church. The labour movement needed the church, for it alone provided the answer to the underlying cause of the social problem and the dynamic for reform: 'Social unrest is aspiration and search after the free brotherhood and the larger life which can only be realised in the spiritual community of love where Christ alone rules and leads into all truth.'[80] To succeed, the church had to free itself from all possible taints of political partisanship, to raise a prophetic voice convicting the world of 'sin, righteousness and judgement' (cf. Jn. 16.8–11) and turn its attention to the demands of the Kingdom of God.[81] For Rees, the Kingdom was fundamentally a moral ideal and was therefore not confined to outward expressions and material possessions. It would be revealed in the world through the establishment of the moral principles of 'justice, peace and joy in the Holy Ghost' in all human relations. 'Thus', he wrote, 'the Kingdom consecrates life, builds character and re-establishes man in his right position with God.'[82]

Such an interpretation insisted that the Kingdom was fundamentally concerned not with society at large but with individuals. The Kingdom transformed men's souls individually by revealing that 'they were the Father's sons' but 'that they were also men's brethren'.[83] This was ultimately the consequence of its moral nature, and the moral principles which it encompassed needed to be accepted and promoted individually. They would have to be adopted willingly and voluntarily or else cease to be moral altogether and become legal instead. Once the individual had opted for a higher morality, he or she was then to affect his or her surrounding society through willing and loving service. This principle for Rees was demonstrated on the cross:

> The cross as it was a life principle in Jesus Christ's daily life is the way and rule of life for us also. Loving souls more than things, and giving ourselves to its [the cross] service whatever the cost – that is the way Jesus lived and that is why he died. We need to stop and notice and recognize this vital living and dying (*y byw a'r marw bywiol hyn*) until they win our intent and our love and our obedience.[84]

In the same way that 'moral principles' were at the root of Rees's criticism of the Liberal Party and the cause of his consequent withdrawal from politics, it was 'principles' which governed his understanding of Christianity. The traditional doctrinal formulations had no relevance to contemporary society. They spoke in a language and in a philosophical style which were foreign to the modern mind. Furthermore, they offered nothing to satisfy the cry for practical religion. No reference had been made to the doctrine of the Trinity to settle the industrial disputes of the 1920s, he claimed,[85] neither had the doctrine of the Holy Spirit been referred to when seeking answers to society's problems, to bring an end to the war or to bring greater unity within the church.[86] Principles alone had the moral authority and inspiration to bring about a transformation in character and, as a result, a change in society. Chief amongst such principles was that of service which involved self-sacrifice as the only path to true reform. This to Rees was the principle of the cross; the decision of the individual conscience to deny itself to save society. This alone would bring true reform both to the individual, in whom self is dethroned, and to society, which is enriched by another life lived in service.[87]

The supremacy of service as the guiding principle to the ethical life required that the demand of the age for 'rights' be qualified by an emphasis on responsibility. In fact Rees argued that rights could not exist without responsibilities and only in the individual recognition of moral responsibility could humankind establish a better society. In pointing to the supremacy of moral principles, and to the need to recognize individual responsibility, Thomas Rees believed he had shown the way towards true reform.

Rees's argument was in sharp contrast to the call for 'rights' within the labour movement where they had been adopted to ensure personal comfort for those sections in society to which it had been denied. He posited that 'rights' could be claimed only to the extent which they enabled the individual to serve the wider community. His argument always centred upon the fundamental place of ethics in human life and indeed in the life of the whole created order. The truly religious life was that which was lived according to the highest ethical principles, in particular that of service. Service, the dedication to provide for the needs of the wider community, was also the way to self-fulfilment. Thus 'rights' were not to be invoked on behalf of the self but on behalf of others. This was basically his contribution to the social-reform debate as he claimed that society could not be redeemed until each individual recognized the call of a higher morality. As a good Nonconformist, Rees would always emphasize the absolute authority of individual conscience. Society, in fact, could not exist until sufficient numbers of individuals lived lives dedicated to service of the other. But this was the path to true fulfilment. The recognition of the higher morality as life's governing principle would not only meet the needs of society but it would also satisfy the longing of the individual heart. The individual was fundamental to Rees's understanding both of social improvement and of society itself, but this was accompanied by his emphasis on the moral purpose of human life on earth:

> But the business of man in society and nation in the world is not to live like a well-fed stallion or a fat pig, but to contribute value and service. There is no reason or meaning in the world for a nation to collect wealth and live luxuriously and no more ... The only argument for social reform and the improvement of man's surroundings rests on the principle that they are to be sought in order to apply men to serve the true life of the world more effectively.

Humankind's whole purpose was to live an ethical life, which meant a life lived in the sacrificial service of other people, and this was to pursue 'spiritual' rather than 'material' principles.[88]

Party politics, in whatever form, concentrated on too narrow an interpretation of life and consequently did not promote 'life in all its fullness'. Instead of sectarian policies, an all-encompassing philosophy was required. As a result, it was not a political system *per se* which Rees advocated but the development of a distinctively Christian society. Such a society needed a firm base which meant the concentration on expressing Christian 'principles' as the governing elements of both individual and social life. In discovering the 'historical Jesus' and believing that the emphasis was correctly placed on the teaching which had been preserved in the gospels, it was inevitable that Jesus would be interpreted principally as a moral teacher. His divinity was reflected in the fact that his morality had reached a far higher stage of development than any other human being who had lived.[89] Thus, the establishment of a Christian society became possible so long as it embodied the social principles which Jesus espoused, namely 'love of neighbour, mutual, loving service, love of enemies and sacrificing personal welfare for the greatest good of the whole family to which we belong'.[90]

Rees's major contributions to the social debate came after the Great War, following his disillusionment with, and withdrawal from, politics. His book *Cenadwri'r Eglwys a Phroblemau'r Dydd* ('The Mission of the Church and the Problems of the Day') appeared in 1923 (Wrexham). This was not an attempt to outline and analyse the burning social issues of the day. Instead, Rees attempted to express the mission of the church to the age in terms that maintained an unbroken link with the centuries of Christian thought while also offering a contemporary interpretation of the Christian message. Rees was convinced that it was through the church and the gospel that society would be transformed. It is not surprising therefore that his book concentrated on the specific problems of ecclesiastical and religious life in Wales.

As would be expected, Rees emphasized the need for each individual to adopt the principles of the Kingdom. This arose from his conviction that God was the sum of the eternal values the true, the good and the real, that Christianity was essentially an experience of those values and that the unique call of the gospel was the requirement to live a moral life based on mutual love and altruistic service. And it is fundamentally the living of this moral life that would see society reformed and renewed. According to Rees, the world was given by God to man for men to develop loving and sacrificial lives towards each other and towards God. 'The world is the medium and the opportunity for man to prove his love for his fellow men.' This vague call to love was, for Rees, the heart of Jesus' message (see e.g. Mt. 22.37–9 and parallels; Jn. 13.34–5). It was to be adopted by men and women but it would not lead necessarily to any preconceived social structure. The form that society should take depended on different factors in each age and in each context. Thus Jesus' teaching offered no blueprint for society. All he offered was the moral absolute that 'no [social] system should make things an end and man a means'. The governing principle should be that all men, rich and poor alike, use what they possess in the service of their fellows (p. 100).

Rees's approach to the subject of social reform was motivated by different concerns from those of Miall Edwards. For Edwards, the primary need that the social problem highlighted was that men and women do not grow to their full potential in circumstances which made life difficult. For Rees, however, the call was to live a moral life regardless of circumstance: 'One can be a Christian in a slum or in a prison or in slavery, but one cannot be a Christian and make slums, or enslave or imprison innocent men' (p. 104). It was the task of the church to convince men and women by transforming their minds, wills and spirits (pp. 211–12) with the call of social service. 'Society could be revived beyond measure, and at once, if each Christian did his duty towards his neighbour in honesty and kindness' (p. 201). Thus the burden of social reform would ultimately lie on individuals who disregarded their own circumstances in order to improve the lot of their fellows, and it was the church's task to convince men of such a need. This brought Rees to the heart of the problem. He recognized that despite the need to rebuild a world rent by war, and despite the suitability of the Christian message to perform the task, his readers needed also to be sufficiently realistic to accept that congregations were declining and Nonconformity's influence waning. In this way, Rees was pointing to the need for reform within the church itself as well as within society. Nonconformists needed to recognize that contributory factors to numerical decline included 'ugly and dreary' chapels, the fact that services were 'too bare, plain and uniform' (*rhy foel, diaddurn ac unffurf*), 'and that preachers of the age incarnate the whole effects of original sin' (p. 131).[91] As a result, the first step was to convince men and women of 'the hope they possess' through a renewed commitment to public worship (p. 132). This is an important point, as some at this time, under the influence of Hegelian monism, claimed that God's presence in the world rendered traditional forms of worship unnecessary (p. 136). Many in the labour movement promoted the moral principles contained in Jesus' teaching and stressed the importance of religious beliefs, but they had also claimed that this was not synonymous with attending chapel. Although himself a Hegelian who believed in the cardinal importance of God's immanence within creation (p. 49), Rees held that such an emphasis led to numerical decline within the churches. As a result, he was convinced that, before attention was given to the social question, men and women needed to return to the chapel. To achieve this end he stressed the cruciality of worship in human life. In this, his argument differed slightly from that of Miall Edwards. Although Edwards was concerned with the numerical decline in chapel attendance, and had also emphasized the importance of religious worship, he was much more at ease than Thomas Rees with the idea that a truly religious spirit existed outside the church. Edwards and Rees would have agreed that God could not be confined to the church, and probably would have agreed that God's presence in the world was a redeeming one. Where they differed concerned the importance of the church *per se*. Although he never said so, and would probably have been horrified at the suggestion, Edwards's viewpoint would lead naturally to the conclusion that the church was unnecessary, except as a particular locus for human worship. Rees tended to emphasize the particularity of church worship as vital for the religious life.

Thomas Rees based his religious contribution on the need to promote moral values. He had claimed that moral values, the good, the true and the beautiful, were alone of absolute worth (*gwerth diamodol*). These moral values were the purpose of life and should promote the human quest for the Kingdom of God.[92] To do so, he claimed, was merely to return to Jesus' own understanding of the Kingdom. Jesus had spoken of God in moral and not metaphysical terms; for him he was Father and King rather than the almighty, omnipotent and eternal one.[93] As a result, Rees advocated a reinterpretation of doctrine which would give prominence to the moral values and imperatives of Jesus' teaching.[94] As moral values were vital to the life of the whole created order, for they found their home in the Divine, anything that impinged upon the development of character and the perception of the good, the true and the beautiful would be a problem for the church. The social question, then, had essentially to do with morals because industrial society had developed on the basis of a false notion of the ethical life. Because it was a moral problem, it also required a moral solution, and a moral inspiration needed to be discovered for social reform. 'The only social reform worth having', he said, 'is the one that turns the whole energy and resource of the life of the *gwerin* to realize its eternal and final purpose.'[95] The social problem was fundamentally one which the church could not avoid because the church's message and its chief task were primarily ethical. The church existed to make Jesus' words that 'they may have life and have it in abundance' (Jn. 10.10) effective in the life of the world. If the church tried to understand the social question and put its energy and resources into promoting a better society, Rees believed it could once again win the trust of the ordinary folk, the *gwerin*.

Rees's criticism of industrial society centred on his belief that capitalism was basically soul-destroying and character-denying. Having been both a farm labourer and a coal miner before his call to Christian ministry, Rees, unlike Miall Edwards, had first-hand experience of the difficulties and injustices of working-class life. He did not openly support Socialism as a political creed, but he claimed that as an economic and political system it was fairer than capitalism 'because there would be more of the general heart and will of mankind behind it'.[96] However, in the end it was not the system that was important but the individuals who made up that system. The church's mission was therefore primarily concerned with the individual. Rees claimed that society could never be transformed by external methods, whether by the government or any other power that chose to begin with the environment. The government could at best only 'express and mark and effectualize the reform that would already have taken place'.[97] It was the church through its regeneration of individuals which therefore provided the key.

Rees's belief that the individual was of utmost importance, and that the systems of government and society should not impinge upon his or her personal development, led him, in the years between the Great War and the COPEC conference on Christian Politics, Economics and Citizenship held in Birmingham in 1924, into the promotion of the concept of 'pure citizenship'. The citizen, he claimed, was central to two complicated relationships; his relationship with the state as it affected him through its law and authority, and his relationship with the other people who made up the immediate society.[98] The citizen's relationship with the state entailed both rights and responsibilities. Those responsibilities involved obedience, service and contribution. The citizen was to obey the state's laws as the rule of a good society. He was to serve the state through paying taxes and through 'giving it any other service *it is just for it to demand*' (my italics). Finally, he was to contribute to the state's activities and organization at least through voting at each election. Also, if appropriate, the citizen should be prepared to offer his or her services to the wider community as a local councillor or as a Member of Parliament or any other community activity.[99]

It is already clear that Rees was wording his argument very carefully. His own obedience to the state had been called into question by the outbreak of war and particularly by the subsequent introduction of conscription. Although he could not advocate civil disobedience on every disagreement between public policy and individual conscience, he also felt unable to deny totally the right of each individual to decide for himself. Thus, he developed his idea of 'pure citizenship'. The citizen who fulfilled the responsibilities listed above could be described as 'an inoffensive and adequate citizen'. But 'pure citizenship' required something more.

The first thing that the 'pure citizen' attempts to do is to 'moralize the whole relationship between man and the state'. In other words he makes his citizenship a matter of conscience. As such, the service rendered is given with good will rather than the 'compulsion of law' (*angenrhaid deddf*). A man's citizenship is only 'pure' when he is obedient and offers his services to the state 'willingly, selflessly, and lovingly'.[100] If the state asks for something with which individual conscience cannot comply, then 'pure citizenship' would seek to reform the state to ensure that the state's demands are always 'just and good'.[101] If this proved to be impossible, then the pure citizen must differentiate in his own conscience between those 'unimportant demands' and those that are of some good to the whole of society. While he could forgo the former it was his duty to fulfil the latter. If he concluded that the demands are evil then the pure citizen must under no circumstances comply.[102]

Although Rees continued to emphasize the right of the individual to follow his conscience, subjectivity and relativism are in the end avoided because the ultimate principle to govern human activity was self-sacrifice. In other words the pure citizen must be willing to give up his or her rights in the interests of humankind. Following the war, Rees's argument differed vastly from that which he had employed previously. He had encouraged opposition to the Education Act of 1902, he had supported conscientious objection and opposed conscription during the war, all of which were apparently imposed by the government in the name of society at large. It could be that Rees had come to realize that the rebuilding of a fair and just world order would require a level of sacrifice on the part of the individual conscience which was at least as great as the sacrifice demanded during wartime. Whatever the inspiration behind it, by 1923 Rees had modified his position on the relationship of the individual to the state.

'Pure citizenship' did not merely exist in the social and political spheres, however. It also had a religious content. The 'pure citizen' is also a citizen of the Kingdom of God and must therefore be led by the will of God as revealed in Jesus. The Kingdom must become the 'final and authoritative aim and purpose' for the whole of life:[103]

> The pure citizen will ensure therefore not only to reject the unjust requests of the state, but will live far above the just requirements of every relationship of service and kindness towards men. And he will attempt through his own sacrifice, and his influence on others to reform the state on the plan of the Kingdom until the kingdoms of the world become the Kingdom of our Lord and of his Christ.[104]

Pure citizenship comprised the service not of self, party or sect, but of humankind under obedience to God. Education was required for the citizen to be able to give his or her best service. This entailed religious knowledge, namely the relationship between God and human beings, and social knowledge, being the relationship of human beings with each other. Alongside this, the citizen needed economic and legal knowledge and will to 'choose high purposes, pure means and the activities of love in every relationship with men in society and state'.[105]

The similarities between Miall Edwards and Thomas Rees stemmed mainly from their common schooling in both philosophical Idealism and liberal theology. Both believed that the individual's claim was paramount. For Edwards, this meant that all things existed for the individual's benefit in order to build his character. Rees, on the other hand, stated that the moral status of men and women would be guaranteed only by the recognition of their responsibilities to serve each other. It was the importance of this moral status which led Rees into pronouncements on public issues in which he thundered Amos-like against the injustice of industrial society and the immorality of a government which had ridden roughshod over the dictates of individual conscience in order to fight an unjust war. For Rees, the only means to discern the highest ethical standard (conscience) had been abandoned in order to pursue the basest of policies (war). Consequently, his duty as a minister of the gospel was to make a stand against government policy. This he did, and though vilified for it (he was expelled from the Bangor Golf Club), history's assessment must be that his stance was courageous, if not prophetic, even though it was, at the time, ultimately unpopular. The major difference between Thomas Rees and Miall Edwards came not so much in theological or social thinking, however, but in their own activities. Whereas Rees had been politically active Edwards had never ventured into the party-political arena. Also Rees's work, especially before 1918, had concentrated far more on specifically theological and doctrinal issues. He was an able scholar and theologian, possibly the ablest of his generation, and argued his theses with vigour and absolute conviction. The quality of his work was recognized by the University of London which awarded him the degree of Doctor of Philosophy for his book *The Holy Spirit in Thought and Experience* (London, 1915). His main contribution to the social-question debate came in the years between 1918 and 1924, particularly during the preparations for the COPEC conference in Birmingham in 1924. From that year he returned to theological work as editor of *Y Geiriadur Beiblaidd* ('The Biblical Dictionary'), which he managed to complete before he died of cancer on 20 May 1926.

John Morgan Jones

John Morgan Jones's[106] interest in social issues and Christianity's response to modern problems was at least partly prompted by his own experience. Born and raised in Garnant, Carmarthenshire, in the heart of the anthracite coalfield, he attended Bethel Congregational Church and was encouraged by the pastor, the Revd Josiah Towyn Jones to enter the ministry.[107] Towyn Jones was a popular denominational and national figure who eventually entered Parliament as a Liberal in 1912. Under his ministry, John Morgan Jones learned that religion had an important contribution to make in meeting the social issues of the day, and that part of the minister's role was to take an active interest in social and political problems. In recollecting his debt to his former pastor he explained that Towyn had revealed 'how the religion of Jesus could touch the social needs of that age to the quick'.[108] Despite his appreciation he was careful to emphasize that Towyn Jones's mission had belonged to his own generation and should not be appealed to in the contemporary situation. It was the duty of each generation of Christians to apply the principles of the gospel afresh to the peculiar context and problems of their period.

Jones went up to Mansfield College, Oxford, in 1896, the same year as Thomas Rees. He concluded his education by spending a year in Berlin, where he attended Harnack's lectures *Das Wesen des Christentums* published in English in 1901 as *What is Christianity?* Jones corresponded with Harnack until 1930, the year in which the great liberal theologian died. In a glowing tribute which he gave to his former teacher, the excitement and thrill of the lectures were still clear in his memory. 'They were not lectures', he wrote, 'but warm, enthusiastic sermons'; Jones thanked Harnack for 'saving one sinner at least, as a brand from the burning'.[109]

On his return to Wales, Jones was ordained as minister of Tabernacle English Congregational Church, Aberdare, where he remained for thirteen years. Aberdare was part of the same parliamentary constituency as Merthyr Tydfil and had been at the centre of Socialist activity since Keir Hardie's election to Westminster in 1900, the year that Jones began his ministry. It is true that there was much mutual respect between Hardie and Jones. Jones considered that Hardie was 'one of the greatest prophets of modern times',[110] while Hardie wrote to Jones in 1913 warmly congratulating him on his appointment to the Bala-Bangor College:

In these days when the spirit of enquiry and also doubt is so much abroad, and especially when such a large number of our young men are taking to serious reading and reflection upon life and its problems, not merely spiritual but also political and economic, it is of the first importance that those who are to have the training of the ministers for the next generation should themselves not only be *au courant* with the best thought of the times, but also have sufficient breadth of mind as to give that thought a full and free interpretation. I trust you will be long spared to be a guiding light to those who will come under your moulding hands.[111]

This appreciation of his talents stemmed from Jones's activity as a minister and local councillor in Aberdare, despite the fact that he did not belong to the same political party as Hardie. He was at this time a fervent Liberal, though he won a considerable degree of genuine admiration from his Socialist opponents following religious and political debates periodically held in Tabernacle Chapel. Indeed, such was the esteem in which he was held that he drew some Socialist adherents to his church services. According to one prominent local Socialist, 'he was so capable, competent and fair in controversy that we were vanquished, though not converted.'[112] He certainly earned the respect of many amongst the labour ranks in the town, an all the more remarkable fact when we discover his political fate. He was elected to the local council in April 1904 but defeated three years later following accusations of having insulted 'labour'. He had been a prominent and active member of the Educational Committee, a post in which he served with such dedication that he earned considerable respect from the townsfolk. It was said that were he to 'come out clearly as a patron of the Independent Labour Party' he would be returned to the council.[113] Nevertheless, he never again stood as a candidate in local elections. Thus, when he was appointed to the chair of Church History at the Bala-Bangor College in 1913, he had first-hand experience of ministry in an industrial area and of the way in which local politics functioned. He was also schooled in the most recent interpretations of liberal theology. This provided him with both the required tools and the inspiration to enter into the social debate with the intention of providing a specifically religious response to current issues. Certainly after going to Bala-Bangor he, like Thomas Rees before him, concentrated on the application of his theological ideals to social issues far more than direct involvement in politics. Unlike Edwards and Rees, however, Jones had very little interest in philosophy. He was more at home in the field of literature and history, his two great interests being New Testament studies and Education. He was prominent in calling for an education system which would fulfil its proper task by producing upright, moral citizens. Education for him was a principal means towards Christianizing society and regenerating individuals.

Although his thinking was formulated by similar theological preconceptions as those of Thomas Rees and D. Miall Edwards, he was completely unconcerned with doctrinal niceties. Instead, he based his faith on Jesus of Nazareth as an ethical teacher and his ability to inspire both personal and social regeneration. The principal themes of Jones's work were the infinite value of humankind, the freedom of the individual conscience, and the universal need for education.[114] All this stemmed from his view of Christianity as a spiritual movement in which the highest moral principles were realized and acted upon. Jesus could be confessed as Lord on the basis of his having embodied these principles perfectly. His divinity was an aspect of his full humanity, irradiated by an exquisite experience of God's nearness which prompted an all-out obedience to the moral law. Nowhere did Jones interpret Christ's divinity in metaphysical or ontological terms. Instead Jesus was, for him, the perfect human embodiment of God's likeness revealed in the natural evolutionary process of human history. After Jesus, the next outstanding example of human obedience to God was St Paul. Like Jesus, Paul's religious experience had also reached an unprecedented height. He was subordinate to Jesus, according to Jones, simply because he had required the prompting and example of Christ to reach his own religious fulfilment.[115] As an interpretation both of Christian history and Paul's message, this is hardly satisfactory. It fails to do justice to Paul's clear devotion to Christ following his conversion. Although it is true that the apostle appears to have had little interest in the human history of Jesus of Nazareth, his emphasis on the death and resurrection of Christ, in which he and others participate through baptism, is far from asserting an inherent religiosity seeking, and ultimately finding, its own fulfilment through dedication to the moral life. Furthermore, it fails to do sufficient justice to the church's conviction that the man Jesus of Nazareth was in a unique sense God incarnate, a conviction which it enshrined in its credal statements at the earliest opportunity. Nevertheless, Jones's interpretation had some consequences for his views on the social question. Both Jesus and Paul had applied their gospel of spiritual principles to their social life. The basic principle was love, which had led them both to 'active, unselfish service'.[116]

Once followers of Jesus had accepted love as the governing principle in their lives, they would inevitably practise it, and thus affect society for the better.[117] The Christian is one who displayed simple, sure, infinite trust in God, as a child's trust in his father, the endless faithfulness to the vision which unfailingly comes from this childlike relationship to God in the life of love and service of men ... the Christian's one aim is to be gripped by these moral and spiritual characteristics, to grow daily in the image and likeness of Jesus Christ, with [these principles] working freely and powerfully in him bringing much fruit in every direction in his personal and social life.[118]

The church's task was to preach this message concerning the need to embody moral principles in life. All else, whether church structures, doctrine, tradition or sacrament, was secondary. Jones believed that each Christian had a duty 'to be able to give some intelligible reason' for his faith, but this involved an explanation of religious experience and not the expression of doctrinal formulations. He had an inherent distrust of, if not distaste for, traditional doctrines. He believed that they were contrary to the proven facts of modern science, an insult to the modern conscience and a stumbling block to the spread of the gospel.[119] This attitude was well expressed in a sermon which Jones preached early in his ministerial career:

We try to get men in our many ways to live for God, for truth, for others in the spirit of Jesus – and they begin to talk to us about the Doctrine of the Trinity and the theory of the Atonement and the infallibility of the Bible. I want to go to men with the Gospel of Jesus – without having these hindrances placed between me and their hearts and souls and conscience. There will be plenty of difficulties it is true – men will fail and sin, and be tempted and despair – they will have evil surroundings to face and fight – but these are difficulties that will help me rather than prevent me from showing what Christ can do for men. I want the difficulties to arise from life and not from the Christianity I offer them as a Christian and a preacher.[120]

Not only were the creeds foreign to the experience of the modern mind, but they were also far removed from the religion of Jesus. As a disciple of Harnack, Jones posited that Jesus' teaching had emphasized the Fatherhood of God, and the consequent Brotherhood of Man. Thus, human beings were of infinite value because they collectively constitute the family of God. The creeds, on the other hand, had emphasized God's absolute sovereignty. Jesus had drawn attention not to intellectual formulae but to ethics and the religious life, to the supremacy of the spirit, and the fundamental principles of love, righteousness, grace and truth. Whereas he had preached the Sermon on the Mount as the guide to the moral life, it was not deemed worthy of mention by those who had formulated the church's creeds.[121] He claimed that the creeds did not represent 'the heart of the Christian faith', which was moral rather than metaphysical. As well as God's Fatherhood and the Brotherhood of Man, Christianity stood for the Kingdom of God and the need for men and women to follow Jesus specifically in accepting his moral teaching and vision.[122]

Jones's condemnation of the creeds was prompted in part by his eagerness to return to the 'historical Jesus'. For him this was not the saviour whose death under Pontius Pilate and subsequent resurrection had effected redemption for the whole of humankind but Jesus the ethical teacher, the rabbi who in his teaching and relationships had outlined the path towards life in its fullness. He maintained the Christian paradox that fullness of life was possible only through the practice of self-sacrificial love which leads to service of one's neighbour in the name of Christ rather than through any selfish and hedonistic quest for personal achievement. In this, Jones simply offered an interpretation of the words of Jesus, namely 'Those who love their life will lose it, and those who hate their life in this world will keep it for eternal life' (Jn. 12.25 NRSV). The question for the social debate was what use would the historical Jesus be in solving the burning issues of the day, nineteen centuries after his death? In answering this question, Jones asserted that Jesus was not a social reformer. It was impossible to glean a definite plan from his teaching which could be applied to the specific problems of modern industrial society.[123] Instead, Jesus was a 'revealer', one who had seen his main task as demonstrating 'the relation of the human soul to God and not to reorganize human society'. However, an automatic result of Christ's gospel, claimed Jones, would be to 'make all his disciples social reformers'. This would not be achieved through the provision of a programme for social reform but through the demonstration of fundamental principles by which Jesus lived his life. He once listed these principles as 'love', 'justice', 'the eternal value of personality', 'the Fatherhood of God', 'the brotherhood of man', 'the forgiveness of sin' and 'faith'.[124] Nothing should be read into this list, as Jones never defined any of these terms. They required a practical or ethical, not a theoretical, response. This entailed the need for Jesus' followers to love their fellow men and live their lives in ceaseless service of others. They needed to have faith in the principles of the Kingdom, to see salvation as encompassing all aspects of human life, to have sympathy for the poor, sick and ignorant, and to co-operate in promoting a moral and spiritual fellowship based on fulfilling God's will in the world.[125] It was essential to emulate Jesus' actions rather than merely to believe his words.[126] Although Jones tended to emphasize the need for individual embodiment of divine principles as the way to true reform, he also recognized the importance of embodying Christian principles in the reconstruction of a fairer and more just international community after the European War. If they did not succeed in this, then a universal economic or political standard would never be achieved.[127] Only the moral principles of religion could give any real meaning and value to social reform and improvement.[128]

Jones believed that the relationship between human beings and God was vital for religion and for any social reform, but a right relationship with God was impossible without a right relationship with other people.[129] The inspiration for this was the life of Jesus. In revealing the centrality of the divine–human relationship, and the inherent link between the two, Jesus had pointed to the importance of personality. He did not merely emphasize the value of personality but its social significance, because, rather than being the product of mechanism, the social order was the product of personality.[130] Thus, by concentrating on the individual, Jesus had taught humankind the principles which would ultimately create a more just, equitable and perfect society.

Jesus' teaching, as far as Jones could see, was always addressed to the individual and not to institutions and organizations.[131] The individual was thus central both to the relationship which God sought with his creation and to inter-personal relationships. As a result, the purpose of the state's existence was to make the arrangements that would allow individuals to live the best, moral life according to their capabilities.[132] The gospel demanded that the state so structure society that each individual had a fair opportunity to develop his or her life fully.[133] Unfortunately, the exact nature of the relationship between the individual and society is not always clear in Jones's writings and the two often become parts of the same whole:

73

I exclude ... any possibility of the absolute isolation of the individual. There is no such thing apart from society. They are mutually correlative terms. It is individuals which give body and soul to society, and it is society which creates individual personalities; when one is properly served so is the other – because they can only grow together.[134]

Thus, in trying to preserve the importance of both the individual and the principle of service, and the need to recognize the significance of society, he seems almost to descend into a monistic view, the wholesale adoption of which is prevented only by the absolute importance which Jones attached to the individual. He never adequately explained the relationship between the individual and the state. The definition of 'individual', 'state' and the relationship of the two belonged to the world of abstractions. He was more concerned with the need to promote moral principles which, in his view, were concrete, practical guides and not to be regarded as abstract. Therefore, the church's task in society was to increase the community's sensitivity to moral and spiritual values. It was the church's responsibility to teach the principles of the gospel, to study concrete problems and gather the required information in order to form an enlightened opinion. Only then could it seek to co-operate with movements and organizations which attempted to improve social conditions and to provide the world with an example of the moral life.[135] Jesus, he claimed, did not simply enunciate principles. He also lived out those principles and by so doing provided an example for his followers.[136] The Christian life was merely a matter of applying these principles. It was for the church, as the fellowship of Jesus' followers, to work out plans and duties according to the mind and discernment which God had provided rather than by seeking direct answers in the words of Jesus.[137]

The first call in the gospel was, then, for each Christian disciple to try to live up to the highest moral principles in the home, the workplace and in all personal relationships. This was because Jones believed that the only way to reform the world was through individual regeneration, for which the gospel provided the inspiration and the dynamic.[138] This was the only way to social reform because there was no 'ready, complete, practical plan' in the gospel which would automatically improve all social evils. However, more than any other part of human life it was the

74

commercial and industrial system which needed to be brought under the gospel's influence. As the only 'evangelical principle' for commerce was that of 'brotherly co-operation' the gospel could never tolerate the profit motive which characterized commerce following the Industrial Revolution.[139] Once again there is a contradiction in Jones's thought which can only be explained by the highly complex relationship between the individual and society which stemmed from his belief in the ultimate unity of reality. He believed that moral principles could only be embodied in individual lives, but 'there is not much hope for the continuation of the gospel if it cannot impress the picture and image of its own principles increasingly deeply not only on the personal life but also on the life of society and its institutions.'[140] Despite the fact that Christianity was a moral and spiritual system and could only therefore be embodied in human life, Jones also believed that a nation could live as a Christian nation. 'If an individual can live the gospel,' he claimed, 'a whole nation can do so too.' To do so it must be prepared to place its faith in the principles of the gospel, but it must also be prepared to embody the highest moral principle of loving self-sacrifice in all its national dealings. It had to be prepared to pay the cost of discipleship. It must always 'serve the world freely, without thanks and without expecting anything in return'.[141]

Jones was well aware of the depth of the rift between labour and the church and was conscious of the two insufficient responses which church people tended to make. The tendency was for them either to offer a 'literal reinterpretation of the economic life of primitive Christians', which meant a call to adopt the apparent communism of Acts 2.44–5 and 4.32, or else to continue to offer philanthropic aid or charity. Instead of this, he claimed that a radical appropriation of Jesus' social teaching was needed. The figure of Jesus, after all, was generally held in respect by both churchmen and members of the labour movement and thus provided a common ground for both groups. Also, the constant task of the church was the application of Jesus' teaching to the needs of modern society. Despite claiming to be 'more or less of a Socialist', he insisted that a Socialist agenda should be followed 'just far enough to give us the best opportunity to establish the Kingdom of God'.[142] Being based on spiritual and moral principles rather than material values, he believed the Kingdom of

God to be something other than the Socialist state. In the light of some of the propaganda of the labour movement, this was an important distinction.

The Kingdom entailed the loving, merciful, forgiving service of all humankind to be established as the governing principle in life and in the economic system.[143] It therefore condemned the current industrial and economic system for having fostered selfish men and placed them in perpetual competition with each other. The system was practised merely for profit and personal gain and needed to be transformed 'into instruments for the adequate natural supply of the physical and spiritual needs of our people'.[144] But the gospel did not offer a plan on which to base a new system of commerce and industry. Jones explained that while the gospel could not give citizens definite instruction by which they could govern their lives, it provided the moral principles which condemned certain practices in society. The gospel witnessed to the inherent and absolute value of men and women. Thus, whereas the gospel did not expressly prohibit the social difference between employers and workers, it did promote the ideals of co-operation rather than competition, and service of others rather than personal gain. The words of Jesus gave no direct guidance concerning the level of wages a worker should receive, or how many hours he should work, but they required that all men have the opportunity to work under honourable conditions which automatically offered the possibility of living a fuller life and not having to work simply to scrape a living. The gospel did not place restrictions on the amount of wealth any individual should procure, but it forbade the possibility of people being controlled through industrial practices. The ownership of coal mines was not forbidden by the gospel, but the gospel did forbid the ownership and totalitarian control of the miners. Although it did not say that no person should be poorer than a mine owner, the gospel insisted that nobody should be so poor that they must sell themselves in order to live.[145] All this stemmed from Jones's belief that freedom was the fundamental moral category within the gospel. This had implications for the social debate, politics and church life where the individual conscience was to be freed from all oppressive struc-tures, from adherence to set creeds and codes of belief and moral life. Individual conscience was sacrosanct, and any impingement on its freedom, as far as Jones was concerned, was to be opposed.

The primary need, in Jones's opinion, was to expound Christian principles which led him to advocate moral instruction as the means to individual moral and social improvement. Throughout his public ministry, Jones always emphasized the importance of education. He had himself enjoyed a wide education having studied in three very different universities under some of the most gifted scholars and able teachers of the age. Like other educationalists at the time, he was keen to play down the specifically personal opportunities which education could provide, emphasizing instead that education had an inherently moral value which improved the quality of life in a general but highly beneficial way. Social improvement was the natural consequence of improving the quality of individual life. As a result it was Jones's contention that specifically religious and moral instruction was required to bring this moral quality to the fore and, while serving on the Education Committee in Aberdare, he attempted to facilitate the process by formulating *A Scheme and Syllabus of Moral and Biblical Instruction* (1905). This helped him to achieve a reputation as an educationalist particularly in the field of religious instruction. He contributed to *Moral Instruction and Training in Schools* (edited by M. E. Saddler and published in 1905) and by 1907 had achieved at least some international recognition. That year, Gustav Spiller wrote to Jones asking permission to quote extensively from his *Scheme and Syllabus* in a report on moral instruction which he was preparing in his capacity as General Secretary of the International Union of Ethical Societies.

Jones's views received their most systematic and detailed treatment in his book *The New Testament in Modern Education* (London, 1922). More than anything this was a handbook delineating the methodology which the Christian teacher should employ. It was undoubtedly a book of its time simply because it was based on contemporary theological trends and on the current educational philosophies. As a result, Jones's book has no lasting relevance in the field of study which it treats, but it does give a valuable insight into Jones's thought. He eschewed the abstractions of education theory, but his own opinions concerning the value and purpose of education, and thus the necessary orientation which should be implanted into the education system, are clearly portrayed in its pages. It is not always clear whether Jones intended education *per se* or specifically moral and religious instruction when he spoke of the need for the church, as an educational institution alongside the school, to be involved in the task. It is clear, however, that he considered education to be necessary to the living of the moral life.

For education to be effective in the pursuit of the moral life, it needed a dynamic ideal 'capable of universal application'. This ideal was to be found in its individual revelation in the 'personality and character of Jesus Christ' and in its social application in the Kingdom of God (pp. 9–10). The need of the age was to provide 'Christian teachers', in the sense both of general educators who were also adherents of the faith, and of 'teachers of Christianity' in order to convey this ideal primarily to the young but also to the world at large. The Christian educator's aim, whether he found himself in the pulpit, Sunday School or in the local classroom, was to bring the life of his student into union with the life of Christ and to ensure that his students were equipped to apply 'the life of Christ' in their own lives and in their social dealings and relationships (p. 23). This meant that individuals needed to 'appropriate the supreme values of truth, goodness and beauty' (p. 47) and the New Testament could be used by the teacher in order to accomplish this. Needless to say, the teacher's approach to the New Testament ought to be scientific and one which welcomed the discoveries of biblical criticism and modern thought particularly where authorship and dating of biblical documents were concerned. Each passage, each image and each concept that came from the New Testament was to be subjected to the strictest examination in order to secure its value and then its best practical application. The fact that he insisted that teachers should adopt a liberal approach towards the scriptures was significant, particularly as he implied that any other method was really a primitive and inadequate, if not wholly invalid, approach to the Bible. While he accepted that schoolchildren should still hear the miraculous and mysterious stories about Jesus primarily because such episodes appealed to the youthful imagination, he also maintained that they should be encouraged to question it all and, if necessary, to reject belief in the unbelievable. Jones did not consider that this was an obstacle to faith for any child, but such an approach led to his own interpretation of Christian faith being particularly open-ended if not at times a little ambiguous. It is almost as if he expected the Christian teacher to adopt this ambiguity whilst attempting to convey the essence of Jesus' life and teaching to his students.

In the scientific approach to scripture the first need was to identify whether the story presented concepts which were central or peripheral to the Christian ideal as embodied in Jesus Christ. Next, its historical context within the New Testament needed to be considered, and finally questions should be raised concerning the nature and value of its ethical appeal to contemporary times (p. 71). Jones's understanding of the gospel was basically ethical. It had the power to transform lives, bringing them into conformity with the laws of love and self-sacrifice in the service of the higher good. These were the only things approaching absolutes in his thought, and all organizations which held the goal of human edification needed to be so administered as to hold moral enlightenment and effort as their ultimate goal. This included education as the sphere of ethical activity which ensured character development through the learning process. And this should be the goal of education both within the church and within the secular education system.

The best time to impress religion as a moral force on an individual was during adolescence. Adolescence was the period when youth faced the challenge of decision-making, when the awareness of ideals, and the conflict of those ideals, was strong. This in turn awakens personal responsibility and finds an outlet in strong commitment to social groupings (p. 146). The youth in adolescence was discovering the truth of common human being while also discovering his own self, and thus it was the ideal time to be influenced in the moral strength of the life of Jesus as it was portrayed in the gospel accounts. In the light of this, the problem facing the Christian educator was to help each person 'to rediscover and to reproduce with Jesus and by his power, the supreme spiritual values which Jesus discovered and provided and which youth alone can conserve and increase from generation to generation' (p. 62).

Jones held to the possibility that someone other than Jesus could be born who would embody a 'life of higher and fuller spiritual values' (p. 93). But until that time Jesus is the gospel. His character and personality reveal the divine attributes in human life at their most advanced. He becomes at once the example to be imitated and the means by which imitation is possible. This gospel, through appropriate education, could help to solve the social problem. Thus, adequate education of the individual would help to alleviate the most pressing needs of the day:

> The world is waiting to hear something more from the church than a proclamation of principles or protests against evils, although even here the Church has lamentably failed in its duty in recent years. No progress, however, can be made with regard to social reconstruction in any direction until Christian teachers can give some positive guidance based on the principles of the Gospel and knowledge of the facts of the situation. It is evading the issue to say that we do not know enough about educational, political, industrial and international conditions to do what is required. It is our business co-operatively or personally to get the requisite knowledge or to see that those who have the knowledge use it in the service of the Gospel. The least that we can do is deliberately to set ourselves to train a new generation that will be more capable than we are of applying the Christian Gospel to the social situation. (pp. 99–100)

As far as John Morgan Jones was concerned, solutions to the problems of twentieth-century life would not, on the whole, be discovered in the New Testament. Instead the scriptures demand 'that we should search diligently for the answers for ourselves and act courageously on our own responsibility' (pp. 102–3). Education was a vital part of the process. Through it, familiarity with the biblical message and principles would develop, and this could be used in conjunction with knowledge of the times to work for overall social improvement. Knowledge would pave the way to wise, relevant and responsible action by making Jesus' teaching and the principles of his life relevant and vital elements embodied in the relationships and structures of contemporary life:

> It must mean in the end to spread the life that was in Jesus in such a way as to make it organically one with all the manifestations of life in our day and express itself in all the circumstances and movements of our life. (p. 117)

Somewhat ironically, John Morgan Jones's activities suggest that he questioned the value of traditional religious activities. Thomas Rees and Miall Edwards had gone to great lengths to demonstrate the importance of the regular practice of worship, not merely for the individual but for the spiritual heart of society as a whole. Jones, on the other hand, rarely mentioned the specifics of Christian practice in its traditional forms. He certainly made no attempt to justify worship to the extent which the other two had. For him Christianity represented a spirit present in the whole of creation, which was revealed through the practice of higher moral values. Thus, the work of Christ was being continued even where men and women were oblivious to his name.[146] Edwards and Rees, aware of the danger of secularizing the faith by overemphasizing the doctrine of God's immanence, had insisted on the importance of worship in human life and had thus, to an extent, maintained the specific role of the church in society. For Jones, however, the more reasonable conclusion was that if moral values were supreme in the universe, then the most important task was not worship but moral instruction. He advocated an education system that would fulfil this task and encouraged the church to put its energy into devising a similar system.[147] But this led him almost automatically to a tendency to dismiss the relevance of the church and its worship, despite his being the principal of a seminary entrusted with training prospective ministers. This dismissiveness came to the attention of at least one of his students, who claimed that it deepened as Jones grew older.[148] This paradox highlighted the intellectual honesty that was Jones's foremost characteristic.[149] Rather than compromise his own thought, his integrity demanded that he follow it to its logical conclusion. Traditional religious activity became almost superfluous to him except to the extent that it offered him a platform for his views, and to the extent that it embodied eternal moral principles and ensured the freedom and ultimate value of humankind. It was unfortunate, however, that in so doing he failed to preserve any status for the church in the world and thus, in an indirect way, contributed to the secularization of society and the loss of Nonconformist influence in Wales.

John Morgan Jones did not seek a social interpretation of the traditional doctrinal formulae. His contribution to the social debate concentrated on interpreting Jesus' teaching and revelation of the eternal moral verities, and applying them to modern needs. Jones claimed the gospel as his authority more so than Edwards and Rees, though it was his interpretation of the content and basic message contained in the New Testament rather than the authority of the written word to which he appealed. Central to the social thinking of all three men was their belief that only renewed individuals could form a renewed society, that only moral reforms could renew individuals, and that the moral dynamic which would do so was revealed in Jesus alone. For Jones this made education fundamental to social reform. Education more than anything else was the passion of his life. As a result, throughout his time in Bangor he devoted much time to the Workers' Educational Association. There is a sense in which this provision of education for the *gwerin* gave him more satisfaction than his position as tutor in a theological college. A chain-smoker, hooked on the Craven A cigarette,[150] he died of cancer of the lung on 7 March 1946 a few months before he was due to retire. He was the last of the theological tutors to hail from the Modernists' camp. His successor as principal of the Bala-Bangor College, the Revd Gwilym Bowyer, represented the neo-orthodox reaction against liberal theology. He had been a student at Bala-Bangor but had been attracted to dialectic theology under the influence of John Morgan Jones's colleague, Professor J. E. Daniel.

Herbert Morgan

Herbert Morgan[151] went up to Mansfield College, Oxford, in 1902 and, on completion of his BA course in theology, studied for a year at Marburg under Wilhelm Herrmann, who was, like Harnack, a major exponent of the Ritschlian theology. Morgan shared with the three Independent ministers the conviction that theological liberalism had correctly interpreted both the gospel accounts and the Christian tradition, and also that the Idealist principles of reason and unity accurately described the natural order. Ordained in 1906, he spent six years as minister of Castle Street Welsh Baptist Chapel, London, which counted Lloyd George amongst its adherents. He was no Liberal in politics, however. He was an early recruit to the ranks of the ILP and became something of a spokesman for the labour cause. He was also one of a number of young ministers who had attended a meeting convened during the Carmarthen National Eisteddfod of

1911 to discuss the possibility of forming a Welsh Labour Party. At one stage he even contemplated a parliamentary career. He was among the first Nonconformists to recognize the importance of the social problem and to highlight the need for a synthesis between the labour movement and the churches as a precondition for creating a better society.

For Morgan, the outstanding task which faced the churches in pre-1914 Wales was to serve the community and its needs in the name of Christ. Although the need for salvation was still paramount, the notion that salvation relied on a belief in metaphysical formulations was rapidly losing its popularity. Rather, salvation was deemed, at least in part, to be the result of human effort based on the practice of specific ethical principles, the service of fellow men being its ultimate goal. Initially, Herbert Morgan appears to have looked outside the church and beyond the traditional interpretations of the gospel in order to discover what the needs of contemporary society were. It was the duty of the church to meet those needs. Considering the importance of the social question at the time, it is hardly surprising that he concluded that the church's priority was to employ itself in social service: 'Real salvation must be achieved by the establishment of a social order which shall embody the greatest possible spiritual good in the widest and fullest distribution.'[152]

Typical of his contemporaries, he too believed in the progressive development of history, with human beings and their environment improving morally as the years went by. As a result, he held that ultimate perfection would come a step closer in each succeeding generation. He was convinced, however, that the future of Christianity depended on its ability to offer a solution to the pressing needs of the day. Its role was vital, as it alone provided the motive and inspiration to act in loving and sacrificial service and so hasten the natural development of a perfect social system. Natural as that development would be, it still, somehow, depended on the willingness of men and women to live lives dedicated to the principle of service. This was 'the first function of a genuine Christianity' and also the source of human salvation. The social impulse therefore had to be 'an inevitable expression of the life and essence of Christianity' and not a mere appendage, an ethical afterthought tagged on to the end of dogmatic assertions. Thus, although Morgan began with the needs of society rather than with an interpretation of the message of the gospel, he concluded with the assertion that the life and teaching of Jesus held the answer to the specific social problems of the day.[153] This order in his thought is important because it demonstrates the ideological basis of his publications, which took the form of social comment from the standpoint of ethical religion rather than a social treatment of theological truth.

It was through his social analysis that Morgan had concluded that the need of the age was to remove the source of evil and not merely tinker with the superficial results. In an address to the inaugural Welsh School of Social Service in 1911, he stated his belief that the church had already learned this lesson. Jesus' teaching was able to answer the social question which meant that the church would be obliged to play a prominent role in improving the material conditions of life. As a theological liberal, Morgan held that these answers were to be found in the ethical values which Jesus had expounded. The essence of his teaching, as Harnack had delineated it in his Berlin lectures, had been the brotherhood of man as a natural result of the Fatherhood of God. It was therefore incumbent upon his followers to do all within their power to establish such a brotherhood. To the degree that human society prevented the development of brotherhood through enmity, bitterness and class war, it stood in need of fundamental reformation. When this had been accomplished the task would then be to establish brotherhood itself.

Morgan certainly succeeded in demonstrating his own conviction concerning the church's responsibility to fulfil this social task, a responsibility which would, in his view, inevitably mean its having to join forces with the labour movement. The moral principles of love, justice and peace which were essential to the gospel would also form the foundations of a perfect society. These Christian principles were not mere abstractions but were intended to form the basis of practical life in this world. Morgan therefore saw religion's primary task as providing means to transform this world in contrast to the traditional pietistic view of life on earth as a preparation for the life of the next world.[154] The church's task was to condemn everything that prevented the development of character and the adoption of moral values. Thus, for example, 'combinations' in industry had to be opposed because they tended to depersonalize the relationship between owner, manager and worker, and instead of considering the worker as an individual personality treated him as a component in a vast productive machine.[155] But in emphasizing this prophetic ministry within the church, it appears that Morgan neglected to encourage a more positive contribution, or a truly Christian philosophy of life.

The two main themes which would recur throughout Morgan's work are apparent in this address. The first was the need to discover the cause of social problems instead of treating the symptoms, and the second was the assertion that the moral development of human personality was central to the Christian message. Although he claimed that 'there can be no life in isolation',[156] such was the importance of character and personality that, like Thomas Rees, Miall Edwards and John Morgan Jones, he seems to imply that the moral justification for social reform was its significance for individual regeneration. Men and women were being prevented from realizing their full potential and living the moral life by adverse social conditions. Consequently, society needed to be reformed in order to accomplish the perfection of the individual and the development of character; that is, social reform was required before people could really be Christians living Christian lives. The individual's relationship to society was highly complex however, which meant that concentration on one aspect of reform would not automatically ensure reform of any other aspect. As a result, both individual and social regeneration needed to be pursued concurrently.[157]

There was a highly radical and challenging element in Morgan's publications which was not so apparent in the writings of Miall Edwards, Thomas Rees and John Morgan Jones. At a time when most Nonconformist ministers were still closely connected with the Liberal Party, Morgan had moved beyond the accepted political stance of his profession and, with an increasing number of the working class, had joined the ILP. Rees, Jones and Edwards would remain Liberals certainly until the Great War and in Edwards's case for many years afterwards. They had initially failed to recognize the significance of Liberalism's loss of popularity and grass-roots support. But there was a further, more important reason behind Morgan's radicalism. As far as he was concerned, principles were mere abstractions until definite guidance was given on how to put them into practice. When faced with a particular issue, a concentration on enunciating abstract principles alone would always result in differences of opinion within the church if no practical guidance for application was offered. After the war, he would support this claim by the further point that individuals could not really be trusted to put the principles correctly into practice. Policies needed to be formed which would specifically guide individuals in the living of the ethical life within society.[158] He believed that the church had attempted to maintain a 'fictitious peace' by leaving its principles as abstractions. Instead, it should have offered a more definite lead.[159] Morgan himself never offered any clear guidance towards defining the minutiae of policies but he did maintain that the church, governed as it was by the principles of love, service, justice and peace, would inevitably have to take sides in social and industrial disputes.[160] This is exemplified in Morgan's own work by a general tendency to criticize the owners and the rich to a far greater degree than the workers and the poor.

The fundamental cause of the social problem was the failure to recognize the moral personality of human beings. The solution therefore would also have to be a moral one. Morgan genuinely believed that an improved social system would never be devised until both the value and the dignity of human personality were recognized. This, for him, was the 'key' to the new world,[161] and would be accomplished by stressing moral 'duty' over 'rights', and by giving a greater degree of responsibility to each worker, both through the control of his industry and more directly for his work. In so doing, human value and dignity would be recognized and established as the axioms on which industrial society should be built. Through the principle of responsibility, men would be taught to live lives of greater service, both of God by man, and of fellow-men through love of God.[162] The way of service was also the way to spiritual development as it perfected individual character and improved society.[163] It also provided the basis for solidarity among humankind, for mutual service 'makes the desire to dominate impossible'.[164]

Dignity could only be claimed for humankind on the basis of religious experience. Morgan held that apart from the religious dimension, such claims were groundless. As Jesus had revealed God to be the heavenly Father, every person was either 'actually' or 'potentially' the child ('son') of God. The basis for establishing a true society with human relationships as they should be was Jesus' proclamation of the Fatherhood of God. This, in Morgan's opinion, was the moral dynamic, 'grounded in divine authority', required to solve the social problem.[165] After having recognized human value and eternal dignity in the light of having God as Father, all aspects of life, including industry and commerce, would have to be moralized. Thus industry's sole purpose should be to serve society.[166] As 'love' and 'service'[167] were the fundamental and universal ethical principles, and consequently the most important duties for humankind, industrial competition would have to be replaced by co-operation. This would benefit industry itself in Morgan's opinion for it would avoid the waste caused by competing for profit alone.[168]

For the church to contribute a satisfactory and effective answer to the social problem, it was essential to promote Christianity as a way of life and not as a dogmatic and doctrinal system of belief. This was practical religion, promoted in Jesus' teaching as the Kingdom of God. The Kingdom was central to the Christian faith. It was in the concept of the Kingdom that morality (human effort) and religion (God's gift) were united.[169] The purpose of Jesus' ministry was the establishment of the Kingdom. This was emphasized repeatedly by those involved in the social debate. The Kingdom was an all-encompassing concept. It primarily concerned God's reign in the individual's soul. As Harnack had put it, 'the Kingdom of God comes by coming to the individual, by entering into his soul and laying hold of it.'[170] As a result, it was not restricted to the confines of the church, but could equally be discovered and realized in the world, even where there was an absence of organized religion. Despite this, it was the duty of the church to realize this reign of God practically in its corporate life and in the life of its members.[171] Jesus' message was not principally aimed at improving society, rather it was directed towards the individual, and the need for God's reign to be established within the lives of ordinary men and women. But this, it was claimed, would automatically effect social improvement: 'Only as individuals can men enter the Kingdom and therefore all the appeal of the Gospel is to men as individuals; but entry into the Kingdom carries with it a new and universal outlook.'[172]

The dignity of humankind and the value of personality were the most important characteristics of the Kingdom. So, wherever those principles were to be found, there also was the Kingdom. As a result the labour movement 'at its best' was, according to Morgan, closer to the Christian spirit than any other contemporary industrial movement, though he was prepared to accept that some of the more enlightened owners, when they practised Christian ideals, also revealed Christ's spirit.[173] The important thing was for industry to conform to the principles of the Kingdom of God which were moral and personal. In order to promote the Kingdom in every aspect of life, the church would have to familiarize itself with details pertaining to economics, commerce and industry, and then present informed policies according to both Christian ideals and the needs of society. The church could be more directly involved by helping to provide leisure activities and education facilities for the working class.[174]

One ironic aspect of Herbert Morgan's work throughout this period was a tendency to be highly critical of the church as an institution. This certainly emerged as a factor in the *Welsh Outlook*'s Church and Labour Symposium in 1918 which Morgan coordinated. He later listed the criticisms of the church as not living up to its confession: 'excessive puritanism', 'obscurantism', 'undemocratic tendencies' and also emphasizing the next world to the detriment of this.[175] But while he always seemed to encourage the church to change its outlook in order to meet the needs of labour and modern society, he never insisted on similar concessions by the labour movement. He never required that its members admit to the existence of the spiritual and its superiority over the material, nor did he criticize the anti-religious element which was rapidly gaining ground. However, nearly three decades later, as president of the Baptist Union of Wales in 1945, he appeared to have come to appreciate the value of more traditional spiritual activities in promoting the values that would create a better society:

And finding ourselves in such awful times with such a great responsibility on such feeble shoulders, should we not consider what sort of men we should be in holy conduct and godliness? Should we not, as individuals and as churches, devote ourselves to love the Lord our God with all our heart, with all our strength, with all our mind, as by doing so we will be enabled to serve our neighbours – through his service – in the spirit of the neighbourly Samaritan who was commended by Christ?[176]

Herbert Morgan's contribution to the social debate was not initially theological. He had insisted that the church's social concern should arise from the conviction that the gospel message itself had something critical to offer to the debate rather than as a response to the growing strength and vociferousness of the labour and Socialist movement. However, he always seemed to prefer to begin with a critique of society. This critique was always religious, as his understanding of religion was fundamentally ethical; it was society's lack of ethical standards, he claimed, which had caused the social problem. His work was primarily to convince the nation, and more importantly the church, of the need to apply the principles of the gospel and the message of Jesus to everyday life, both personal and social, and to attempt to ease the general suspicion which had developed among the working class and the labour leaders towards the church. It seems that his efforts did not produce much fruit, and although his 'theology' would always maintain the importance of even secular education, certainly from 1920 when he was appointed director of Extra-Mural Studies at the University of Wales, Aberystwyth, the task became too difficult for him. He may have regarded this move, and his standing for Parliament in 1918, as an extension of his work as a minister.[177] Others saw it as leaving the ministry to 'preach economics'.[178] From the beginning of his ministry Morgan had expected to be called to an educational post within his denomination. This never materialized. When he applied for the position of principal of the South Wales Baptist College in 1928 he found himself placed third on the list following the vote. Exactly why he was never offered the position of theological educator which he had confessed to be the desire of his heart is unclear, though most commentators considered that his heterodoxy, particularly in his youth, accounts for the suspicion in which Morgan was held in denominational circles. One of his friends, Nathaniel Micklem, one-time principal of Mansfield College, Oxford, remarked:

Had he been a man of less Liberal and decided views he might have pleased his co-religionists in Wales and been appointed to some ecclesiastical office worthy of his abilities. But he preached every Sunday and was known and loved by all manner of people up and down the Welsh valleys, and that, it may be, was better still.[179]

In one of his last public addresses to the Welsh Baptists in 1945 he recognized that the outlook for rebuilding the world after the destruction of war appeared to be bleak. Youth had none of the idealism that he perceived to have existed in 1919 and which had been strong and enthusiastic certainly until the COPEC conference held in Birmingham in 1924. Morgan did fail to realize that this was a fundamental ideological shift from a positive and optimistic view of human nature to a reappropriation of the doctrine of human depravity. The events of the 1930s, the economic depression, the rise of Fascism and Nazism and the horror of war all played a part in strengthening the grip of this 'new' ideology. This was a far more vital issue than the liberal theologians realized. They had all, including Morgan, believed that this new ideology, or rediscovered orthodoxy, had sprung from the pessimism of the preceding years. Ironically, on the home front at least, this 'pessimistic' outlook would be greeted with a greater resolve after 1945 to provide social welfare and governmental help and control in industry. Herbert Morgan did not live to see this, however. Another heavy smoker, he died on 22 December 1946 after a short illness.

Welsh Liberal Theology

The evidence of the thought and practice of these four leading Nonconformist theologians illustrates the nature of the social consensus in progressive Welsh theology at the time. These main protagonists of a social interpretation of the gospel all held firm to the image of Christ as the perfect man who revealed the supreme, divine, moral principles in his life and teaching to a higher degree than any before or since, and thus deserved the title 'Lord'. It was Jesus the teacher of righteousness and not Jesus the saviour from sin who was central in their message; thus moral instruction became the means to both social and individual salvation and, implicitly, more important than worship *per se*. The goal of Jesus' teaching was the creation of the Kingdom of God, which was both a religious phenomenon, the gift of God in the heart, and an ethical task to which men's lives were to be dedicated. The Immanent God whose essential being was fatherly love replaced the distant sovereign king, whom the liberals believed orthodoxy worshipped, and in so doing conferred status, value and dignity on humankind as the object of his love. This, in turn, established universal brotherhood to which all men and women belonged and involved them in the exercise of responsibility towards each other. Human beings, according to the liberal theologians, became the sole object of both Christ's existence and God's existence and, thus, also the central figure in theology. This in itself was enough to influence the church in favour of social reform as all conditions which degraded men and women were to be authoritatively opposed as contrary to the divine righteousness.

Although the principal precepts of their theological understanding were basically the same, the four men tended to emphasize different aspects. Edwards stressed the need for a doctrinal expression of the faith which took social needs and modern knowledge seriously, and allowed them to influence dogmatic formulations. Rees believed moral principles to be at the root of the universe. These principles were to be adopted and practised by men and women as they strove to develop their 'pure citizenship'. For Jones, it was the inspiration of the person and teaching of Jesus which provided the dynamic for the moral life. Morgan, however, stressed the need for an answer to society's problems and a need for the church and the labour movement to be reconciled.

One of the major weaknesses of the social theology of the period was its individualism, that it primarily spoke to each human being as an individual personality. The development of character and the practice of personal ethics were defined as being basic to the religious life. But neither the terms 'individual' and 'society', nor the ideal relationship between the two, were ever really defined, and this despite Miall Edwards's somewhat hollow claim that society was no 'mere aggregate of individuals'.[180] On reading their work, it is difficult to know what exactly it was. Such was the emphasis which all four placed on personal value and individual responsibility that at best the implication was that society consisted of an aggregate of individuals dedicated to loving service of their fellow human beings.

Similarly, a lack of an adequate definition of the state's role in contemporary life, other than to provide for individual development, was a major weakness in Nonconformist theology at this time. With the introduction of conscription during the Great War,

Rees, Jones and Morgan had all challenged the right of the state to impinge on individual conscience. When the war was over, however, Rees sought to remind everyone that, unless the state demanded something that was thoroughly evil, it was the citizen's duty to serve it in whatever it demanded. Rather than bringing clear guidance, such a generalized statement left men and women the potential victims of arbitrary interpretation, for even the war could have been justified on these criteria.

Despite differences in detail, the liberal theologians were entirely in agreement concerning the relevance of the Bible to the modern situation. Nothing could be found in the words of the scriptures to speak directly to the social problems of the twentieth century.[181] Instead the church, and the followers of Jesus, had to interpret and then apply his words to the contemporary situation as part of their moral duty. This was a major weakness, for agreement, particularly on practical measures to counter the social problem, proved by and large to be impossible. Herbert Morgan came to believe that individual men could not be trusted to give concrete and practical expression to eternal truths, and his desire was to see definite guidance offered by the church. John Morgan Jones alone seems to have retained an unwavering faith in the right of the individual conscience to follow its own lead, providing it did not encroach on the freedom of others, though even he came to expect more guidance from the church than the mere enunciation of principles.[182] Our problem does not concern the accuracy of their philosophical and theological claims, but whether or not they were consistent. Critically, they never offered the clear advice that they had claimed was required, and at the same time demonstrated an inherent weakness in their thought, namely that the very principles which they espoused, particularly individual freedom of conscience and the absolute importance of human character, did not ultimately lend themselves to social reform without a certain amount of reinterpretation. As in Christian orthodoxy, the development of individual character was judged to be bound up with a commitment to self-denying service. But such a commitment itself was almost certain to affect individual freedom. The inevitable result was a weakening of the claim that 'individual freedom' was a moral principle of eternal significance, and its replacement with the need for sacrificial service. Despite the promise and optimism with which they advocated

social interpretations of the gospel and recommended moral principles 'guaranteed' to draw men's attention towards their social
responsibility, they went no further. In practice, the churches
as denominational institutions, as well as the majority of
Nonconformist ministers, did not proceed beyond the stage of
withdrawing from worldly institutions into the stage of challenging the presuppositions of the status quo.

The stress on responsibility and the moral principle of service
was summed up in Thomas Rees's idea of 'pure citizenship' and
is what John Vincent has more recently called the pattern of
'cultural insiders'.[183] It was the duty of Christians to infiltrate
business, government, education and all other areas of human
activity and to persuade the adoption of a superior morality by
personal influence, witness and example. Yet the action of the
church as a whole in this period seemed to aim for what Vincent
calls 'radical discipleship'. Nonconformist ministers, including
the four mentioned above, came to believe that their role was not
to involve themselves directly in overtly political activity but to
challenge society with an all-pervading interpretation of the
gospel, which would naturally reform society and solve social
problems without necessarily directly targeting specific issues.
Such a Christianity would automatically challenge the status quo.
However, it became important for several reasons to sustain the
two views which, if not mutually exclusive, proved to be hardly
compatible. It has to be said that, far more than eschewing politics, the stance of the 'cultural insider' should have prompted the
corollary of a politically active church. Herbert Morgan in fact
encouraged such a more radical input from the church, but most
Nonconformists, particularly after 1918, felt that they could not
comply even when they were certain that to do so would be in
support of gospel principles rather than party politics.

In some respects, the problem stemmed from the enthusiastic
adoption of the doctrine of God's immanence. As God existed
everywhere, humankind could gain benefit, and be led along its
developmental path to the goal of perfected individual character,
under any condition and in any situation. Thus, while God was
not to blame for the social conditions which prevailed, he could
use them to fulfil his own purposes. A possible result of this was
to claim that while every effort should be made to improve living
and working conditions it was to be noted that adverse conditions

build character.[184] The Idealist notion of the unity of all reality would ultimately become a hindrance to the prophetic task of the church, for even when they had identified singularly evil social and personal practices, these theologians had also to admit that they could not be wholly bereft of virtue.

At the basis of their thought, all four men demonstrated a superficial theological exposition of Christianity's social teaching. Although Edwards and Rees had both treated doctrinal topics, when they discussed Christianity's social mission their tendency was to ignore doctrine totally. Instead of a doctrinal expression of the Christian truth applied to the social needs of the day, these progressive Nonconformists tended to rely on familiar, inspiring motifs. As a consequence, they offered no real ideological basis to the existence of the church, either as the society of the redeemed or as the means to preach salvation. They offered no doctrine of sin, whether personal or structural, to support the claim that sin was the cause of social problems. Although 'man' figured prominently in their work, it was man in whom the potential for redemption already existed through the influence of the immanent God, rather than man in need of redemption. All in all, their message depended on the recognition of responsibility by human beings to employ the highest morality in their personal and commercial dealings. It was wholly individualistic and lacked any real definition of society. But, more importantly, it undermined the need for a church and the need for a saviour.

The question of technical orthodoxy, which certainly did not concern Miall Edwards,[185] is demonstrative of the problems which Welsh Nonconformity faced in attempting to provide an adequate social theology. The doctrine of God was obviously of great interest to theologically minded Nonconformists, with the doctrine of the Trinity being in the centre of attention during the 1920s. Thomas Rees appeared to adopt the Modalist position of successive revelation while Miall Edwards tended to mirror Paul of Samosata's heresy that Christ grew progressively in divinity. Both denied that the relationship in the Godhead was of necessity to be restricted to three 'persons', while also questioning terminology such as 'substance' and 'person' which they considered foreign to the mind of modern men and women.[186] Edwards was a particularly careful thinker whose theological claims were tightly argued from the basis of Hegelian idealism. His logic was impeccable, yet in choosing Idealism as his starting-point he appeared also to adopt a nonchalant attitude towards traditional orthodoxy. In a tribute to Thomas Rees he wrote:

> I used to chaff him with being a Sabellian and he would retort by calling me a Samosatene or even an Arian! I think we were orthodox in spirit and intention, though somewhat heterodox in form. But we knew that theological labels solve no problems, and that technical orthodoxy is a matter of little importance in comparison with the experience of God in Christ which the orthodoxies and even the heresies endeavoured with varying degrees of success or failure to safeguard.[187]

Both Rees and Edwards had discovered precedents in the Early Church for their theology but had done so in the thought of men condemned as heretics. This did not bode well for the production of an acceptable social theology.

It was not theological difficulties and considerations alone which prevented the formation of a better society during the optimistic years which followed the Great War. Other considerations such as the control which the capitalists exercised through political contacts and economic domination, the lack of real vision and political will, together with the genuine difficulties of government all conspired to ensure that no great steps were taken. But it should be clear that there were inherent problems within the prevailing religious thought of the time that made such a realization all the more difficult. The theology which was intended to support social reform was weak. It did not take traditional doctrine sufficiently seriously and as a result tended to rely on assertions that were often unscriptural and based on what individuals considered to be theological 'common sense'. The liberal theologians had adopted a particular philosophy (Idealism) and used it to interpret theology and social needs. They relied far too much on the use of words and phrases which they thought conjured up the right kind of image without really defining what they meant. In the case of the Kingdom of God, they were hardly faithful to the evidence of the gospels in overemphasizing the ethical interpretation. Perhaps liberal theology, with its inherent weaknesses and contradictions, did not lend itself to social concern and reform. Certainly the failure to achieve anything concrete would appear to point to such a conclusion.

A Social Gospel?

As has been noted, the basis of most progressive Welsh religious thought during the 1920s was liberal theology as interpreted by Ritschl and Harnack and undergirded by Idealist philosophy, which particularly emphasized the fundamental unity of all things and the governing force of reason in the universe. But to what extent can this be claimed to have been a social gospel?

According to Rhondda Williams, the justification for a social gospel was that 'The organization of industry and commerce makes it impossible for even the best men to act upon the essential ethical principle of Christianity embodied in the words: "Thou shalt love thy neighbour as thyself."'[188] This would suggest that the basis of the social gospel was the moral relationship between human beings. Its initial task was to assess critically the social and economic environment and decide whether or not it impinged on humankind's ability to accomplish all moral requirements. Although the four Welshmen mentioned above would have agreed that moral relationships formed the basis of the religious life, and probably also recognized social criticism as a necessary function of religion in the modern world, on this criterion only Herbert Morgan offered a social gospel, because his work alone had concentrated on a critique of society. For Jones, Rees and Edwards, even a description like 'liberal theology with a social conscience' would be inaccurate. Their interpretation of liberal theology, with its emphasis on the Kingdom, was inherently conscious of human society even if they ultimately concentrated on the need for individual improvement and moral effort in the conviction that Jesus' teaching dealt naturally and simultaneously with both individuals and society. However, their ideas only constitute a 'social gospel' in the sense that the application of Jesus' message, although not necessarily directed towards social systems, would naturally reform society. Usually this would occur through the reform of the individual.

Rhondda Williams is probably a poor example of a 'social gospeller'. He was far more concerned with the reinterpretation of religious truth along modernist lines than with offering a specifically social application of that truth. As a convinced Hegelian, he believed in the fundamental unity of all truth and consequently he saw Socialism as the practical application of Christianity, and both were simply expressions of the one, single Truth behind the universe. He was one of the first in Britain to publish a book under the title *The Social Gospel* (London, 1902), but the volume merely encouraged the church to support Socialism. It was not therefore an attempt to state clearly the social teaching of the gospel *per se*. And there was no shortage of Nonconformist ministers who looked to the political movements of the ILP and to Socialist politics in the period leading to the Great War to bring about social redemption. At least initially, Herbert Morgan was of this opinion. He still recognized the *a priori* importance of the church and its religious mission but he longed for a union between the church and the labour movement in the years before 1914. The Revd Herbert Dunnico[189] also came to the attention of the Welsh public in those years as a politically minded Nonconformist minister. He was an early example of a liberal theologian, close to the mainstream of church thought and life, and yet at too early a stage to develop a specifically Christian understanding of the social question. He was, in reality, a Socialist supporter but his message appears to have been moderate and one that therefore appealed to chapel men whose disaffection with the Liberal Party was only gradually developing.

Although born in Cefnybedd, Wrexham, north Wales, Dunnico never ministered in his home land. He joined the Labour Party while minister at Kensington Baptist Chapel, Liverpool, and demonstrated an ability to hold his political and religious views in balance, being president of both the Liverpool Free Church Council and the Liverpool Labour Party. He established a 'Socialist League' during the National Free Church Council conference in Swansea in 1909. Although seventy-one ministers and forty-three laymen subscribed to the league, its influence appears to have been minimal. It was no more than peripheral to the activities of the Free Church Council conference which had concentrated on the principal Nonconformist shibboleths of education and disestablishment.[190] After this, politics *per se* gradually became more important for Dunnico than specifically religious activity. His life and career, as with some of the Welsh

Nonconformists involved in the ILP, are testimony to the blurring of the divide between the sacred and the secular that Idealism made inevitable. To follow conscience, to work for the betterment of the human race and to pursue such a calling outside the church, could all be interpreted as within the remit of ministerial vocation. Dunnico's radicalism came not so much in the ideological stance that he adopted but in the fact that he decided to leave the ranks of the ordained ministry in order to place his energy into creating a new society through parliamentary methods. He became a Labour MP and was later knighted. Although Herbert Morgan once stood for Parliament, and Thomas Rees and John Morgan Jones were at one time local councillors, they never contemplated any further 'direct action'. Indeed, their absolute trust in didactic methods resulted in a tendency to appear nonchalant regarding more practical activity towards social improvement.

In 1913, the *Merthyr Pioneer* published an article recording Dunnico's views on the subject 'Why Christians should be Socialists'. He concluded that not only do Socialism and Christianity have similar objectives 'but in reality they are one'. He described the New Testament message in classic liberal terms as being concerned with God's Fatherhood and man's brotherhood and the advent of the Kingdom of God. Christianity was the 'union of all who love in the service of all who suffer', and stood for personal righteousness, social progress and the establishment of the Kingdom. Instead of leading to the development of a social Christianity, this reasoning led Dunnico into accepting Socialism whose object was 'the reshaping of human society upon such lines as shall secure equality of opportunity for all and freedom to live the largest and best of all possible lives'.[191] For Dunnico, both Christianity and Socialism were primarily moral forces. They advocated the sacrificial service of the community with the establishment of a perfect state based on a common brotherhood as their goal. He had adopted Socialism because it sought to remove all obstacles to true brotherhood. It was not, therefore, an economic doctrine. Nationalization and the principle of state control were advocated simply as 'the most expedient method' to arrive at the goal of the 'fullness and unity of life'. At this time, Dunnico considered that Socialism held a greater similarity to the religion of Jesus than did the religion of the church. The church was too passive, concentrating on the need to believe certain doctrines and trust that this was sufficient for eternal salvation. Dunnico believed that there was a need to be active, to 'do' rather than merely to 'believe', and he saw the labour movement as offering the opportunity to exercise a more practical vocation. It is hardly surprising, therefore, that he should enter Parliament.

Similar messages to that of Herbert Dunnico were propounded in Wales in the period before 1914. The romantic poet R. Silyn Roberts, until 1912 a Calvinistic Methodist minister initially in London and then at Tanygrisiau, Blaenau Ffestiniog, had advocated the ILP's Socialist message as not merely compatible with Christianity but the practical outworking of Jesus' teaching.[192] The Revd D. D. Walters (Gwallter Ddu), Congregational minister at Newcastle Emlyn, had embarked on a tour of the western coalfields in June 1908 to spread the Socialist gospel and had become the most committed of all Socialist firebrands.[193] Perhaps the most celebrated Nonconformist Socialist in the period before 1914 was the Revd T. E. Nicholas, Congregational minister at Glais in the Swansea Valley. His persuasive articles in Y *Geninen* (between 1912 and 1914) and his Socialist poetry brought him to the attention of the Welsh public and he was soon in great demand as a speaker throughout the country. All three had recognized the ethical nature of the Socialist message and emphasized nationalization as its primary economic tenet mainly because it would help establish justice in the economic system through common ownership and fairer distribution of wealth. And because it sought justice, fairness and equality, it was compatible with Christian faith and indeed it was the practical application of Jesus' teaching.

Much of what Herbert Dunnico said in the years before the Great War found echoes in the work of Thomas Rees, D. Miall Edwards, John Morgan Jones and Herbert Morgan. But despite some obvious similarity, Dunnico's 'social gospel' in reality was the Socialist message as propounded by the labour movement rather than a specifically social interpretation of Christian truth. This was a common response before the Great War. Nonconformist ministers were attracted to the labour movement for its prophetic criticism and moral dynamic which would see the social evils of the day vitiated. But while supporting Socialism naturally meant the propagation of *a* social gospel, it did not necessarily mean a social interpretation of the *Christian* gospel. This was where the opinions of both Rhondda Williams and

Herbert Dunnico were inadequate. They had both been led, at least initially, to place their hope and trust in the labour movement to establish a new and more just society. They, like other Nonconformists who had been wooed by Idealism, would have seen Christianity and the labour movement as two possible responses to the single truth behind all reality. But in doing so, they could no longer justify claims to Christian uniqueness and, in the long run, they contributed to a secularization of society. It is not without significance that Dunnico became a Member of Parliament, that both Silyn Roberts and T. E. Nicholas eventually left the ordained ministry. For them, as for the four principal Welsh theologians, it was not simply the attraction of the Socialist message which inspired their thought and prompted their call for social reform. These men, influenced by Idealism and by Kant, found true religion in the truly moral. As a result, it was the religious spirit, as it was revealed in the labour movement, that attracted them and justified their involvement. The exception to this appears to have been D. D. Walters who later renounced his Socialist affiliation and concentrated on the preaching of an evangelistic gospel. However, the 'social gospel' as far as it was expounded by these men, or by Miall Edwards, Thomas Rees, John Morgan Jones and Herbert Morgan, was ultimately inadequate. These men had largely eschewed directly political activity in favour of a more obviously religious and theological standpoint, which had no direct means of accomplishing its goals. Dunnico had at least entered the sphere which would ultimately dictate social policy but in so doing the inherent dangers of a socially orientated gospel were clearly demonstrated. It could mean that traditional religious forms were to be deemed inadequate and consequently to be abandoned. Nonconformist ministers at this time were forever battling against the temptation to be involved in politics while at the same time trying to influence society and economic practice towards a more just and wholesome way of life. It was in many ways an impossible situation.

The Wider Theological Context

It was not in their originality of thought that the Welsh Nonconformist theologians contributed something to the social debate. In fact they can be viewed in the broader context of British theology, particularly that of the Nonconformists, at the time. The writings of Will Reason, T. Rhondda Williams, Alfred Garvie, S. E. Keeble and Ebenezer Griffith-Jones all display a common dependence on the claims of liberal theology.[194] For these men, the social implications of Christianity were to be worked out as an essential part of the individual's faith, where true love of God would issue forth in the love of fellow human beings. Thus, their theology was essentially moral and individualistic. It affirmed the motifs of human 'value' as a direct result of God's Fatherhood and the consequent brotherhood of man. Because of this fraternal relationship, the salvation of the individual and the salvation of society had to be viewed as 'two sides of one endeavour' and thus the brotherhood formed would create the new age which could only arrive through the sanctification of men and women to the moral task. This therefore affirmed the moral responsibility of the individual which was to be revealed in the world and established in society through the practice of love. The church was then to pursue these policies on a personal and individual level, as well as in its corporate witness and influence.

None of this adopted the specific title of a 'social gospel' despite claiming to be the basis of social reform. This is significant because the title was in common usage certainly by the 1920s and may consequently have been rejected by the majority of British theologians, certainly the Nonconformists, possibly on the grounds that it suggested a sectional interest on the part of the gospel instead of the whole picture of the redeeming power of Christ. If this was the case, then it should be remembered that 'redemption' by this time was largely perceived to involve a moral transformation in the individual character far more than the idea of salvation from eternal damnation. More importantly, Nonconformists tended to be adamant that the Christian message was first and foremost addressed to individuals and not intended to reform society. The term 'social gospel' had been popularized initially in America.[195] The question is, therefore, whether the American social gospel offered a pattern and a precedent to which the Welsh models complied, and whether it offered an inspiration for the Welsh theologians.

Even in America, the term 'social gospel' was not common until the years following 1900. Previously, those who were concerned to present a social understanding of religion referred to 'social Christianity'.[196] As Rhondda Williams's definition implies, the social gospel developed from a recognition of the injustices inherent in industrial society and the practice of economic Capitalism. It was inherently political and while not all American social gospellers recommended Socialism as a fairer economic system, they all desired an economic and political change to establish a social system based on fairness and justice. Its theological roots were certainly in the liberalism prevailing at the time, particularly as defined by the Ritschlian School. Thus it, too, laid particular stress on the value of individual personality as a child of God, that men and women, being essentially or at least potentially good, had the ability to bring about social reform, that such reform could come about through the sanctification of individuals and that the ideal to present before the world was that of the Kingdom of God. In all this, human beings become partners with God in creating a better world. The social gospel called for all individuals to recognize not merely their social rights as citizens but to realize and exercise their social responsibilities. This was usually accompanied by a stress upon 'Christ's way of love', as that would lead all people into service for the good of society as a whole. The role of the church was consequently to multiply the number of individuals who would live their lives dedicated to service of the wider community.

Although neither the first, nor the only, social gospeller, the American theologian most closely connected with the concept, and the one who systematized his thinking most cogently, was Walter Rauschenbusch.[197] Though a church historian by training and 'intellectual liking',[198] his eleven years' pastorate at 'Hell's Kitchen' in New York City had opened his eyes to the injustices in society. It was this experience which made him formulate a social interpretation of Christianity.[199]

Rauschenbusch drew heavily on the work of Ritschl and his pupils, and presented the same ideas as those listed above. Although, like many liberals, his theology was ethical rather than metaphysical, he is significant because of his insistence that doctrine was important. He had by the 1890s turned against the concept of automatic improvement and progress in the history of humankind, and begun to emphasize the need for individuals to know the presence of the spirit of the risen Christ, to recognize the immanent God, who held the dynamic to transform them into socially conscious, serving, Christian people.[200] For Rauschenbusch, the very essence of Christianity was the dynamic which it provided to create a new society. This would be achieved through the regeneration of human relations.[201] Each individual would contribute his own changed personality and so 'realize a new type of Christian manhood' which would overcome evil and build the Kingdom.[202] The evil inherent in the social order itself meant that environment and circumstance played a role in individual sinfulness.[203] The need was therefore to Christianize the social order which would build the principles of love, justice and sacrificial service into the social system and would also link Christianity 'with the highest objects of statesmanship'.[204] In the face of the social embodiment of sin, it was simply insufficient to recommend that men and women love their neighbours. This assumed that they had the ability to choose to do right.[205] This was not the case, as the unchristian social order was causing good people to do evil things.[206] The need was for human commitment and sanctification, through communion with the immanent God, and to live lives of service of the Kingdom. The Kingdom dealt with the physical needs of humankind and offered redemption through a commitment to service.[207] It required 'good sense' and 'holy will' far more than dogma and speculative theology.[208] But as it was central to the religion of Jesus, the church would have to change its system of practical theology, its ritual, prayers, hymns and its evangelism in order to encompass it.[209]

The essence of religion was morality, resulting in the promotion of both ethical values and duties. This, together with a concentration on immanence, made it a natural development for Rauschenbusch to insist that religion could be found outside the church. Religion included the ideals of love, tenderness and longing as well as the willingness to sacrifice self for the salvation of others, as in the labour movement in America.[210] Thus, where men and women were engaged in meeting the practical needs of society inspired by the great principles of Christianity, they were living the truly religious life, even though they may have lost all specific religious consciousness.[211] Religion is therefore dependent on the fulfilment of moral duty[212] and this brings Rauschenbusch back to the image of the Kingdom which 'establishes organic unity between religion and morality'.[213] This

Kingdom must be central or else the redemption of the social order becomes an 'annex to the orthodox conception of the scheme of salvation'.[214]

The similarities between the American social gospel and the work of the progressive Welsh Nonconformist theologians are obvious. Although there was often a sympathy towards some kind of collectivism amongst both American social gospellers and the Welsh theologians, and they shared the belief that political reform was required, it was not the case that their theological understanding was bound to political Socialism. Rauschenbusch's work certainly seems to have emphasized the need for political measures to a greater degree than that of the Welshmen. No doubt they would have recognized the need for such measures, but their work emphasized the regeneration of individuals connected to personal morality and responsibility, with the belief that such a scheme was unavoidably social and more uniquely Christian and religious.

Despite the similarities, it is unlikely that Rauschenbusch himself had any direct influence on either English or Welsh theology at this time. Miall Edwards, for example, had certainly read his work and had used *A Theology for the Social Gospel* in preparing a Christian witness questionnaire.[215] But Edwards had been moving in this direction for many years, even having hinted at it in his ordination service. In answering questions concerning the content of his gospel, Edwards recognized the need to preach Christ. By this he meant three things: to preach Christ directly, to preach about contemporary problems and issues in the spirit of Christ and to apply the religion of Christ to all aspects of life, both personal and social. Thus, the basis for Edwards's involvement in social issues later in his career was already laid by the time he was ordained to the Christian ministry at Salem Welsh Independent Church, Blaenau Ffestiniog, in October 1900.[216] Herbert Morgan has been quoted already as seeing the Kingdom as the union of religion and morality[217] and Miall Edwards made the point that the Kingdom was both a gift to be received and a task to be accomplished.[218] But far from quoting Rauschenbusch, all three were quoting from the work of their theological mentors, Ritschl and Harnack. Industrial problems, together with the rise of a strong, vocal and political social movement, had inspired theological developments in Britain towards a social understanding of

Christianity that was ultimately bound to the most recent theological formulations. This was echoed in America where similar industrial developments had taken place. Although Rauschenbusch is probably the theologian who made most use of the title 'social gospel' in this period, his basic tenets were echoed in Britain by those who had been influenced by the works of Ritschl and Harnack. What these Welsh Nonconformists offered was merely the individual, moral regeneration of liberal theology. But this was meant to be inherently social in character.

3

A Crisis for Faith

But as for you, teach what is consistent with sound doctrine. (Titus 2.1 NRSV)

The vital issue facing Welsh Nonconformists at the end of the 1920s and beginning of the 1930s was the formulation of an adequate theology, one that was not too divorced from the historical faith of the church while also being sufficiently contemporary to speak directly to the needs of a modern industrial society. There were still liberal radicals who continued to challenge the church with a provocative message that associated the gospel almost exclusively with social critique. Usually this included a, by this time inevitable, criticism of the church and its failure to respond to the needs of the age. During this period, Herbert Morgan continued to claim that the church should pay more attention to the physical aspect of life and to worry less about church attendance. Wales was in a far more perilous state than England regarding issues of health, particularly the incidence of tuberculosis and death in childbirth. This, and not full chapel buildings for Sunday services, should be the major concern of the churches.[1] The Revd J. H. Howard, a Calvinistic Methodist minister, looked to Jesus as the 'agitator' whose ministry consisted primarily of a protest against the status quo. It was the church's task in every age to follow the master's example. The church needed to recognize and to affirm in its theology and worship not only that the very fact of 'life' was far more important than material possessions but also that 'vacant cupboards are not unrelated to empty churches'.[2] Simply put, his message was that society had to be renewed before the churches could reach the masses with the gospel. This was merely the reaffirmation of the kind of socially orientated religious message promulgated by Nonconformists since the Great War. For men like Morgan and Howard,

Christianity could only be a credible force in society when it proved its practical value in its moral effect on men and women, both individually and socially. Such a standpoint was becoming increasingly difficult to maintain, however, and this was in some respects a result of the attitudes developed under the influence of liberal theology. The liberals had argued that the church's business was to discover timeless values and pronounce eternal principles. As a result, the church's task was not to identify and solve the specific problems of any particular age but to proclaim the general principles which, when adopted as axiomatic in daily life, could bring about a transformation in individual human beings and in society as a whole. The point was well expressed by the Revd D. H. Davies, Brynaman, who argued that although conditions of life and work should be improved, to do so was not the explicit task of the church. The church's calling was to ensure that the men and women who would inhabit such an improved environment would be 'developed in the spiritual sense'.[3] In other words, the church existed to ensure that individuals adopt the eternal principles of love and self-sacrificial service. This was the church's mission in every age and could be effected whatever kind of social conditions prevailed. The implications of such a stance for the future of Welsh theology were highly significant. Davies had perceived that social renewal had been overemphasized and that somehow this was not the religion of Jesus Christ. The Christian gospel concerned greater things than specific problems associated with a particular period in history. The emerging dissatisfaction with official theology would draw support from the development outside Wales of dialectic theology as an alternative to liberal Modernism. Before too long, the propriety of expounding a social interpretation of the Christian message at all would be questioned and found wanting.

The 1920s proved to be the heyday of social theology amongst Welsh Nonconformists. Their social ideology, unsophisticated as it was, had been developed through an involvement in various organizations dedicated to social renewal along Christian or religious lines. Perhaps the most important were the Welsh School of Social Service which was inaugurated at Llandrindod Wells in 1911, and *Urdd y Deyrnas* (the Guild of the Kingdom) which was established after the Great War to draw on the optimism, vision and energy of youth in the task of rebuilding a war-torn continent.

In the early 1920s, the Welsh Nonconformists attended the national Conference on Christian Politics, Economics and Citizenship (COPEC) held at Birmingham in 1924 and the International Conference on Life and Work held in Stockholm the following year. Despite the absolute dedication of most of the delegates at Stockholm to the application of Kingdom principles in social life, the conference was far more important for marking the first signs of a definite shift in theological reflection that would soon challenge the prevailing liberal interpretation of Christian faith. The Welsh liberals had viewed the Great War as a historical blip, a minor setback on the path to ultimate perfection. The task after the armistice was to return to that path as quickly as possible. For others, however, the war had demonstrated the untenability of such a neo-Hegelian philosophy of history. It was the young Karl Barth, recently departed from his village pastorate at Safenwil, Switzerland, for the chair of Reformed Dogmatics at the University of Göttingen, who would forcefully draw attention to the inadequacies of theological liberalism. As time went by, he would construct a viable theological framework which would ultimately replace liberalism and provide a basis from which theologians could discover a revitalized meaning to religious truth.

Barth's reaction came to light in his commentary on the Epistle to the Romans published in 1919. His own theological education had been at the feet of the great Modernists and leading exponents of the Ritschlian theology, Adolf Harnack at Berlin and Wilhelm Herrmann at Marburg, and, initially, Barth was attracted to their humanistic and ethical approach to theology. But both Harnack and Herrmann offered unmitigated support to German militarism at the outbreak of war in 1914, and this led the young Swiss pastor to discern a fundamental weakness if not a thoroughgoing bankruptcy inherent in their liberalism. He looked again at the teaching of the church fathers, to Kierkegaard and Dostoevsky, and to 'the strange new world of the Bible' and in the light thus gleaned he led the attack on liberal theology that would soon become a positive reaction against it. Instead of the parity of moral substance between humankind and God, Barth proclaimed that the two were dialectically opposed. They existed in different spheres. Human beings were sinful and finite, while God was holy and eternal. Men and women could not of themselves reach God

but depended on God's self-giving revelation for all their knowledge of the divine. Men and women could not, if left to their own
devices, reach the moral heights necessary to live godly lives; only
the transforming grace of God in their lives could count their
efforts as righteous, not in virtue of inherent goodness but because
of the vicarious suffering of Christ for human redemption. The
Hegelian dialectic by which a dynamic relation of opposites
would lead to a perfect synthesis, had been abandoned in favour
of Kierkegaard's dialectic for which the opposition between things
finite and infinite and between human beings and God was
axiomatic. Synthesis was still possible, but only in the God-man
Jesus Christ who alone effected atonement in his very person. For
Welsh theology, which at that time was largely based on the dual
foundation of ethical Idealism and a social interpretation of the
gospel, the implications of Barth's critique of liberalism were
profound. For too long the principality's theologians had been
encouraged to believe that salvation, whether personal or social,
was a human task. Now they were challenged over the very basis
of their theological system. Dialecticians such as Barth demonstrated, in a way that had been lacking in mainstream theology for
years, that men and women need God. Without God, all efforts at
social reconstruction would come to nought. And God was the
creator, sustainer and redeemer known in traditional Christian
theology as eternal Trinity of Father, Son and Holy Spirit.

Although Barth's ideas were originally published in 1919, they
did not reach Wales until the mid-1920s. They came to the notice
of Welsh Nonconformists partly as a result of the International
Conference at Stockholm. During the deliberations ideological
differences came to light between the theology of the German delegation on the one hand and Anglo-American theology in general
on the other. The differences became particularly evident in
connection with the doctrine of the Kingdom of God and the
human responsibility of establishing it. If, as the German delegation had insisted, the Kingdom belonged to a different realm from
the material and physical, then God alone could bring it into existence. The liberals, who had called the conference, saw this as
defeatism. They perceived that the needs of post-war reconstruction made a concerted effort for human improvement vital if war
was never to darken the continent again. As a result, all people of
good will needed to commit themselves to the construction of a

social system based on justice and righteousness. In their view, this could be nothing but the Kingdom of God. Behind the alternative view of the Kingdom which the German delegation proffered, there was a feeling that liberalism was an inadequate expression of the truth of the Christian faith, a conviction which had been moulded by the horror of the Great War. Far more than revealing humankind's incessant, progressive development towards perfection, the War had revealed the primitive corruption at the base of human existence which had traditionally been described in Christian theology as 'sin'. This had tremendous consequences for the social application of Christianity. Men and women could no longer be trusted to opt for the good and to work for the higher ethic of love of neighbour commensurate with love of self (see Mt. 22.37–9 etc.) and achieve personal fulfilment through so doing (see Jn. 15.13).

The second source of dialectic theology in Wales was a more direct and didactic one. In 1927, J. D. Vernon Lewis published an exposition of Barth's thought in the students' periodical *Yr Efrydydd*.[4] Vernon Lewis's articles testify to the excitement that Barth's commentary on Romans effected by breaking away from the hackneyed means of biblical interpretation hitherto employed. His complaint concerned the way in which the higher criticism had become an end in itself rather than a means of approach to the scriptures. He recognized the value of biblical criticism but pointed to the fact that its worth had been overestimated.[5] When discussing biblical topics the need was not to be made aware of modern scholarship but to be challenged directly by the Word of God.[6] This is what Barth had succeeded in doing. His commentary had therefore brought a freshness into biblical study that, for Lewis at least, was long overdue. He, for one, could understand that Barth's commentary had sent a 'thrill of surprise' through the ranks of biblical scholars on the continent and had caught the imagination of a younger generation of Christian theologians and ministers who were searching for a way out of the dead end into which liberalism had led them. Despite the ripples of interest Barth was causing in Europe, Lewis noted that very little had been published in Britain discussing Barth's contribution, while none of his work had been translated into English. This in itself was not to be a hindrance, however. Lewis called for a Welsh translation of Barth's books. The Welsh needed to have access to the greatest thinkers of the age in the vernacular. He was convinced that such a task could be accomplished, there having been a theological faculty in the Welsh university for a quarter of a century. It was time that the Welsh broke away from their dependence on the English in theological matters. For that reason he accepted the invitation of Miall Edwards, the editor of *Yr Efrydydd*, to write on Barth's theology, convinced that Barth had much to say to correct the misunderstanding of religion and revelation prevalent in modern theology.

Being strong on paradox, Barth's literary style was difficult to convey. Despite this, Lewis was convinced that, after reading the dry and lifeless work of the liberals for so long, the Swiss prophet would be an inspiration: 'It is as if he [the reader] is suddenly overtaken between sleeping and waking by some dawn which shakes us back and forth to lead us along new and uncharted paths before slipping again in quicksand.'[7] Lewis said very little about the content of Barth's theology. Instead, he listed the influences on Barth, ranging from Schleiermacher, against whom Barth reacted, to Kierkegaard, whose system of dialectics he accepted and expanded. He noted that Barth had rejected the idea that the gospel could be summarized as religious feeling or experience. The stress on human experience, prevalent in theological reflection since Schleiermacher, was the cause of theological apostasy. Rather than offer an accurate portrayal of the divine object it gave a far clearer picture of the human subject. In fact it was no more than the parade of human wisdom which is foolishness before God. It is striking that Lewis described Barth's objection to liberalism and its stress on feeling and experience. Yet, inexplicably, he did not explain what Barth regarded as the positive content of the gospel.[8] It could have been that, for Lewis, Barth's message was unclear at that time. Despite the consequent tendency towards criticism rather than construction, Lewis was certain that Barth, like Schleiermacher, was 'beginning a new era in the history of theology' but that he would take a completely different direction from that of his predecessor.[9] Clearly, Lewis believed Barth to be offering something new and different from the liberalism then in vogue, and that the Welsh reader would be inspired by his commitment to the task rather than persuaded by the effectiveness of his argument.

For his part, D. Miall Edwards noted the significance of the articles first as an alternative to the theology which prevailed in Wales at the time, and second as the most thorough treatment of Barth's work to appear to date in either Welsh or English. Edwards's footnote to the articles is interesting. He considered that Lewis's articles were an 'important contribution to Welsh theology and a means to bring us into closer contact with the thought and life of the continent'. Edwards believed that 'we should all give the best consideration to the teaching of this school, whether we agree with it or not'.[10] He certainly held no sympathy with the Barthian position. In fact he may merely have seen this as an opportunity to familiarize the religious public with a theological position against which they would have to fight if a new world was to emerge from the ruins of the old.

The Modernists on Karl Barth

Perhaps at this stage it would be helpful to look in a little more detail at the Modernist response to dialectic theology in Wales. This will help us to see more clearly what Barth was proposing and why the liberals objected so vehemently to his theological scheme. But first a word of warning. It is not primarily Barth who speaks but the liberals, and one liberal in particular (namely, D. Miall Edwards), in their response to him. Also, the Barth whose work is criticized is the young pastor-cum-theologian of pre-*Church Dogmatics* days. It is not the sophistication so much as the novelty of his thought which was important. In this, his rise to prominence is all the more significant. Virtually overnight, he became a theological celebrity on the basis of a rejection of the prevailing liberalism that was accompanied by attractive, though not always explicit, proposals for theological reconstruction. Doubtless the despair felt in Germany when the war was lost did contribute to a general suspicion that neo-Hegelian influence on religious thought had ended in an ideological cul-de-sac, and that the only course of action was to turn around and rediscover the basics. Barth provided the framework for a theology which was far removed from the principles of liberalism. The almost instantaneous recognition of his importance demonstrated the effect which his commentary had caused. It had indeed proved to be a veritable bomb which had exploded in the theologians' playground.

The undeniable fact and nature of the Welsh response to Karl Barth's work has been chronicled by Dewi Eirug Davies.[11] Perhaps the most significant reaction was that of D. Miall Edwards. Two years after his commendation of Vernon Lewis's articles he published a more detailed response in *Y Traethodydd* entitled 'The gospel according to Karl Barth' which later appeared as an appendix in *Bannau'r Ffydd* (1929), Edwards's most systematic theological treatise. It took the form of a review of Barth's book *Das Wort Gottes* (published in English as *The Word of God and the Word of Man*, London, 1928). In this Vernon Lewis had the advantage over Edwards. Lewis was sufficiently versed in German to have access to Barth's work in the original; he had in fact studied for a period at Leipzig, having been awarded a travelling (Proctor's) scholarship from Mansfield College, Oxford. Edwards, alas, had to wait for the appearance of an English translation.

For Edwards, *The Word of God* was not Barth's most important book; that honour belonged to his epoch-making commentary on Romans. It was characterized by 'energy rather than balance and order' and was far more 'a prophet's manifesto' than a 'neat body of theology' (*Bannau'r Ffydd*, p. 383). As a result, it was not easy to understand. Despite this, and despite an inevitable disagreement on fundamental theological principles, Edwards considered it to be of vital consequence that Welsh people read the work. They needed to 'know about important and influential movements which are happening beyond the narrow limits of our own land'. For this reason he actively sought a translation of the work of continental thinkers into Welsh. Edwards was a nationalist. He had recognized, and expounded, the value of language and culture and emphasized the differences which existed throughout the world and within the United Kingdom. But he was no narrow partisan. Differences in culture and outlook were to be put to the common good as all nations contributed to the drama of history as it is acted out on the world stage. Wales and the Welsh people, for him, should be no exception to this rule. It was this, and his pragmatic recognition that the written and spoken use of the Welsh language was to be encouraged, that led to his call for major philosophical and theological works to be translated into Welsh. He had himself translated Descartes's *Discours de la méthode* (*Traethawd ar*

113

Drefn Wyddonol) in 1923. Furthermore, he believed theological reflection to be a peculiar attribute of the Welsh mind and psyche. This had to be fed. Hence the Welsh needed Barth to speak their own language, even if ultimately his views should be rejected.

The first point that Edwards made was that Barth's style made the book particularly opaque. Vernon Lewis had previously indicated that Barth's theology was not easy to follow. But whereas for Lewis the freshness of Barth's literary style, in contrast to the moribund liberal approach to biblical study, was one of the attractions of his system, for Edwards this was clearly a serious weakness. It was Barth's dialecticism that was ultimately to blame, with the reader left confused 'at the speed of his nimble movements from one pole of thought to the antithetical pole, without revealing the path which leads from one to the other' (p. 383). Perhaps this was Edwards's greatest blindness. He could not accept that no such path could possibly exist. He wrote lyrically of Barth 'jumping as a squirrel from one tree to the other and back again, until he surprises you by his skilful feats, or causes you to catch your breath worriedly in case he falls between the trees!' He demonstrated Barth's literary style and his theological method with a quotation from *The Word of God*:

> *This* No is really Yes. *This* judgment is grace. *This* condemnation is forgiveness. *This* death is life. *This* hell is heaven. *This* fearful God is a loving father who takes the prodigal in his arms. The crucified one is the one who was raised from the dead. And the explanation of the cross as such is eternal life. No other additional thing needs to be joined to the question. The question is the answer.[12]

Though not entirely invalid, Edwards's criticism of Barth's method and literary style somehow missed the point of the Swiss theologian's work. In the dialectic argument Barth was offering something completely different from the prevailing Idealist view of harmony and unity. Far from offering a new theology, Barth claimed that he was offering a corrective through emphasizing a great truth revealed and accepted long ago but since become lost in the ideological maze of theological liberalism and philosophical Idealism. Barth's theology was Christocentric, demonstrating the universality of God's love and redemptive action through the particularity of the life, death and resurrection of the man Jesus

Christ who was God incarnate. This, too, struck at the heart of liberalism, which had emphasized the generality of God's presence through immanence within the creation and human existence, by nature rather than by grace. By attacking harmony and unity on the one hand and stressing the particularity of Christ on the other, Barth broke away from liberalism and offered a cogent basis for theological construction. Edwards's article demonstrated the problem to good effect. He and Barth were two theologians representing two fundamentally different theological traditions, whose thought was based on different axioms and, as a consequence, they were conscious only of the truth of their own interpretations. They had, of necessity, to consider the other's view to be false. Despite his attempt to be descriptive, it is in Edwards's description of Barth's critique of contemporary theology that the philosophical distance between the two men becomes apparent. Since Schleiermacher, emphasis had been placed on the authority of religious feeling, with theology and the creeds of the church seen as expressions of that religious experience. Religion itself had been seen in historical terms as man's search for God. The Bible was simply the chronicle of that quest. For Barth, this had overemphasized the human role in religion, life, the universe and everything else. The objectivity of God's revelation from beyond experience and breaking into history in apocalyptic fashion had been forfeited. The greatest failing in liberal Modernism had been to subjectify religion totally, becoming real only in the depths of human being, in a person's feelings and psyche. He repeated the dictum that all human attempts to find or to reach God were mere 'towers of Babel'. The process could only be one of revelation from God to humankind. By realizing this and accepting the gracious judgement which it involved, men and women are able to receive God's revelation, and that revelation was found in the Bible.

It is clear, however, that Edwards had seen the human search for God as in itself a kind of revelation, or at least as part of the revelationary process. His familiarity with Descartes is significant as he appears to adopt as axiomatic that *cogito ergo sum* (I think therefore I am) offered the formula on which to base all perception of reality. The ability to reason validated existence, but the concept of existence required the exploration of the depths of the self. As man looked in on himself, which was after all the basis of

all he could consider as real, he came into contact with the immanent God as the ground of his being and of Being itself. More than
this, however, he recognized two equally important dynamics.
Knowledge of God depended on God's act of revelation but also
on human preparedness to act in interpreting the information
conveyed in the revelation, thinking about it and, in the light of
the knowledge thus gleaned, subordinating oneself in obedience
to the divine will. As far as Edwards was concerned, Barth had
refused to see these human actions not only as relevant but as
vital in religious faith. Edwards wrote:

> It will be seen that Barth does not aim for balance, otherwise he would
> be more prepared to recognize that the Bible contains man's thoughts
> about God as well as God's thoughts about man, man's history as well
> as God's history, men's standpoints as well as God's standpoint ... But
> a prophet, it is said, does not aim for equilibrium. Through his one-
> sided emphasis on some truth, he challenges his fellow-men to listen to
> him, forcing them to awaken and to rub their eyes in amazement, to
> see what is going on! (p. 385)

Ideologically, Edwards and Barth were simply poles apart.
Barth, in his reactionary stage, could not conceive that human
beings had any part to play in the process of revelation. Later, he
would develop the idea of 'awakening' whereby human beings
responded to revelation in a way inspired by the revelation itself.
So, the possibility of man knowing God is actualized in God's
revelation of himself. As he later wrote, 'man is capable of
perceiving the God who meets him and reveals himself to him;
that he is capable of distinguishing him from himself and *vice
versa*; that he can recognize his divine being as such and his word
and his will.'[13] For the moment, however, Barth simply
contrasted human weakness and helplessness with God's gracious
action on behalf of his creatures. For Edwards, the idea that God
alone could bridge the gap between the divine and the created
order was unhelpful and philosophically unconvincing. In order
to be effective, even Barth's scheme required that something exist
on the human side that would provide firm supports on which the
full weight of revelation could be held. Edwards's argument is
attractive and reasonable. But, convinced as he was of the fundamental union between human beings and the immanent God,

Edwards in fact went further than pointing to the reasonable claim that divine revelation requires a human response in order for something to have been revealed. For him, the divine and the human always overlap, which tended, in his thinking, to depreciate the concept of a unique incarnation in Christ. God, for Edwards, may be searching out lost human beings, but human beings, as Augustine himself had prayed at the beginning of his *Confessions*, were naturally predisposed to search out God: 'Thou hast made us for thyself, Lord, and our hearts are restless until they rest in thee' (*Confessions*, I/ I (I)). In rejecting this, Barth had been too Calvinistic for Edwards's taste.

The sum of Barth's positive contribution to theology, according to Edwards, was his insistence that only through death to all things of the flesh and the world could men and women enter into eternal life. It was the discovery of hope through and beyond despair. To Edwards, this sounded remarkably close to the liberal insistence on self-sacrifice as the principal ethical demand on followers of Jesus. But, for Barth, the discovery of that hope did not require a reconstruction of Jesus' perfect humanity as the ideal for the Christian life. Barth had discounted the importance of the quest for the historical Jesus, and therefore the need to discover an inspiration to live the moral life, in favour of an emphasis on his death and resurrection as a single incident, concurrently a negation and an affirmation, the 'No' and 'Yes' which belonged together. Furthermore, it was not the historical event of the cross that was important, but the spiritual truth which it encompassed. In Edwards's words describing Barth's position; 'the cross represents the No, judgement, death, despair and man's bankruptcy, and the resurrection represents the Yes, life, hope, grace and God's sovereignty.' In Christ's resurrection a new world was created which simultaneously destroyed and replaced the old. In this, God breaks into human history from his position of transcendence and sovereignty. Edwards discerned that Barth had returned to Calvin's doctrine of *soli Deo gloria* (to God alone be glory):

> The pitiful failure of man on the one hand, the sovereignty and all-sufficiency of God on the other hand, that is the two parts of his mission. And these two are one. The Yes and the No are one. Man's need is God's opportunity. (p. 387)

Edwards's objections should be obvious. In emphasizing God's 'otherness' and holiness, Barth had rejected his closeness, his immanence and his Fatherhood. In an attempt to emphasize their depravity and sinfulness, he had neglected to see anything of God's image in human beings. Thus, instead of recognizing their moral value and potential for goodness, Barth's scheme required that men and women recognize the futility and worthlessness of their state and their efforts. Rather than centring on the fact that man had been made 'a little lower than the angels' (Ps. 8.5 KJV) he chose to remember that he was 'a worm and no man' (Ps. 22.6 KJV). Barth had rejected the internal, experiential and psychological aspects in religion which were the very aspects Edwards had always considered to be of vital importance. Even if liberalism had neglected revelation, God's transcendence and, to an extent, his objective personality, this was an insufficient justification for replacing the positive methodological process and the sources of authority which had been identified and promulgated by the liberals. Experience and human understanding were in fact vital to the concept of revelation if it was to have any real meaning in human life:

> Barth wears himself out (*ymorchestu*) in speaking of 'God's truth' as something 'incomprehensible, unpsychological (*anfeddylegol*), unhistorical' (p. 69) ... Barth talks of God breaking through to man's life. But with respect I say that the infinite cannot, or at least does not wish, to break into man's life except on the lines of the laws of man's mind, which he himself ordained. (p. 388)

This was, of necessity, a presence and revelation that had to be worked out on the stage of history, in physical, material terms, processes and frameworks. Thus to speak, as Barth had done, of 'non-historicity' in the Bible was foolish. The Bible itself was written in just such a worldly framework, and consequently belonged to history rather than eternity. According to Edwards, this demonstrated the development of religion from a lower to a higher ethical form. It is probable that it was the early Barth's apparently nonchalant attitude towards history which worried Edwards more than anything. For Barth, at this time, it appeared to be unnecessary for Jesus to have been a historical figure at all. Despite his own emphasis on the two 'non-historical' events of crucifixion and resurrection, the former as humankind's 'No' and the latter as God's 'Yes', Barth deemed that they gained no greater significance if shown to be historical incidents. The question for Edwards was clear and important: if the crucifixion and resurrection were not in some sense historical events, that is occurrences that took place at a particular point in the past which somehow have saving efficacy for the present, what exactly were they?

Despite Edwards's criticisms, however, and despite the fact that his objections shine forth from every page of this review, Edwards was far too circumspect an author and too liberal-minded a scholar merely to make the point. He recognized Barth's value in recalling attention to the 'sublime pinnacles of the gospel' according to Paul, Luther and Calvin, particularly his continuous references to human failure and God's grace. Furthermore, Edwards considered the restatement of God's lordship, sublimity, majesty and transcendence to be a timely one, providing that theology did not lose sight of God's immanence and Fatherhood. Barth had also called theology back to contemplate God's being 'with his essence in himself' rather than in human experience of him. In this he was prepared to see that liberalism had overstated its case. But, for Edwards, it was the Roman Catholic Modernist thinker Baron Friedrich von Hügel who had succeeded in doing this rather than the 'one-sided, unbalanced and extreme' Barth, and he advised that his readers consult von Hügel's work. Edwards's reference to von Hügel is particularly significant. He had recognized previously that von Hügel was, at best, an eclectic thinker whose work had received little attention in Welsh publications and whose name would mean nothing to the ordinary chapel-goer. 'As a saint and thinker', wrote Edwards, von Hügel 'reaches such brilliant heights that I can do no more than say in the words of the Psalmist "such knowledge is too wonderful for me; it is high, I cannot attain unto it"' (Ps. 139.6). Like Barth, then, von Hügel's work was not easily understood, yet Edwards was clearly far more appreciative of this Roman Catholic mystic than the ultra-Protestant, Reformed theologian from Switzerland. In fact this was hardly surprising for, despite differences in detail and ecclesiological allegiance, Edwards had recognized in von Hügel an intellectual effort and pilgrimage similar to his own. Von Hügel had attempted to bring together modern learning in the fields of biblical criticism, science and philosophy with the 'wealth of truth and religious experience' of which the Roman Catholic Church was safeguard. This was far closer to the theological task for the contemporary church in Edwards's view than Barth's attempt to deny all the discoveries of Modernism.[14]

By the time that Barth's thought had arrived in Wales, dialectic theology had become a more viable option than merely an ideology of despair inspired and fuelled by the total defeat of 1918, which was the common perception concerning Barth's early work. Even if not yet in the ascendancy, Barth's theology was being claimed as a feasible alternative to liberalism. Having said this, there were still liberals whose allegiance to Hegelian Idealism was unflinching and who consequently did not know how to cope with the inherent pessimism which they discerned at the heart of the Barthian dialectic, particularly in its view of human helplessness and the consequent inability to work for the common good and the establishment of the Kingdom of God. For them Barth and company had merely reacted to defeat in the war and in so doing had given expression to the degradation and despair of a whole nation. Miall Edwards had voiced such an opinion on his return from the International Conference on Life and Work where it became clear that dialectic theology had deeply influenced the German delegation. 'There was', he wrote, 'the colour and taste of the bitter experiences of the last few years on the ideas of these Germans. A deep undertone of disappointment and hopelessness was heard in their words'.[15] But there were others who would repeat similar allegations even as late as 1938. In that year, Rhondda Williams published his autobiography, *How I Found My Faith*. As the title may suggest, the book is a chronicle of how his theological views developed and changed through his life, replacing an orthodox, Calvinistic, dogmatic religion with neo-Hegelian philosophical faith. Needless to say, he also launched a hostile attack on dialectic theology:

> This movement is not without a touch of that fanaticism that arises from despair. One can understand its rise in Germany in the post-war years when people felt as if all humanity had become devil possessed, and where Germans had lost confidence in themselves, feeling that the heavy foot of the conqueror had trodden them down. That this

condition gave strength to the appeal of Bart [sic] is pretty evident in the fact that now, when the Germans have become more hopeful about themselves, Bartianism [sic] is on the wane in that country. How English ministers became infected with it is past my comprehension. The more I look into Bartianism [sic], the more impossible it becomes ... I hope I live long enough to see those who have been infected by it recovering their sanity. (p. 215)

For Williams, it appears that Barthian theology became the victim of Nazism, which he interpreted as the result of increased German confidence. Hindsight of course is an unfair advantage which we have over Williams and his generation, but his own words appear to condemn him. The absolute horror of Hitler's regime has been proved since 1945 as the thoroughgoing evil of his 'final solution' and the concentration camps have been revealed. Yet, even in 1938, it should have been clear that Hitler's government represented a far more insidious and dangerous force than that of merely over-exuberant Germanic confidence. The Nazi dictatorship had been established as early as 1934, with anti-Semitic legislation following in 1935 with the passing of the Nuremberg Laws. In 1938 Hitler annexed Austria and the Sudetenland, with Czechoslovakia to follow, sacrificed on the altar of appeasement. Historians will always have to consider the guilt and naïvety, or even culpability, of those holding political power and religious authority at this time, for many the darkest period in the twentieth century. The signs were there if only those who had eyes would see. The truth is that most, still traumatized by the memory of the previous conflagration, probably did not want to see. In the light, or otherwise, of all this, Williams's comments appear naïve to say the least. If Barth's theology was to fall victim to Nazi posturing and oppression then this would now appear to be far more a commendation than a condemnation.

The Revd Morgan Watcyn-Williams, Calvinistic Methodist minister in Merthyr Tydfil, Glamorgan, expressed the belief that liberalism had been corrupted by individualism and that it needed to be reformed rather than rejected. 'We shall remember too', he said, 'that Marx was no Marxist, and hope that Barth is not Barthian.'[16] He recorded this in an article which, by implication, linked the trend in German theology with totalitarianism. Thus, for Rhondda Williams totalitarianism had rendered Barthianism

121

unnecessary, while for Morgan Watcyn-Williams totalitarianism and Barthianism represented the same spirit in different spheres. Such an accusation was ironic to say the least. Barth was a Swiss democrat and a leading figure in the German Confessing Church that had been established in opposition to the totalitarianism of the Nazi regime. Liberals like Rhondda Williams and Morgan Watcyn-Williams were absolutely committed to their Modernism and refused to be shaken from their ideological foundation simply by being presented with Barth's corresponding assurance that in fact they were misguided. It was this rather than a clear perception of dialectic theology that inspired their initial response to Barth. Of the four main social gospellers identified earlier, Miall Edwards's view was clear. Thomas Rees died before the arrival of a cogent explanation of Barthian theology, but he, like Edwards, would have opposed it and probably for similar reasons to the Brecon theologian. Herbert Morgan was virtually silent on strictly theological topics during the 1920s and 1930s. In his address to the students of the Presbyterian College, Carmarthen, in 1945, he hinted that his objection to Barth was similar to that of Edwards. Barth had argued against the inherent religiosity of human beings, restating the maxim that they were fundamentally sinful and therefore unable to reach God by their own efforts. God was the 'wholly other', beyond the means and grasp of creaturely men and women. But if so, asked Morgan, 'how can it [the divine] be even appreciated or known in any degree by an understanding so tainted and infirm as that which is attributed to men?' It was not the 'wholly other' God who was revealed in the New Testament but the 'God and Father of our Lord Jesus Christ'. Jesus encouraged his followers to approach this God with the paternal acclamation of 'Abba, Father', the one who was ready to forgive man's sins and weaknesses and receive him as a son.[17] John Morgan Jones, Bangor, believed that the dialectic school represented the theology of 'panic' and was in danger of undermining all the progress which liberalism had achieved in the political, social and religious spheres. Despite all this, the Modernists failed to realize the one important factor. Dialectic theology was pointing to the far more significant possibility that liberal theology was at heart inadequate and that this, rather than its corruption, had led to the theological reaction.

Liberalism or Christianity

One of the first books to offer a critique of the prevailing liberal interpretation of theology was *Christianity and Liberalism*, published in 1923 by the American John Gresham Machen (1891-1937).[18] Machen was a Presbyterian minister and assistant professor of New Testament Literature and Exegesis at Princeton Theological Seminary, New Jersey. After the Great War, he found himself embroiled in the controversy that erupted within his denomination between the protagonists of liberal theology on the one hand and the stalwarts of Calvinist orthodoxy as enshrined in the Westminster Confession on the other. Machen was a leading light among the latter group. He perceived that the danger facing the church was far more insidious than that which denominationalism presented, because division was now occurring within ecclesiastical bodies over theological understanding and outlook. Although sales of his book reached the 5,000 mark in 1924, it is difficult to measure its effect and it is unlikely that it was influential in Britain. But it provided a cogent objection to liberal theology at the very time that Anglo-American theological optimism was at its height. Simply put, liberalism had transferred the emphasis in theology from God to man (p. 154). For Machen, liberalism did not take historic Christian doctrine sufficiently seriously and consequently it had no claim to the name 'Christian'. The liberals had been so busy *applying* Christianity that they no longer had any conception of the content of the Christian gospel: 'The Liberal believes that applied Christianity is all there is of Christianity, Christianity being merely a way of life; the Christian man believes that applied Christianity is the result of an initial act of God' (p. 155). Hence, for Machen, the Christian life was not merely the application of the 'Golden Rule' of selfless and serving love in personal and social fields but was fundamentally concerned with the relationship between human beings and God, a relationship that had gone awry and was put right only by the atonement made by Christ. Those who knew him, and agreed with him, recalled a humble man whose intellect and broadness of mind allowed for disagreement and disputes of opinion. To his Princeton colleague, Caspar Wister Hodge, he was 'the greatest theologian in the English-speaking world [and] the greatest leader

123

of the whole cause of Evangelical Christianity'. Those who found themselves representing a different standpoint and understanding often vilified and dismissed him as an intolerant bigot. Though uncomfortable with the title 'fundamentalist', his defence of 'historic Christianity' emphasized the relation of Christian doctrines earmarked as axiomatic for faith, and he in fact built his argument upon a naïve fundamentalism which rejected the propriety of interpretation in favour of rigid acceptance of the perceived kerygma of the early church. The original Christians, those who had written and then collected the scriptures, were closer to Jesus in time and were consequently more likely to present correctly both the words and the implications of his teaching. Having said that, Machen showed, more effectively than most, that the application of ethical principles as the sum of Christian life, which was the cry of the liberal Modernist, was a policy which was seriously flawed. Based on the Kantian theory of ethical imperatives, it had been assumed that the necessary 'ethical principles' belonged to the realm of common knowledge and had been hailed as moral maxims by popular consent. It was equally averred that they found their origin in the life, death, teaching and example of Jesus Christ. In reality, however, these principles were neither generally recognized nor commonly prac- tised in social structures and institutions. They belonged to a particular philosophical world-view which was then undergirded with proof-texts or with the call to recognize in Jesus the first truly moral human life. The fact was that men like Machen were questioning that world-view and found it to be grossly inadequate and incompatible with their understanding of Christian truth.

Although initially unaware of the full significance of the chal- lenge of dialectic theology and the bankruptcy of liberalism, at least one prominent British Nonconformist theologian quickly realized that it was no longer possible to present a social and ethical interpretation of the Kingdom of God without the nagging suspicion that something was not quite right. Alfred Garvie (1861–1945), the Congregational theologian and principal of Hackney and New College, London, had played a prominent part in the decade's social Christianity debate.[19] He was vice-chairman at the COPEC Conference and, due to his mastery of the French and German languages, he had also played a prominent part at Stockholm. Though he would always remain firmly in the liberal camp in theology, Garvie had come to doubt the propriety of using Kingdom imagery in the context of the social question partly through the persuasive effect of the German delegation's dialectic theology. In Garvie's case, this was all the more significant as he had formerly been one of its most fervent advocates. In his lectures to the students of Mansfield College, Oxford, in 1899 he presented 'The Ritschlian theology' as a possible Christian response to current problems. Garvie had endorsed Ritschl's interpretation of the Kingdom as an 'evangelical idea [which] will enable the Church to meet the social demand made upon it'.[20] In his opinion, Ritschl had removed the individual as the object of God's love and replaced him with the community. Although he considered this to be an overemphasis, Garvie recognized that this was also the necessary inspiration for social reform.[21] Thus the emphasis on the Kingdom placed God's love and attention firmly on humankind collectively instead of on each individual human being, and the search for salvation on humanity as a whole. This, Garvie believed, would give the churches the imagery, as well as the moral dynamic, they needed to contribute to the social discussion.

That was in 1899. Garvie's most important theological works were written after the Great War, by which time it was clear that he had changed his mind. This change in his theological understanding was most apparent in his book on ethics, *The Christian Ideal for Human Society* (London, 1930), part of which had been delivered as public lectures in the University College of North Wales, Bangor, two years earlier. Initially intending to refer to the Kingdom in the book's title, he rejected it because it was unclear whether it should be seen as an eschatological or ethical concept (p. 42). Instead of the term Kingdom, Garvie suggested the image of the 'family of God' as being the closest concept to the Christian moral ideal, namely 'God revealed in Christ as Father, and man redeemed in Christ as child of God' (p. 44). Garvie made no change to the ideological basis of his social thought. He still believed that society could be reformed through the adoption of moral principles in national policy and institutions, and that this required the Christianization of its citizens (pp. 52–3). Instead of a change in policy, the Stockholm conference merely changed the terminology which Garvie was prepared to use. The ideal was still brotherhood, but brotherhood would lead to the establishment of a family rather than a Kingdom.

125

Different theological interpretations of the Kingdom at this time caused sufficient concern for an Anglo-German conference to be convened. The direct result of the differences in theological interpretation encountered at Stockholm, the conference met at Canterbury, between 14 and 19 April 1927 and consisted of six German representatives and six British theologians. Amongst those present was C. H. Dodd who, if not inspired by the conference, was certainly aided by the discussion as he came to formulate his proposals for a Realized Eschatology. The proceedings of the conference were recorded in *Theology* for 1927.

In Wales, no such modification was made to the liberalism which had offered the Kingdom as the ultimate goal of human effort. Instead, there were the representatives of fundamentalism and of the reaction to theological liberalism, both of which became prominent in the late 1920s. Time and again, the call to rewrite theology was heard during that period. It was claimed that the young suspected systematic theology on both philosophical and ethical grounds.[22] Nonconformists were called upon to define their politics, social thinking, theology and churchmanship.[23] However, events seem to have conspired to ensure that this never proved to be the case. Apart from Miall Edwards's systematic treatise, *Bannau'r Ffydd*, published in 1929, no theological reconstruction along liberal and Idealist lines was attempted. In place of this, theological controversy ensued as a rediscovered orthodoxy attracted younger Nonconformists. The work of two, Martyn Lloyd-Jones (1899–1981) and John Edward Daniel (1902–62), was of particular significance for Welsh religion generally but also for social Christianity in particular.

Lloyd-Jones[24] had left his career as a surgeon in London in order to preach the true, evangelical faith to his countrymen. The result, in his first pastorate at Aberafan, was nothing short of a revival. His fundamentalist approach to scripture, and his preaching of the need to escape the coming judgement by fleeing to Christ, were in sharp contrast to the moralistic approach of the Modernists steeped as they were in a so-called scientific, critical approach to the Bible. Daniel,[25] on the other hand, was a far more subtle and sophisticated theologian than Lloyd-Jones, and he spent the 1920s and 1930s not in pastoral charge of a church (in fact he was never ordained) but as a tutor at the Bala-Bangor Congregational theological seminary. He developed an early critique of liberalism that condemned the Modernist concentration on human beings as moral creatures able to make their own decisions and able to affect their environment and consequently able to achieve their own salvation. Liberalism had dethroned God and in his place had deified the human race. Both Lloyd-Jones and Daniel vilified the liberal concentration on social issues to the detriment of the church's task, namely to preach the gospel of Christ's redemption of the whole creation from the fatal grip of sin.

Perhaps the most remarkable contemporary conversion from an extreme social gospel to a renewed orthodoxy was that of the unconventional Congregational minister (and later Anglican priest) D. R. Davies (1889–1958).[26] His book *On to Orthodoxy* chronicled the sea-change of theological view which occurred in his life. Initially, he had espoused a Christianity that involved the application of social principles and required that the church translate them into the structures of society (p. 131). This had brought him into involvement in COPEC (p. 107), it had led him to read the work of Walter Rauschenbusch (p. 130), and it had resulted in his commitment to socialist politics and the Labour Party. Later he, like Daniel, insisted that the gospel did not consist in the application of moral principles to social institutions but that it was the good news of God's redemptive plan fulfilled in Jesus Christ and instituted for the salvation of humankind. The gospel, he claimed, was highly personal and addressed people, not systems (pp. 17–18). Society would only be Christian when all people became Christians through personal confession and commitment and not through the embodiment of so-called Christian principles in social, political and industrial institutions (p. 132). Although he had at one time believed that the Kingdom of God was a social utopia which would be established in history,[27] he came to believe that the Kingdom had been weakened by linking it to human activity alone and thus losing its other-worldly aspect (p. 16). Although Davies argued that the Kingdom enters into history through redeemed lives (p. 135), it is not even finally established by the regeneration of all men and women, for it depends totally on God's will. It did not belong to the realm of evolutionary (or, for that matter, revolutionary) activity but to the apocalyptic realm. It had to be revealed, it could not be constructed.

Davies linked the ascendancy of liberalism to the particular historical situation of the time, and he further believed that historical phenomena had proved its insufficiency. Clearly he held a close interaction to exist between theological formulation and environmental conditions, almost to the point of suggesting that different theological preconceptions were necessary in order to face the world as it was perceived in different periods in history. Such had been the call of the theological liberals. They had seen the need to relate their faith to the needs and philosophical concepts of the age. Dialectic theology had not made such a claim. It was a reappropriation of the eternal gospel of Jesus Christ. For Davies, however, dialectic theology too depended on the exigencies of the day, as he showed with regard to the Barthian dependence on a pessimistic world-view:

> Christian Liberalism was, to a considerable degree, the working of an unconscious historic need, namely, the need of a social system to expand and grow. That is the significance of its doctrine of progress and its doctrine of man. Its heyday coincided with the prosperous, ascending years of capitalist civilisation. With the coming of crisis and decline, Christian Liberalism has gone into shadow and become discredited. We are witnessing the rise of new tendencies, which, in fact, are a return to some classic, traditional ideas of Christian orthodoxy. Barth is one of its symbols – and symptoms. Harnack was the expression of a proud, prosperous Germany. Barth was the expression of a Germany and a whole system in defeat. (p. 24)

For Davies, then, his rediscovered orthodoxy did not simply empower him to proclaim the eternal gospel but offered a more adequate interpretation of the gospel for the needs of the day. This corresponds with his own religious preconceptions held from the days of his liberalism, and it corresponds to his stress on *his own spiritual journey* during which he reclaimed his faith through a profoundly disturbing experience of God while suffering in the depths of depression and attempting suicide. His experience had been that despair had allowed him to come 'face to face with God'. It was only when an individual was brought to his or her lowest point, recognizing his or her own worthlessness and depravity, that the truth of the gospel could be grasped and the love of God be experienced or known as real. This experience of divine reality then raises the individual to a status of dignity and infinite value.[28]

Extreme as Davies's views were, this was a personal appropriation of the Barthian emphasis on discovery of hope beyond despair, but it seemed also to depend on the liberalism of Davies's early years as he searched for an adequate expression and conceptualization of his newly confessed orthodoxy. However, in Davies's view it was not Barth but the neo-orthodox Reinhold Niebuhr who offered the most satisfying explanation of Christian faith. Niebuhr had shown him 'the fatality of radical sin'. For Niebuhr, it was impossible to *achieve* social utopia because of sin, but he still emphasized the need to work towards a better society under the grace, forgiveness and acceptance of God in Jesus Christ.[29]

Within the context of a naïve reaction against liberalism and towards dialectic theology, where Modernists threw up their hands in horror at the backward step about to occur, the neo-orthodoxy represented by Davies, Lloyd-Jones and Daniel was gradually achieving a credibility amongst younger Nonconformists. The days of liberalism with its inherent social gospel were drawing to a close. During the 1930s, less and less was published in the denominational and secular press insisting on the application of Christian principles to political, economic and social structures, and this occurred despite the obvious need for improvement in the international situation and for relief from the depressed economy at home. The situation inspired pessimism far more than optimism. It may also be that political and social pessimism compounded the popularity of this 'new theology'. But if this is the case, then it merely highlights Modernism's inability to speak clearly and powerfully to a generation that could find no optimism either for its social and political future or for its spiritual life. Events had demanded a modification of certain liberal axioms such as the inherent goodness of humankind and the unavoidable progress of history towards inevitable perfection, but this need had been largely neglected by the liberals. As a result, there arose a crisis for faith. What now could Christians in general and Welsh Nonconformists in particular believe? As the liberals and the dialecticians faced each other from opposite poles a debate arose around this question, though finding an answer would prove to be an impossible task with an elusive goal.

John Morgan Jones

Towards the end of the 1920s, dialectic theology had begun to pose challenging questions to the prevailing liberal understanding of religious faith. This was a period of theological controversy and the figure who found himself at the centre was John Morgan Jones. Jones had been appointed principal of the Bala-Bangor Theological College in 1926 following the untimely death of Thomas Rees. Of all the Modernists it was he who most fearlessly applied the discoveries of biblical criticism and investigated the theological claims of the orthodox creeds. He took his answers to their logical conclusions and, as a result, came to emphasize the need for education to supplement, if not replace, the attempts of religion to lead men and women towards the ethical life. In this he eschewed metaphysics, and held an inherent distrust of creeds and dogmatic formulations. That he would find himself at odds with the new Barthian theology is hardly surprising. It was, however, his rejection of older orthodoxies which initially brought him to the midst of controversy over the case of Tom Nefyn Williams.

Tom Nefyn Williams (1895–1958) was inducted as minister of Ebenezer Calvinistic Methodist Church, Tumble, Llanelli, in 1925.[30] His unorthodox style in leading worship as well as his heterodox theology soon brought him into conflict with the patriarchs of the faith in Welsh Methodism. Dr Owen Prys, principal of the United Theological College, Aberystwyth, who had supervised Williams's ministerial education, was the one appointed by the Connexion to pronounce judgement on Williams's theological views. His report, though expressed in a kindly spirit, was ultimately damning. Williams had 'lost faith in the Trinity, the incarnation – apart from the incarnation inherent in every man – and in the divinity of Christ – apart from that divinity of which every saint partakes. Jesus Christ was not the only Saviour; he was one amongst others who have left their mark on mankind. It is true that Jesus' influence was wider than everyone else's but he was not the unique Son of God. He denied completely Jesus' atonement'.[31] The result was in many respects an inevitability. Williams was prevented from ministering in the Methodist church at the Nantgaredig Association in August 1928.

On the surface at least this incident had nothing at all to do with John Morgan Jones. It was simply a matter of internal discipline within the jurisdiction of a different Nonconformist denomination. Yet Jones, who had recently become the editor of Yr Efrydydd, the Welsh journal of the Student Christian Movement, found it impossible to remain silent. This, for him, was no mere question of theological orthodoxy but one of freedom: freedom of religious belief and theological expression. And this was fundamental to his understanding of the Reformed and Dissenting traditions as well as his understanding of the Christian gospel. More than anything else, Jones believed intensely in the right of the individual to express his or her faith according to the dictates of conscience with no reference to external authority, that of the Pope or of an official Confession of Faith. Thus, to excommunicate a minister on the grounds of a confession was 'the most important and most accursed (melltithiol) incident to occur in Welsh church and religious history'.[32] As editor of Yr Efrydydd, he used its pages not only to support Tom Nefyn Williams but also to protect and defend the valid approach to the truth of God. In so doing, he unwittingly contradicted the broad-minded axioms of his own liberalism, for while no person and no religion could have a monopoly on the 'truth', the way to that truth can be highlighted and followed. But the implication is that there was only one way and that the liberals had discovered it:

Yr Efrydydd believes without any doubt that the only way to save Wales and to save her churches from blight and curse is to release Christ from the theologian's iron fetters and from the grip of dead ecclesiastical traditions about him to do his own work in his own way.[33]

Jones had discerned this release within Williams's work. He was attracted instinctively to the minister from Tumble and the result was that he was labelled a heretic for his pains. Peter Hughes Griffiths vehemently protested that Jones had no right 'to pronounce his curses upon our church'.[34] D. J. Lewis, the theologically orthodox Welsh Independent minister in Tumble, lost all sympathy with Jones and refused to support the Bala-Bangor College so long as he remained principal.[35]

The whole incident was unfortunate. Whatever Williams's shortcomings, the Methodists would merely appear intransigent and completely void of compassion in their dealings with an ordinary and popular minister. Williams himself remained in an ecclesiastical wilderness for a few years before returning to the Methodist Connexion in 1931. He resumed his ministerial vocation during the following year. His supporters at Tumble left the Methodist Church and formed their own fellowship, Llain y Delyn, membership of which was open to all and not prescribed by an official Confession of Faith. The members of Llain y Delyn invited Williams to become their pastor, a request which he declined. It was they perhaps who were the real victims, having been inspired and led by a man whom they later perceived to have betrayed them. Jones himself came out of the incident relatively well. He had demonstrated great courage in supporting a man deprived of his livelihood simply through an inability to adhere to what he perceived as an outdated and ethically unacceptable creed. He had recognized that religious leadership can require a crossing of denominational boundaries, and he was prepared to stand alongside Tom Nefyn Williams rather than isolate him in the outer darkness beyond the church to which the ecclesiastical authorities have always sought to banish the theologically heterodox. Controversy in this instance had not come directly through Jones's expression or defence of liberalism but from his genuine compassion for those whom he perceived to be suffering from oppressive authority and from his absolute belief in the freedom of individual conscience. When such issues were at stake, Jones's support could always be relied upon. This is the classic position of the Reformed and Independent theologian, but Jones's intervention in the Tom Nefyn Williams controversy was not unproblematic. Methodism was based on different axioms, finding its unity in a Confession of Faith and in its administrative order. John Morgan Jones did not recognize the importance of this and was guilty of transferring the principles of *Annibynia* (Independency), which he considered to be the kernel of the gospel, into the Methodist church. Other incidents occurred when Jones reacted against the claims of other Nonconformist theologians when he perceived the principles of Modernism to be under threat from more recent theological developments. The first man to suffer this criticism was the Revd W. D. Davies.

John Morgan Jones v. W. D. Davies

William David Davies was born in 1897, the son of the Revd
Isaac Davies and Margaret Jane Davies.[36] From Friars School,
Bangor, he progressed to Jesus College, Oxford, via the Meyrick
Scholarship which awarded him £80 a year. He had been a
student at Oxford for one year when the government introduced
a Bill to conscript men to the armed forces to fight in the
European war. Davies declared himself to be a conscientious
objector and spent the remaining war years working on the land.
He was able to return to his studies in 1919 and graduated with
First Class Honours in Theology in 1922. At that time, it is said,
Davies was offered a fellowship in the college accompanied by a
lectureship in Divinity in the University on the condition that he
join the Anglican Church. His Nonconformist convictions proved
to be too strong and, instead of embarking on an academic career,
he was ordained within the Calvinistic Methodist Connexion and
became minister of Shirland Road church in London in 1923. At
the same time he undertook work for the degree of BD in the
University of Oxford. When he sat his initial examination, he was
one of the first two Nonconformists to be allowed to matriculate
for that degree in the ancient university. He was awarded the
degree in 1927. Following two years as pastor to Cathedral Road
church in Cardiff, Davies was appointed to the chair of
Philosophy and History of Religion at the United Theological
College, Aberystwyth.

Davies belonged to a different theological generation from John
Morgan Jones. He was almost twenty-five years junior to the
principal of Bala-Bangor and had consequently developed as a
theologian under different ideological presuppositions. According
to John Thickens, Davies was a 'neo-fundamentalist'. He was
entirely orthodox on all aspects of the creed including the
doctrine of the Trinity in which there was no 'hint of Sabellianism
or any other "ism"'.[37] Although Davies identified certain dogmas
as being unimportant for faith, such as the Virgin Birth, he generally asserted the orthodox faith of the creeds, which was reflected
in the title of his BD thesis, 'The sufficiency of the doctrine of the
person of Christ in the definition of Chalcedon', which won him
a share of the Ellerton Theological Prize in the university.

Having said that, it is not insignificant that Thickens could only commend Davies as a '*neo*-fundamentalist'. His years of academic training had not gone entirely unheeded because he had accepted philosophical Idealism as a way of describing both the content of faith and religious experience. He was also willing to accept the discoveries of biblical criticism so long as they did not compromise the basis of the faith. Thickens noted that this tendency in Davies's work related particularly to the authorship of the Pentateuch and the book of Isaiah. Nevertheless, despite this compromise with recent academic claims, as far as Thickens was concerned, Davies was the ideal person to train recruits for the ranks of the ordained ministry.

Four years after his appointment as a professor at Aberystwyth, Davies published his first book, *Cristnogaeth a Meddwl yr Oes* ('Christianity and the Thought of the Age', Caernarfon, 1932). In the book Davies made it clear that the Great War had struck a fatal blow at the philosophical and theological categories popular in the period 1904 to 1914 (p. 57). He perceived a weakness in contemporary liberalism and its claim of offering a social gospel. The cry for social amelioration had led to the conceptualization of Christianity as a moral force with the church as one means amongst many to reform social and economic structures, thus raising the standard of living. But this description totally obscured the essence of the gospel as the 'reconciliation in Christ between God and man' (p. 184). As a result, theologians had to rediscover their source-material in the salvific work of Christ from the theological formulations of the past which liberalism had eschewed. With such an agenda, it is hardly surprising that Davies was attracted to the new movements in Europe as he sought a valid basis from which to construct a theology adequate for the age.

Not surprisingly, the book incensed John Morgan Jones, and in two articles in *Yr Efrydydd* he proceeded to explain why. The crux of the disagreement was the nature and task of Christian theology. Davies had entitled the fifth chapter of his book 'What is Christian Theology?' and his remarks so infuriated Jones that he then used the title in quotation marks in a review of the book published in *Yr Efrydydd*. The choice of title in itself reveals the nature of this debate. Two theologians were approaching their task from different directions. It is this difference in theological stance, far more than a real misunderstanding or misuse of terminology, which becomes most clear in Jones's articles.

There was much which Jones disliked about the book. Davies's literary style, he claimed, was verbose and unclear, while his use of terminology was ambiguous. Davies had initially implied that the only thing of true value in Christianity was its theology. This theology was 'wholly familiar and final and changeless. It is beyond reason and it cannot be understood. It can be "believed" or not, but it is impossible to be a Christian without believing it.' Elsewhere, however, Davies's views were not quite so definite. Theological formulations could change. He sought to differentiate between theology, which can change, and the 'truth as it is in Jesus' which remains constant. The latter was the truth, the former an expression of that truth. Expressions can change, but the truth remains the same forever.[38] For Jones, this was an impossible distinction. Where, he asked, is the line between 'the Christian truth' and 'Christian theology' to be drawn?

Reasonable as such an objection may appear prima facie, on closer inspection John Morgan Jones's criticism becomes untenable. This was due not so much to the logic and relevance of Jones's point but to the fact that he would have expressed the case in similar terms. Jones's only real objection could be that Davies was unclear at this point. The principal of Bala-Bangor himself often claimed that there was a difference between the truth of Christian faith, in his terms spiritual experience leading to the moral life, and the way the truth of religious experience is expressed, namely theology. It is far more likely that his objections arose because of his suspicions concerning Davies's theological viewpoint. Davies had confessed that the theology of the dialecticians, Barth and Brunner, was 'Christian theology, if not the Christian theology'. It was his suspicion that this was the case that led to Jones's problem with the title 'What is Christian Theology?' He perceived that Davies, under the influence of Barth, sought to separate revelation of God from human discovery of God. For him, 'the Christian Truth is at the same time a revelation from God by God, and a discovery by man for man.'[39] Thus, it was not that Davies made a distinction between truth and the expression of truth which Jones found unacceptable, but the fact that he separated the act of God in revelation from the human act of discovery or apprehension of that revelation.

Jones considered that his own theological standpoint was clear:

I myself am quite sure in my mind what constitutes the spiritual and moral characteristics of revelation, namely simple trust, sure and endless, in God, as the trust of a child for his father, endless faithfulness to the vision which comes without fail from this filial relationship with God, in a life of serviceable love for men. Man overtaken by these moral and spiritual characteristics, and growing daily towards the example and image of Christ, and [these characteristics] working powerfully in him bearing much fruit in all directions in his personal and social life – that, for me, is the essential characteristic [*nod angen – sic*] of the Christian. And Christianity is the movement which is keen to spread these characteristics, this spirit and this life amongst men, and towards establishing human society on their foundation. Everything else is second-rate and changeable and finite – every doctrine, every church structure, and every sacrament, and the value of each one [of these] is to be measured according to their service to the growth and spread of 'Christ's spirit'.[40]

For Davies, on the other hand, the task of theology was to discover 'the fundamental truths of Christianity and then to prescribe them for people to believe. According to Jones, he had identified the Virgin Birth[41] and the bodily resurrection of Christ as *essential truths* because they show how the divine and human could be united in Jesus. As such, they were not *essential doctrines* of the church. Instead they held the status of beliefs retained in support of the Chalcedonian doctrine of Christ's person which was one of the *essential doctrines* of the faith. The Trinity, on the other hand, was an example of 'changing forms of the eternal Thing (*y Peth tragwyddol*)'.[42] The only reason for this, as far as Jones could see, was that it was 'the claim of the Christian faith'. Jones desired to know simply on what grounds and on whose authority. Davies's insistence that there were particular creeds which had to be believed as received was for Jones a denial of the fundamental freedom which Jesus had offered to all men and women and was the heart of the gospel. It was thus an unacceptable proposition.

In his second article, Jones regained something of his composure and qualified the largely condemnatory critique of his first article. He praised Davies's treatment of the modern thinkers, Barth, Brunner, Otto, Bertrand Russell and others. The age was marked by crisis in public life, particularly regarding the fields of thought, politics, international relations and ethics. Davies was well equipped to speak on the subject and had a wide knowledge to contribute to the debate. This more conciliatory tone was vitiated, however, when Jones admitted to getting the impression that Davies was simply panicking. In order to face the philosophical challenges of the day he had simply fled to the 'positivity of the authority of *unreason* under the shadow of revelation which is beyond man's grasp'. Jones could not see how Davies could conclude with Barth that there is no way to God except in the way God has broken through in Jesus Christ to save the world. In an amazing leap of logic, John Morgan Jones claimed that if Davies truly believed this, then he should also have agreed that the only way for this to be effective is that the church, or Pope, alone held the authority to preach and offer salvation, and salvation was possible only through obedience to the church.[43] He underlined, in this second article, that God reveals himself and people discover God as part of the same process. Men and women come to know God through their human experiences, and this led Jones to emphasize the importance of Jesus' humanity. Through the fulness of his humanity, Jesus became a full revelation of God – 'of the mind, of the heart and will of God, of the character and spirit of God'. Davies on the other hand had denied Christ's humanity. He had claimed that the 'I' (*Myfi*) behind the 'body of flesh' was in fact the 'eternal Word'. If this were true, according to John Morgan Jones, then Christ was human only in a docetic sense. This 'divine I' could only put on flesh, according to Jones's interpretation of Davies's argument, through a Virgin Birth, and equally could not leave the flesh except through resurrection on the third day. For Jones, it was reasonable to hold both together but he could not understand why Davies had offered no argument in favour of the importance of these dogmas but simply held them *a priori*. Furthermore, Jones recognized a fault in Davies's work as he placed no importance on the character of Jesus' life and the human characteristics which he portrayed.[44] It was the morality of Jesus' human character which alone held any appeal as far as Jones was concerned. For Davies to have ignored it meant that he had failed to comprehend adequately the significance of Jesus of Nazareth.

According to John Morgan Jones, there were two major areas

which should be profoundly affected by any study of Jesus' life. The first came through a correct perception of the character and work of Jesus as a historical person. The life of Jesus was central to the history of humankind as a whole and, more specifically, to the religious life. Christ had an important place in the movement which he inaugurated. Although they could argue over details, he agreed with Davies that his teaching presented the ideals and principles of love, forgiveness, simplicity, purity, sacrifice, complete dependence and confidence in the Father. There was no ambiguity in Jesus' teaching. These principles radiated from the picture of him found in the gospels. The second aspect was the rich and varied experience of Jesus' disciples concerning their master's value and saving power. It was this expression, developed by the early church, which recognized him as Lord. Thus, the theologian's task was to seek an expression of the person of Christ which took seriously the moral character (as opposed to the ontology) of his humanity, but recognized the importance of the doxological claim that he is *saviour*. Such expression could only be 'incomplete and imperfect' at best. Davies had committed the great sin of replacing the actual, historical person of Jesus with an abstruse dogma about the Christ.

Perhaps this picture should be placed into its context. Jones had merely represented the theological task in terms of his own interests. His two principal theological interests were the interpretation of the New Testament with its necessary and complementary tool of literary criticism, and history, the teaching of which was his responsibility at Bala-Bangor. It is hardly surprising, then, that Jones considered the actual events of Jesus' life and teaching to be of vital significance, rather than speculative notions about Jesus' person. Unlike Miall Edwards, Jones did not believe that the importance of Jesus' teaching could give added significance to a doctrine of his person. W. D. Davies's interests were far more doctrinal and philosophical. It was therefore quite natural that he should present the theological task in dogmatic and epistemological terms. That the two men would disagree was inevitable.

In responding to these articles, W. D. Davies admitted that he could perceive no common ground between himself and the principal of the Bala-Bangor College. In this he accurately portrayed the initial controversy between liberal and dialectic theology.

There simply was no point at which the two systems converged. Davies drew attention to the 'meaninglessness' *per se* of Jones's favoured expression 'The Spirit of Christ'. It was not easily comprehensible but required some kind of doctrine of preconceived foundation. For Davies, theology had always tried to say *something* about the 'truth as it is in Christ' however inadequate, lest men and women conclude that 'there is nothing to be said'.[45] This truth went far beyond the ethical terms employed by the liberal Modernists to speak of Christ and the significance of his life. They had recognized Jesus Christ as the 'perfect man'. But for Davies '*moral* terms cannot exhaust the truth of Christ's gospel's saving power. A moral ideal will not make a sinner a saint.' The power of God unto salvation must be given an intellectual treatment far above that of the best moral categories known to human beings. This perhaps demonstrates the fundamental contribution of the Barthian neo-orthodoxy gradually reaching Wales at this time. Davies wanted to return to the description of God known through the revelation of Jesus Christ rather than through the anthropological process of discerning (and living out) ethical principles. This was another way of expressing the same criticism that liberal theology had replaced God with man.

Davies sought to correct Jones over the issue of the Trinity in a way that revealed the assurance, if not the arrogance, of youth, together with the zeal of a man fighting for what he believed the Christian truth to represent. The Trinity had arisen precisely as the church's experience had forced it to do theology. It was an attempt to recognize God as Father, Jesus' divinity and the presence of the divine in a special and unique way in the church 'and in every true believer in his personal experience'. This was a vital part of Christian belief and was not therefore part of the 'changing forms of theology'. Davies began:

> If these words are themselves an example of my poor Welsh, the flow of the book throughout should ensure that any fairly honest and sensible reader would not make such an unfair accusation. I would prefer to believe that the Principal has not yet read my book except (as we all do, from the least to the greatest, when reviewing books) choosing a sentence or paragraph here and there than to accuse him of a lack of honesty or philosophical sense![46]

Davies took exception to Jones's insistence that the old theological building had crumbled under the findings of modern thought and science. His efforts were not merely reactionary, an attempt to rediscover former truths and rebuild a dated building on foundations of sand, but were made in the belief that theological truth rested on 'the Rock of Truth'. This was no gradual and progressive discovery of God and God's ways in the history of humankind. Instead it was the belief that God acted differently in Jesus Christ and it is from him that all else acquires meaning. Despite his failures, and his inability to expunge entirely the philosophical Idealism that prevailed at the time, there was at least this to commend Davies's work. He had perceived, in a way that the liberals could not, that Jesus Christ, for Christianity, is a unique figure and that the theologian's task was to retain that uniqueness and proclaim it as truth in each age.

This incident was more the result of Modernism meeting dialectic theology, or at least a more orthodox interpretation of Christian faith, than about true theological debate. The ground was marked. There could be no compromise between the two positions. There was no meeting-place for Jones and Davies, an ironic side-effect of a liberalism which claimed harmony and progress but in fact could find no unity with the aims and claims of neo-orthodoxy and dialectic theology. It is, finally, interesting to note that, despite his ability and wide knowledge, Davies never really achieved much prominence as a theologian. An air of controversy surrounded him from the beginning of his academic career. His obituary notice referred ambiguously to clouds gathering ever more ominously above his head during his years at Aberystwyth, leading up to his resignation from the post in the summer of 1933. Oral tradition has it that Davies had a weakness for alcohol which certainly would not have ingratiated him with the patriarchs of Welsh Methodism with its particular leaning towards temperance at that time. After his resignation, Davies's life was unsettled. He worked for *Y Cymro* for a time and he took pastoral charge of Methodist churches on two further occasions while frequently moving house around Wales. He added the initial 'P' to his name which could have referred to his wife's maiden name of Palmer but which he suggested stood for 'pechadur' – sinner. He published one other book, *Datblygiad Duw: Efrydiau Diwinyddol* ('The Development of

God: Theological Studies') in 1934, but appears really to have faded into obscurity, his intellectual promise unfulfilled.

John Morgan Jones v. J. E. Daniel

The relationship between John Morgan Jones and J. E. Daniel as colleagues at the Bala-Bangor Theological College from 1926 proved to be a most interesting one for those men who studied at the college between the wars. One of those men, the Revd Trebor Lloyd Evans, recalled the students' pleasure whenever a debate between the two tutors would arise, whether during official classes or in the common room. When discussing theology, Evans recalled that the inevitable result would be agreement to disagree, each man matching the other in ability and erudition.[47] There can be little doubt that a relationship of mutual respect and affection existed between the two men. In a glowing tribute to his principal on the day of Jones's funeral, Daniel confessed that 'part of my life went into his grave'.[48] Yet the theological convictions of the older man were unacceptable, if not anathema, to Daniel. For his part, Jones had hoped that Daniel would follow him as principal. But while he held a great regard for his junior colleague, he had little trust in or time for his theology.

In a radio address he planned to give in memory of D. Miall Edwards, John Morgan Jones explained how he had lived through a period which had seen four schools of theological thought grow to fruition only to be replaced by the next phase in the continuous development of understanding and truth. Jones's youth, he said, was characterized by Calvinistic orthodoxy in religion, and no one represented the age better than the Revd H. A. Davies, Cwmaman, Aberdare. Davies 'was a man of firm conviction, with no doubts and for that he was a dangerous man in debate'. He represented a dogmatic orthodoxy which held that those 'who could not agree with the plain doctrines of the church on the Trinity, the incarnation and the atonement were in dreadful danger concerning their eternal fate'. There followed a reaction to this dogmatism inspired by scientific theories such as Darwinian evolution, and philosophical developments, such as Hegelian Idealism. This reaction was led by the 'generation of revolutionaries' such as the Revd David Adams. For Jones, these men were happy neither with the old theology nor with the new learning offered by science and philosophy. Their 'world of thought was in pieces and they groped blindly for an intellectual background (*cefndir meddyliol*) in its place but without finding it'. Jones and Edwards belonged to the third generation of liberal Modernists who attempted to give intellectual and practical expression to Christian faith in contemporary language using the insights of current scientific discoveries and philosophical formulae. Daniel, however, belonged to the fourth generation. This was the 'reactionary' generation who wanted to rectify the excesses of theological liberalism which had replaced God with man. The call was to go back: back to Calvin and the creeds; back to rediscover the absolute difference between humankind and God; back to a recognition of human sin, the Fall and the existence of original sin. For Jones, this demonstrated the 'serious decision' facing the modern world:

> That choice is – between following our convictions until forced to reconsider not only the form and details of the ecclesiastical theological tradition but also the meaning and purpose of the gospel itself, the relationship between religion and every theology, the meaning and value of every church organization and the meaning of authority of the New Testament itself. Modernism has only gone half way. And Wales' choice, and, I believe, the world's choice, is between completing the Protestant Reformation or going back to the creeds of the church and their authority as a final revelation of the full truth of God and man and life.

There can be little doubt in which direction Jones would wish Wales to go. This task of completing the Reformation was constantly put before the church by Jones throughout his career. In this he echoed the teaching of Dr Joseph Warschauer, who had come to prominence during the New Theology controversy over thirty years earlier. Warschauer too had advocated the development of a truly immanentist and spiritual religion and eschewed most credal formulations as attempts to enslave the spirit to the word.[49] Perhaps because Jones hoped that the theological reaction which Daniel represented would not last, or simply because of the time restriction, these remarks concerning Daniel's theological position and the religious choice facing Wales and the world were omitted from the actual broadcast.[50] Either way, it tends to suggest that, for Jones, Daniel's theological standpoint was not particularly important.

The theological controversy which had existed between Daniel and Jones, would have been restricted mainly to private debates in the Senior Common Room. But it became public in 1933 following an invitation extended to Daniel to give a radio address, which he duly delivered early in the year. In his address, Daniel complained at the way that the modern 'arrogant (*praff*) pagans' spoke so much of 'the spirit of Christ' (which was, it should be noted, an expression oft-quoted by John Morgan Jones) and put so much energy into all kinds of humanistic and socialistic movements but tended to depreciate connections with the church and chapel. For Daniel, the church was vital for Christianity. 'It is not the church's work today, or in any age to come,' he said, 'to lose itself as leaven into the life of society, but a completely different thing, to try to turn society into a church.' Because the church is so vital, Daniel identified denominationalism as one of the critical evils of the age. Unlike the general clamour for organizational unity which has always dominated ecumenical discussion, Daniel believed that unity could only be established on the basis of a common creed. Although the churches sought unity, it could never be secured unless church representatives knew the answers to important doctrinal questions. Thus, Daniel averred, it was not important whether a Christian was a Methodist or Congregationalist, but whether he or she was a Barthian or a Ritschlian; whether he or she believed that men and women needed God's revelation and salvation in Christ or saw human moral regeneration and effort as the crux of the Christian life. This certainly is an odd argument when ordinary church members would have been far more familiar with denominationalism than with the intricacies of theological formulation. But, Daniel insisted, the lack of doctrinal definition had led to a religion which was 'all things to all men'. It was in fact a 'spineless religion'. Thus, denominational unity would be little more than superficial. The only ecumenism worth working for was a unity of belief which crossed the denominational barriers. Denominationalism was suffocating the efforts to Christianize the nation. The churches were concentrating on their internal affairs and not on the need to spread the gospel. In his criticism of denominationalism, Daniel's hyperbole knew no limit: 'Our fate will be that of the Cheshire cat, everything will disappear but the smile of treasurers and secretaries and officers, and the end of our denominations will be an address by the treasurer on the financial situation of the Union [of Welsh Independents].' For Daniel, the church ceased to be the church when its beliefs became clouded. It must know what it believes or else it will die. The dual threat of Communism on the one hand and Catholicism on the other were surrounding and smothering the church and true religion.[51] They were providing a definite and positive mission which only served to highlight the lack of purpose within Nonconformity. The chapels too needed to fly their banner high and fight beneath and for it. This banner should be that of the Christian faith, rightly expressed, and not that of denominational nicety. The denominations had been too busy trying to meet the social needs and solving the problems of the age instead of preaching the gospel and winning converts for Christ. The 'foundation of the church is its creed, and beside that its whole organization and decisions are nothing but a clanging gong or a tinkling cymbal'.[52] In the fifteen years or so since the war, Welsh Nonconformist theology had been concerned almost exclusively with the applica-tion of Christian truth to social needs. All this was dismissed by Daniel as a side-issue, and one which had caused the church to neglect its true mission.

The BBC were quick to recognize that Daniel's address was a strong challenge to the theological status quo and decided to exploit the situation. In a letter dated 4 February 1933 Sam Jones, on behalf of the regional director of the BBC in the west, invited John Morgan Jones, Daniel's colleague and principal, to respond to the original address. Sam Jones wrote:

> The talk aroused much interest, and I believe there is much divergence of opinion regarding the conclusions drawn by Professor Daniel. That being so, we think it would be an excellent idea to broadcast a reply to the talk, not necessarily opposing the sentiments, but bearing directly upon them. We believe you could be the very man to give this talk.

John Morgan Jones was offered a fee of four guineas and duly broadcast his reply 'Anghenion crefyddol Cymru' ('The religious needs of Wales') on 25 March 1933. Significantly, Jones's address was later published in *Y Dysgedydd*, the Welsh Independents' monthly journal. This probably reflected the popularity of the liberalism to which most Nonconformist ministers in Wales still adhered. Daniel's address was not printed, though any reason for this can only be speculative. It could merely be down to his own unwillingness to submit it for publication, the consequence of his notorious dissatisfaction with the articles which he produced. On the other hand, it could reflect the deliberate editorial policy of *Y Dysgedydd* during these years. Whatever the reason, Jones's address was ensured a wider audience than Daniel's by its appearing in article form.

It is clear that Jones differed with Daniel over the very nature of religion in general and Christianity in particular, though this may have been a distinction that would not have occurred to Jones. Although he recognized that the experience of God and eternal life in human history found its climax in Jesus Christ, he was unwilling to accord this any absolute authority over and above other religious claims. Christianity may offer the most developed of religious experiences, but religious experience itself was the property of all human beings. Religion simply became the way different people explained that experience and worked it out practically. All the structures of organized religion were necessary but of secondary importance. This included all creeds and theological formulae. Consequently, Jones believed that Daniel's emphasis was misplaced. Instead of placing theological belief as of seminal importance it is the historical person of Jesus which takes centre stage, for in him there is 'the most certain clue we have to the fullest and completest human and divine life, the ever open door to the divine reality, in whom alone we can find our peace and salvation, the dynamic, I hope, and consummation of all Truth, Beauty and Goodness'. Following Christ as his disciple would automatically involve the gradual acceptance of and co-operation in God's will in loving and serving one's neighbours. The outcome of religious experience, then, was the provision of a moral and practical dynamic. Because of this, Jones believed that the religious need in Wales was not for a more Christian *religion* with accurate creeds and doctrine, but a more Christian *life* in which individuals 'become more Christian in spirit and disposition, in the motives that control us, in the ends we serve, in all our thinking, feeling and willing'. The moral and the spiritual were to be supreme, dependent solely on individual conscience rather than on a set of dogmas and belief: 'I object ... to allowing any system of theological doctrines or formulated theological creed to usurp the primary place of the Christian life and experience and therefore I object to identifying the church itself with any one theological creed whether orthodox or heterodox.'

It is unclear what Jones meant by the 'Christian life and experience' apart from living according to the ideals of self-sacrificial service. In eschewing credal statements, Jones also sacrificed clarity and definition in the terms he employed. Despite this, his radicalism is plain to see. While he spoke of humanity in social as well as individual terms it was clear that the latter was of greater importance to him than the former. He believed wholeheartedly in the right and authority of individual conscience in all matters, for true life (without any qualifying religious adjective) was fundamentally moral and spiritual and the conscience could be its only guide. When he mentioned social organization it was society at large which he meant rather than the church. The church, for Jones, was the result of human weakness and mortality – a strange indictment, considering that weakness and mortality are both inevitable characteristics of human existence. His tendency to see life as the goal of religion, and his willingness to see the moral values of 'eternal life' displayed in all kinds of people in all walks of life, would lead inevitably to a low view of the church and its creeds and its apparent desire for uniformity. Its only justification was to teach men and women to become more Christian, interpreting that term in an entirely moral sense. Religion for him concerned religious experience as the motivator and inspiration for the moral life. So long as men and women were living that life, all else was secondary:

> Its particular form of ecclesiastical organisation, whether it be Trinitarian or Unitarian, the particular ritual it may employ, whether sacramental or symbolic, the type of ministry it may have, whether priest or preacher, these are valid or true or good only in so far as they serve the purposes of the Christian Gospel, that is in so far as they enrich the Christian experience of God, help it to grow in the direction of Jesus Christ, that is in so far as they promise an even fuller and richer religious experience, life and personality in men and human society.

Jones's radio address saw him at his most positive, his most militant and his most Modernist. He confessed that he saw more religion in Wales in that age than was often admitted. Despite the fact that the church was losing adherents, there were more people than ever seeking to live a truly moral and social life in recognition of the needs of their fellow human beings. He once again made his opposition to dialectic theology known. It was nothing more than a reaction against all the liberal movements of the nineteenth century and it was to be hoped that it would be short-lived. It could be seen in the social and political life of Europe, in Germany and Italy, and it could be seen in the theological realm:

> We are called back to uniform organizations and external authorities from the Middle Ages in politics and theology. In my opinion, this is nothing but the fear of panic, like raising a weak rampart of sand against the flow of the sea – in the world of religion as in the world of politics.[53]

The argument came down to a more personal level when Jones identified Daniel as a protagonist of this theology and referred directly to his broadcast. Daniel had emphasized the importance of 'credo' in religion, particularly in ecumenical discussions. In as far as the word 'credo' originally meant 'I believe', Jones concurred wholeheartedly with Daniel. However, he suspected that in fact Daniel was looking to set a 'more definite and authoritative theological creed' as the way to salvation. In this, Jones believed he had to respond 'NO'. For Jones, this would destroy four hundred years of theological development and intellectual progress. The very foundation of the Protestant Reformation was at stake, in which human value and the freedom of individual conscience were endorsed as fundamental to the life of the Christian church. Dialectic theology would, he said, 'be no more than to lead us in religion to the muddy, deceitful, deathly bog for all true and full human life – the bog where Mussolini and Hitler and Stalin live in politics'.[54]

Jones could not see which creed should be adopted. Jesus himself had left no creed but in fact promised eternal life to the man or woman whose love for God is absolute and whose love for neighbour is comparative with love for self. There were countless creeds, those of Paul, the Jerusalem church, the Apostles, Nicaea,

Chalcedon, Augsburg, Trent and so on. Rather more significant than this was Jones's naming of the Methodist Confession of Faith and the creed contained in *Cristnogaeth a Meddwl yr Oes*, thereby calling to mind the views exchanged in two religious debates in which he had been involved, as well as demonstrating his abhorrence at the insistence placed by many within the churches on creed and dogma. This reflected the church's error that God had intended a 'body of theology to be the foundation and condition of his grace and the life of the Christian church'.

Jones's positive contribution required that clarity and certainty be located not in dogmatic assertion but in human experience. Humankind itself was blessed with a fundamental religious nature. This could then lead to good or evil depending both on the use made of it and on whether or not it had developed to maturity through adequate education. For Jones, the religious life was lived to the full by Jesus Christ. Thus in him, human experience of God, or God's revelation to humankind depending on your theological terminology, reaches its most perfect expression in the history of the world. This life could be summed up in a sentence rather than in the creeds. For Jones the essence of Christianity was easily expressed. 'At its best', he wrote, 'this religion is a simple and sure trust in God the Father, and free, loving activities towards men.'[55] The strength and reality were in the experience of this life, but that experience could be described in various ways, as faith, morality, as the good, the true, the holy. The Christian life exists where these characteristics are put into practice both personally and socially. This life, the spirit of Christ himself, may be found in people such as Gandhi and Julian Huxley, and Jones believed that Jesus 'would prefer his spirit in them than his name on them'.[56] Jesus wanted to create men and women, offering them the means to live life to the full. He had not sought the development of a personal clique for himself. This too should be the church's desire. All sectarian and denominational interests should be subordinated to the creation of men and women, living the Christian life of humble discipleship to Jesus. This was not going to be a sudden, miraculous conversion but was the ongoing task of the church in history. And to secure it, and prevent the 'curse of false religiosity', then 'a patient, wide, effective Christian education' was required.[57] Jones then outlined the need for changes in ecclesiology to encourage a willingness to share resources and co-operate denominationally to ensure that this education was provided.

Of course, there are grave implications here for any understanding of the content and significance of Christian faith. The emphasis on personal experience, whatever form that takes, leads inevitably to subjectivity. Not only are experiences different, but often the interpretations given to those experiences support individual and personal differences. This leads to an inevitable problem of identification. To combat this, Jones identified a particular moral outcome as the living out of a Christian way of life. This outcome is not necessarily based on some kind of mystical religious experience but can be taught to succeeding generations when the education system is geared towards such an end. The question is, why is such a moral outcome necessarily Christian? Many were living an ethical life regardless of such an identification, as Jones himself was well aware. But if men and women could live ethically without a spiritual understanding, and even while denying a spiritual dimension, what was the point of being a Christian? All Jones could do was hint at a kind of 'anonymous Christianity' though he never articulated such a doctrine because Christianity for him did not have any particular salvific significance. Void of that, and seen exclusively in terms of a dynamic and inspiration to live the moral life, the fact was that, in Jones's interpretation of it, Christianity ultimately lost any unique status for, and even any real relevance to, humankind.

A Crisis for Faith

During the 1930s, there were new theological claims coming to the fore which threatened the belief-system and world-view of Welsh Nonconformity. The prevailing liberalism which had achieved the status of general orthodoxy amongst Welsh Nonconformist ministers was being challenged by a valid alternative argued with passion by its protagonists that represented a completely different approach to theological truth. The result, for the observer at least, was a crisis for faith. How should the truths of Christianity be expressed? Was it better to use the anthropocentric and ethical framework offered by liberal Modernism and its attempt at a social gospel or was this in fact inadequate?

Was God immanent in the creation and human beings consequently endowed with an inherent religiosity which made the search for God and the quest for truth both possible and inevitable? Or was dialectic theology accurate in its demonstration of God's otherness to creaturely life, God's diametric opposition to human sin and thus each individual's need for redemption which is only possible in Christ? Was knowledge of God impossible apart from a specific act of revelation on his part? Was truth, then, a starting-point and not a destination in the Christian pilgrimage? Perhaps the greatest crisis was the result of the polarization which had occurred in religious thought. The dialecticians and the neo-orthodox as represented by Barth, W. D. Davies and J. E. Daniel were ranged in opposition to the traditional liberals like Miall Edwards and John Morgan Jones. There could be no convergence between the views advanced by the two groups. No longer was a Hegelian synthesis to be sought. There was no common ground. It was one or the other, and once the choice was made then the rejected option, naturally, was to be condemned.

Certainly the reaction of dialectic theology was a timely one. John Morgan Jones had by this time assumed the role of elder statesman within Welsh Nonconformity because Thomas Rees was dead and Miall Edwards was incapacitated by illness. He argued his theological case vigorously, but the implications were grave for the Christian faith as it had been known and adhered to for centuries. The naturalism and Idealism which he displayed, looking always to the importance of the ethical ideal and human ability to accomplish and embody it, deprived the Christian religion of its salvific content and, as a result, depreciated it to the level of one other philosophy of life. Nonconformists were facing increasing secularism where church membership was falling and the chapels were gradually but surely losing adherents. Men and women were shifting their interests and even their religiosity into other movements, some political, some social and still others established to provide leisure facilities. Perhaps the protagonists of Welsh theology would have better served their denominations and the Christian faith by reasserting the gospel of Christ's unique sacrifice for the redemption of all creation. At least this new theological movement maintained a particular sphere as the exclusive domain of the church, leaving no room for confusion about the nature of the Christian message. It preserved the uniqueness of the church's role and of Christ's work, maintaining that no other organization could fulfil the task of turning a sinner into a saint. For the liberals, however, the church could be viewed as one other educational or reforming establishment among many. J. E. Daniel, perhaps, had grasped the crisis facing Nonconformity in particular but Christian religion in general to a far greater degree than Jones. For Daniel, the loss of adherents and the decline in membership were probably linked to the all-pervasive, and ultimately corrupting, influence of liberal theology. Liberalism had sought to ameliorate the conditions in which people lived without speaking directly to the human condition. It had neglected the teaching of human sin, Christ's redemption and the church's evangelistic and nurturing functions. It is likely, then, that Daniel saw the crisis as having arisen owing to the decline in traditional religious forms as well as in the lack of a specific Christian theology and Christian teaching amongst the churches. Jones could not have been unaware of the situation, but he was not prepared to view the crisis as the loss of religious forms. For him, human beings were inherently and instinctively religious. The forms of worship, ecclesiology and theology developed by Nonconformity (and by other denominations and even other religions) were simply expressions of human religiosity. It was imperative, he claimed, that new forms should now be found to complete the movement started at the Protestant Reformation. Thus, for Jones, the end of religious practice as it had been known was merely a natural consequence of grasping the fundamentally ethical nature of Jesus' message and the need to see those ethics practised and embodied in the whole of society and not just in eclectic religious clubs. There simply was no common ground. Although both Daniel and Jones (and, for that matter, Martyn Lloyd-Jones, D. R. Davies and W. D. Davies) used the same words and referred to the same people and institutions, they were clearly talking about different things.

But even though there was a theological crisis, its extent was not far-reaching. There were too many other difficulties facing Britain and the Welsh for anyone but the theologians to get excited over theological formulae. The world was once again poised for a fight as the deadly menace of Fascist dictatorship raised its ugly head in Germany, Italy, Spain and Japan. As the nations first of Europe and then the world went headlong into war, greater crises arose to face the churches and Christians than a valid and adequate expression of their faith. And in this aspect at least the perceived social gospel of liberal Modernism had won the day, for the Modernists had averred that human conditions far more than cognitive process were of ultimate significance even if this went against their inherent Idealism. The universe, and therefore life in general, was governed by an idea. Providing the idea was the right one, all else would come right. The Modernists had argued for the ethical and practical imperative of love of neighbour to be installed as the basic axiom for individual life and for the social structures. In this they gave a minimalist interpretation of Augustine's dictum 'to love God and do what you like', believing love to be incapable of doing anything that did not lead to the good, the true and the beautiful. The fact was and is that human beings do not find it easy to love, and certainly find it difficult to love all of the time. This called for a more adequate ideology, and a more pro-active ecclesiological strategy, that recognized the weaknesses (sins) of human life, the need for and accomplishment of redemption, and a guide to living the moral life. Instead, liberal theologians tended to call for practical application of principles. More often than not, these principles were left as abstract references to the eternal verities of goodness, truth and beauty, while the need to recognize the sanctity of individual personality and freedom of conscience resulted in a lack of directly practical advice. And this constant cry to be practical led inevitably to the downfall of the liberals and must, in part, have contributed to the overall decline in traditional religious observance. To be effective, liberalism required a well-established Christian base. People needed to know what they believed and why they believed it in order to be attracted to the call to ethical living. When such a religious base disappeared, liberal theology's call to the moral life lacked power and appeal. Ordinary people were losing interest in chapel life, and this lack of interest appears to have been, at least in part, the result of an absence of clear guidance. Initially, the decline in chapel attendance appeared to be the result of identifying the chapels as impractical organizations unable to ameliorate the conditions of ordinary life. Later, however, there came the charge that they were no longer fulfilling their proper role of preaching the gospel. There was a common expectation that the church was to fulfil a particular role in its own activities and in the society in which it was located. When this was not forthcoming, ordinary people perceived something to be amiss. If it was solely the protector of ethical living, the church no longer had a unique message to offer society. Men and women found that they did not need religious teaching and forms in order to be moral citizens.

But if these arguments were ever considered to be vitally important, certainly by the late 1930s there was little or no interest being shown in them. In the face of the international crisis which confronted that generation, Daniel's separation of people into Barthian and Ritschlian camps became unimportant. Rather, it was once again the importance of winning a war which was foremost in people's minds, particularly as this time the enemy was far more insidious and recognizably evil than during the previous conflagration.

4

The Question of Context

*I have become all things to all people, that I might by all means save
some.* (1 Cor. 9.22 NRSV)

From the late 1920s there was a growing number of younger
Nonconformist ministers who were reacting against the claims of
the prevailing liberal theology. This growing vocal and youthful
caucus was arguing quite convincingly that liberalism was at best
an inadequate interpretation of Christian faith and at worst a
gross misrepresentation of the faith once delivered to the saints.
By the outbreak of the Second World War Welsh theology was
'limping between two opinions'. Liberalism still held sway at
denominational assemblies and to a large extent at the theological
colleges. But the next generation of Nonconformist leaders, those
who would come to prominence after the Second World War,
would not be theological liberals. Partly because of the decline of
liberalism, and partly because of the inherent weaknesses within
the theological systems promulgated by the liberals, there has
been a tendency either consciously to discount or merely to
neglect their truly remarkable achievements in the years before
1930.

Between the two world wars, there appeared a tremendous
amount of published matter which dealt with various theological
subjects. This included a plethora of books and articles concerning the church's duty, both in its theological formulations and in
its practical compassion, to contribute something towards the
social rebuilding, which was both the necessary consequence of,
and the opportunity presented by, the devastation of the Great
War. Apart from the books, popular theology continued to reach
a wide readership through the monthly journals and weekly newspapers published by the different religious denominations in
Wales. But perhaps the crowning achievement was the publication

154

of *Y Geiriadur Beiblaidd* ('The Biblical Dictionary') which was complete by 1926. The bulk of the editorial work had fallen upon Thomas Rees. He succeeded in preparing the final pages for the press but died before they actually appeared in print. The ethos of the articles is stringently liberal in theology and Idealist in philosophical outlook, simply reflecting the fact that the majority of contributors had developed as theologians in a period when those ideologies were in vogue. Theology has certainly moved on since the publication of the Dictionary, and it has also moved far beyond the limitations of the liberalism of 1926. Nevertheless, these articles are still a source of scholarly information on biblical topics while the publication of such an immense work in the Welsh language was an exceptional accomplishment. In Miall Edwards's words, 'it will probably be agreed that this Bible Dictionary is by far the most elaborate and scholarly work of the kind that has ever appeared in the Welsh language.'[1] Although succeeding generations have tended to dismiss the Dictionary because of its theological stance, Edwards's words have remained true in the seventy years since its publication.[2]

Theological emphases, along with primary social and political concerns, have changed in the last fifty to sixty years. The ethical and anthropological axioms of the liberal theologians were displaced rapidly as continental theologians urged a rediscovery of God's essential otherness. Nevertheless, the stress on moral duty, conscience and the absolute value of the individual person laid the basis for all future campaigns for social reform. The liberals certainly succeeded in demonstrating that the church had to address itself to moral and social matters as well as primarily religious and soteriological issues. In some senses the church had always been a moral guardian. But whereas in the past the general idea had been that the church's pronouncements should dictate how people lived their lives in society, the liberals demonstrated the necessity of first of all finding out *how* people lived their lives. They gathered the necessary information to speak authoritatively about social problems and, as a result, they ensured that the church's moral message had to be relevant to empirical conditions. In other words, the church must speak to the context in which it finds itself. The first need was knowledge, then came ethical judgement. When the church spoke its informed message, transformation would ensue. The result of this was that the protagonists of the neo-orthodoxy which came in liberalism's wake could not deny the need for, and even the duty of, the church to address issues of justice and peace. But the argument for Christian social concern would become stronger later in the twentieth century owing to a far greater emphasis on Christology, particularly following the challenge of Latin American theology, which has suggested forcefully that the correct image for Jesus is that of 'liberator'. This highlights what has to be a fundamental and damning criticism of the liberals. They tended not to look to the New Testament picture of Jesus in their call for social reform, nor did they engage in much New Testament exegesis to extrapolate the necessary dynamic for social renewal. Instead, they used their knowledge of philosophy and a critique of industrial society to make a social claim on the Christian gospel. The gospel was perceived as representing the highest good and existing wherever that good could be discerned. As a result, all things deemed to be wrong or evil could be criticized and transformed in its light. But it all remained conceptually vague and practically ambiguous.

The New Testament certainly is not void of images for a social message. Jesus' words offer at least some teaching which can be used to condemn social practices and insist on a better way of life in any generation and not just that of the first century. Some of the best-known passages in the New Testament offer inspiration for just such a social message, such as the Sermon on the Mount (Mt. 5–7); the advice to the rich young man (Mt. 19.21; Mk. 10.21; Lk. 18.22); identifying the two great commandments of love for God and love for neighbour as central to the requirements of the law (Mt. 22.37–40; Mk. 12.29–31); the issue of identifying my neighbour ('the Good Samaritan': Lk. 10.36–7); the warning that you cannot serve both God and mammon (Mt. 6.24). These are all useful sayings, but have been notoriously difficult to interpret and to apply to succeeding generations. Yet there can be little doubt that the imagery found in the New Testament may be used to present a picture of a perfect society, one in which relationships are as they should be between human beings, one with another, and between humankind and God; relationships in which there can be no oppressors and no victims but only equals upheld, served and inspired by mutual love. As such, the New Testament offers at least a basic inspiration for social reform. The motifs of the church, the Kingdom of God, a New

Heaven and a New Earth, the New Jerusalem, all imply social rather than merely individual aspects of existence that were indelibly linked with the new faith as it developed in the first century after the life of Jesus. To answer exactly what was intended by these images is a far more difficult problem. The Kingdom, for example, was promulgated by the liberal theologians, and by those concerned with the state of society, as the goal of creation, yet biblical hermeneutics suggests at least two aspects to Jesus' view of the Kingdom, namely the ethical and the eschatological, to which a social interpretation cannot do full justice, even when an early version of realized eschatology is adopted. Sometimes the Kingdom is seen to be present amongst or within men and women, while at other times it is to break in at the end of time. Furthermore, it was claimed that the Greek term *basileia* did not in fact imply a social interpretation at all. Primarily it denoted kingship, i.e. 'rule' and only secondarily, if at all, Kingdom, i.e. 'realm'. Thus the social gospellers interpreted the 'reign of God' in ethical and individual terms. It required a 'spiritual' conversion and the acceptance of Christ's rule in the heart. It was therefore *entos humōn* (cf. Lk. 17.21) very much 'within you' rather than 'in your midst'.[3] Such a rendering of the Lucan term, though not entirely beyond justification, certainly owed something to the axiomatic acceptance of God's immanence within creation, and particularly in men and women, effecting their moral duty to strive for the good, the true and the beautiful.

Of course, the problem that the liberal Nonconformists recognized was that Jesus did not immediately effect a radical and revolutionary reform of his society. New Testament imagery, particularly certain words of the apostle Paul, may suggest a social structure based on mutual love and the recognition of human value as in Galatians 3.28, 'There is neither Jew nor Greek, there is neither slave nor free, there is neither male nor female; for you are all one in Christ Jesus' (RSV). There is no evidence, however, to suggest that relationships were redefined on anything but a personal level. Social, legal and cultural distinctions remained firmly in place. More importantly, human relationships were transformed only by their being *en Christō*: 'in Christ'. Acceptance of the redemption wrought by Christ enabled the believer in some way to reach a level of intimacy with his or her saviour, an intimacy from which the believer's attitudes to others should stem. Being 'in Christ' is inherently social, as the author of the Epistle to the Ephesians grasped when he wrote that 'we are members of one another' (4.25). The fact is that Jesus' life and death made no direct impact on the social structures of his time with the exception that his followers, those who were 'in Christ', formed a community in which previously acceptable relationships are invalidated and replaced by God's grace, with the development of radically different attitudes towards others. Believers were to discover the fact that love of God was impossible unless it existed alongside a love of neighbour, and that this was the meaning of the whole law. According to the liberal theologians this community was based on a common Fatherhood and consequently a general brotherhood. The New Testament pattern, then, would seem to be that individuals *in Christ* adopted a different attitude and orientation concerning their social dealings, while as a group they offered an alternative social identity and praxis as they called others from the world and into the *ekklēsia*, into the church. It appears to be the case that the author of the book of Acts intended that we see this early community of believers as offering a radically different behaviour pattern, which included a communistic aspect, from those outside the church. The emphasis in Acts is placed firmly on the unity of the community of believers: they were one with each other, and sought to meet each other's needs, while their goods were considered common property (cf. Acts 2.44–6; 4.32). The Welsh liberals appeared to want something of the communistic attitude while playing down orthodox views on redemption and traditional understandings of the importance of the church. Human beings did not need redemption from sin but needed the moral strength of character to aim for the good. When they did so the world, and not the church, became the community to which they brought a high moral standard to affect all aspects of life.

These two views are quite different. On the one hand there is the formation of a new community with different values and goals from the rest of the world (cf. e.g. Gal. 3.28; Acts 2.44–6), while on the other there is a sending of individuals, with no social vision but dependent solely on their personal moral standard, into the world to do what they can in transforming it (liberal Modernism). Whether or not the two are compatible, there was a sense in which the liberals had moved away from the social ideal of scripture, namely the creation of a worshipping community which exists in self-giving love and through that stands before the world as a witness to the grace of God. While men like Thomas Rees, D. Miall Edwards, John Morgan Jones and Herbert Morgan did, prima facie, appreciate the need to generate ethical and loving individuals, they missed one crucial factor. This could only be done within a particular social context, and within Christian faith that context had always been the church. These men tended to view the world rather than the church not only as the primary ethical sphere for human beings but also as the locus of *divine* activity. That in itself is in accordance with an orthodox view of God as loving creator involved in the life of God's creation. God's existence in the world is not at issue. But because the liberals had eschewed any sense of God's redemptive action requiring *metanoia*, a turning away from the natural way of the world, their sense of God's gracious, redeeming presence within the bounds of a society recognized as in dire need of reform appeared to be a contradiction of immense proportion. They struggled to have it both ways. As the Idealists had suggested, God's presence in the world would have to be a redeeming one, constantly transforming and renewing sinful and fallen forms in a process leading towards a perfect consummation. But the immanence of God within an unjust and immoral social system would ultimately validate that system and call into question the quest for reform. In denying the significance of the church, they lacked a social organism through which they could promulgate their religious, social and political views. They tried to address too great an audience and convince them of the claims of ethical living. They discovered that when all was said and done the world, with its various institutions of political and social power, was not interested in their message.

It would be appropriate to mention here that the social problem, as it was perceived in early twentieth-century Britain, was fundamentally concerned with men and had very little to say to women. Though Galatians 3.28 sets out three different sets of relationship which supported qualitative or hierarchical distinctions between different groups of people and which are to be radically reviewed by those who are 'in Christ', St Paul only ever demonstrates his willingness to reinterpret two of them. More than any other in the early church, it was Paul who recognized that Christ had destroyed the division between Jew and Gentile. His passionate defence of Gentile converts against the Judaizers over the issue of circumcision demonstrates his belief that old social, cultural and racial distinctions count for nothing when one is grafted into Christ. His relationship with Philemon and with his servant Onesimus brought the second distinction home to him as one to be broken down in the Christian community. In the realm of personal relationships, the community of the church was intended to be a pioneer. It could do very little about slavery as a legal, social institution in the Roman Empire. But it could accord dignity to slaves in each congregation by treating them as full members with the respect due to an equal. It is the oneness of male and female which Paul appears to deny in other passages in his epistles (cf. e.g. 1 Cor. 14.34–5; 1 Tim. 2.11–12).

In some ways this is reflected in the social problem as it was interpreted in early twentieth-century Wales and in the theology offered to help solve it. Welsh society, despite the legendary status and power of wives and mothers as home-makers, was androcentric. The social problem was seen as bringing justice to men and equality between the capitalist and working classes. The possibility of equality between the sexes was never really part of the social vision either for the agitators of the labour movement or for the Nonconformists, though they certainly would not have believed that inequality *per se* existed between the sexes or that an unequal share was in fact a correct social pattern. If they considered the matter at all, then it is likely that they held the biological differences to imply a social difference and that society simply reflected this. Only later in the century would the need be voiced for women's liberation from hierarchical and patriarchal constrictions embedded within the social, economic and political systems as well as in the church, and questions be raised over the assumptions which lay behind stereotypical roles. A far different kind of 'social gospel', or message of liberation, would then be adopted and proclaimed from that which was promulgated at the height of industrialization, one where God's *Fatherhood* and *man's brotherhood* were recognized to be correlative terms but were equally deemed to be unacceptable because of the implication they contain that God is male and that women are 'non-persons', with masculine terms and androcentric forms representing all humankind.

The question remains why such interest developed in a social theology at this point in time in the history of the church. Certainly there was considerable pressure to reform and then rebuild society in the years immediately prior to, and following, the Great War. Primarily, this stemmed from the propaganda of labour and Socialist organizations, both of which grew in strength and increased adherents in these years. To offer this as the sole reason for the church's involvement in the social debate would, however, be inaccurate. Rather, we should look to the more general humanistic developments that stemmed from the Enlightenment in the eighteenth century as a common source for both the proliferation of social movements and the attempt at a social interpretation of the Christian message. Despite the fact that much can be gleaned from the New Testament, it is possible to see this more general ideological shift as the major source of social concern. In a sense, the New Testament was used in support of these humanistic developments, though it is also true that the New Testament's message was particularly predisposed to being interpreted in that way. The call for a social interpretation of Christianity, then, had more to do with the social condition of the time than with a particular interpretation of Jesus' teaching. What, if any, was the significance of Jesus' teaching and how was it seen to be relevant in an industrial context?

It is true that, frequently, different cultures and periods can view Jesus according to their own requirements and design. Thus, it is not only the New Testament's presentation of the life, teaching and effect of Jesus which is useful in supporting social reform, it is also true that Jesus, as an inspirational figure, has been claimed as leader by those convinced of the need for social reform. Jaroslav Pelikan has argued that each succeeding generation and age tends to emphasize different perceptions of Jesus in order that he may somehow project the right image for that time. Jesus was the 'Rabbi' in the context of first-century Judaism; 'King of kings' as his lordship was contrasted with that of Caesar in the second and third centuries of the Christian era and so on.[4] The principal title for Jesus in the twentieth century has been 'liberator'. Pelikan's thesis tends to emphasize one pervading image as representative of the thought of a particular age. It is also true that the same period can produce different ideas of Jesus owing to differing but coexistent contexts. As a result, 'black

161

theology' and African Christians in their struggles for freedom in the twentieth century have pictured Jesus as dark-skinned, while Hollywood-style films have presented him as the archetypal Western man: blue-eyed and white-skinned. (Another, slightly different, version of this is the emergence of Christa as a female version of Christ adopted by some feminists who perceive the need to have the salvific figure in their own image.) In this whole process Jesus becomes subjective, primarily the projection of one's own needs, ideas and enculturation, rather than the objective, historical person behind the gospel accounts, or for that matter the credal, universal Son of God, who died, arose from the grave and ascended to glory. The point, then, is not are we Jesus' people, but is he *one of us?* His belonging to us becomes more important than us belonging to him. And it is this that very often leads to perceiving him as a social reformer. He reforms society not because that was his desire or necessarily because that was the natural effect of his teaching, but because society needs to be reformed. Thus, it is not necessarily a theological claim which accords to Jesus the ability to reform society, but the perceived need of the day. In short, Jesus is far more likely to be seen as a social reformer in the context of social deprivation than in the context of material comfort. This is at least one of the reasons why the early British labour movement was associated so closely with Christian ethicism. The original Socialist agitators often drew on a store of religious imagery designed to appeal to a generation which, if estranged from the churches, still maintained a certain degree of religious belief and had been raised on religious symbols and a belief in Christian hope. Their appeal to the figure of Jesus and his teaching owed more to his status as an inspirational and authoritative figure than to his directly social message. In other words, he was appealed to in order to give voice to the Socialist message.

The liberal interpretation of theology should have led to exactly this kind of reasoning. Liberal theologians had recognized Jesus to be the ethical teacher and the instigator of eternal moral principles, and they had insisted that his ethics and his principles could be applied in each age. This required that they familiarize themselves with the conditions of contemporary life in order that principles could be applied correctly. But the liberals rejected the idea that Jesus was a social reformer. In rooting him in what they considered to be his historical context they discovered that he had no direct message which would rebuild modern industrial society along lines of justice and fairness. As a man, Jesus of Nazareth could not be blessed with the attribute of omniscience which allowed him to know how the world would develop years before events actually took place. Therefore, Jesus knew nothing about capitalism, industry such as coal mining and steelworking or the kind of working conditions and slum living conditions endured by the masses in the wake of industrialization. He was rooted in his own socio-economic context. It was the church's responsibility to find and articulate a moral message to contemporary society. But in finding and articulating such a moral message they were promulgating the spirit of Jesus. As a result of this view, there always appeared to be something forced about the liberals' social theology as, for example, with Miall Edwards's reformulation of doctrine at the Welsh School of Social Service in Llandrindod Wells in 1913. The liberal theologians' positive contribution was to offer a kind of enlightened individualism, strengthened by the conviction that social reform required the dedication of every high-minded citizen. Society could only be reformed through the moral renewal of individuals and their consequent determination to improve their lifestyle and their treatment of their fellows.

The liberals had promulgated a weak social ideology based on the whims of current philosophical trends. Thus, it was the need for reform rather than Christianity's reforming dynamic which was important. In this they were merely reactionary, giving vent to the frustrations of modern industrial life with its inherent injustices rather than demonstrably offering a naturally religious critique. This may have been the result of their acceptance of the Kantian theory of ethical imperatives. In a particular historical, social and cultural context, they believed that there was an eternal moral reason for acting in a certain way, whether they wanted to or not. The problem was a theological one. Rather than basing their response on the Christian message itself they found themselves using current philosophical trends in order to meet the needs of the time and the industrial situation against which they were reacting. In all this, liberal theology proved to be good at criticism, but its vision was at best blurred and questionable, and at worst there was no constructive input at all. It had no positive conception of a better society on offer, save the minimalist answer of individual ethical reorientation. Charmed by the claims of philosophical Idealism, it was over-sure that one move, namely the placing of self-sacrificial love at the heart of all relationships, whether political, industrial or religious, would transform society from the unfair and unjust state created in the wake of industrialization into a more utopian social structure in which men would act properly towards their fellows. This was always doomed to failure because far more factors are involved in structuring society than personal relationships, which themselves are far more complex than a call to love neighbours may suggest. Furthermore, religion, for the Welsh liberals, was almost exclusively about living life in the correct way. Although this stemmed from their Idealism and the view that reason was at the heart of nature and reality, there was still a pervading sense in which they attempted to promulgate a fundamentally practical message, something that seemed impossible if Idealism was the prevailing philosophy. In other words, the Welsh liberals believed that it was the ethical imperative, and thus a fundamentally practical concept, which formed the basis of universal reason. Nonconformists felt therefore that they could not, and should not, be over-concerned with theology in its more theoretical aspects. But ideas and ideology are important. They give a basis to action and praxis and offer a significant means of criticism and evaluation once a course of action has been decided. Only when ideology and practice come together can any claim be made for fullness of life. The Christian life is about knowing the truth of Jesus Christ which liberates (cf. Jn. 8.32) and that truth must be worked out with minds and in lives (Phil. 2.12). Unfortunately, the liberals had started with an ethical philosophy and a humanistic world-view. Theology suffered. There was an inadequate ideology behind the projected action, and the result was no action at all.

Although the liberal theologians were reacting to their social and political context, it is also true that they failed to realize that the world, and Welsh Nonconformity with it, was in crisis. Historical events were beginning to cast doubt on the adequacy of philosophical Idealism with its confidence in human development and goodness. The 1920s was a decade of increasing industrial dissatisfaction and unrest. Despite the optimistic conferences organized by the churches in Birmingham in 1924 and in Stockholm in 1925, the actual situation soon appeared to be deteriorating. Not only had this generation faced and survived the Great War but they were now facing the threat of insidious and pernicious political philosophies in Europe that would lead ultimately to a second war. For David Tracy, it was the tempests which rocked 1930s Europe which sounded the death-knell for liberal theology. His critique is worth quoting:

> As progress faded into apocalypse, the liberal had finally to face the fact that not all human beings – perhaps not even he himself – were reasonable and well-intentioned. As suggested symbolically by the still pathetic figure of Prime Minister Chamberlain returning from Munich, umbrella and hope still in hand, liberalism – by its stark refusal to face the fact of evil – could no longer understand, much less control, such demonic outbursts of the human spirit as Nazism.[5]

A distinction must be made here between the older liberals and the younger Nonconformist ministers taking their place. Tracy is accurate when he asserts the requirement for, and the ultimate failure of, the liberal to face the problem of human evil as it raged and held sway about him. But it was true only of the younger generation who had learnt their theology from the liberals but had questioned its treatment of human sin and need of redemption. Men like J. D. Vernon Lewis, J. E. Daniel, D. R. Davies, Martyn Lloyd-Jones would lead the way back to a more orthodox conception of the relationship between an infinite and holy God and mortal and sinful human beings. In this way they, too, looked to context, but it was the metaphysical context into which men and women of every age are born, namely the radical alienation from God. But their tutors, and many of the older denominational leaders, remained adamantly within the liberal and Idealist camps. There would be few converts amongst the liberal Modernists to the renewed orthodoxy. Even Nazism could not persuade them to forgo their optimism. It is ironic to note that while the liberals had claimed the need to make theology relevant for each successive age, in fact they acted as if they had discovered an eternal expression of religious truth. They did not take account of world events when those events appeared to contradict the fundamentals of their theological position. Their silence ultimately came not through the horror of world events as they transpired, but through illness and death. The liberals maintained a loyalty to their vision and a confidence in their theological method which appears now to be remarkably misguided, if not highly foolish, following the experience of the two world wars. The liberals had developed a way of approaching social issues from a vaguely religious perspective. But, by the 1930s, though the church may have found a social message, it was struggling to give it a voice and, apart from its liberal leaders, it almost certainly had a very small audience.

The churches in Wales were facing grave difficulties. Although membership figures had increased following the Great War and up to 1926, church leaders continually voiced their concern at the decline in numbers attending worship during these years. Before the war this was generally perceived to be a move by the young men in industrial districts out of the church and into the labour movement. This had been one of the factors that led the Nonconformists into a consideration of social theology in the first place but it had not retrieved the situation. Alongside this, it is clear that the end of the 1920s marked the beginning of a decline in Welsh theology. This was a particularly fruitful period in Welsh literary and theological history with a large number of able men involved in theological debate through the medium of the Welsh language. Very quickly this golden age came to an end. Perhaps symbolic of the crisis facing Welsh theology was the failure to build on the achievement of the *Geiriadur Beiblaidd*. The intention was to publish *Y Geiriadur Diwinyddol* ('The Theological Dictionary') and discussions continued for twenty years from 1929 but to no avail. In that period the chief editor for the project, the Revd D. Francis Roberts, and two of his assistant editors, John 'Gwili' Jenkins and Principal John Morgan Jones, all died and this, together with the failure of many of the 107 contributors to complete their articles, ensured that no such dictionary ever appeared. A similar fate awaited a promising project whereby the most productive Welsh theologian of the time, Miall Edwards, accepted the task of editing a book commissioned by the theological branch of the Guild of Graduates of the University of Wales. *Yr Efengyl yn Ei Pherthynas â Meddwl a Bywyd* ('The Gospel in its Relation to Thought and Life') was to be the first of a trilogy of books bringing modern scholarship to Welsh people in the Welsh language. The others were to deal with *Y Ffydd Gristionogol* ('The Christian Faith') and *Iesu Grist* ('Jesus

Christ'). Nine contributors were approached including C. H. Dodd, John Morgan Jones, J. E. Daniel, Herbert Morgan and Edwards himself. Only five of the nine articles were written, one of which was lost in circulation owing to Edwards's insistence that all contributors read and comment on each article. In all, the project continued for four years but never saw the light of day. Edwards finally resigned his position as editor.[6] It may appear wrong to place too much significance on the failure to produce these works. Yet they do point to the fact that something was happening in Welsh intellectual life during the late 1920s that ensured the end of the ascendancy of liberal theology. Modernism's optimism, the belief in human ability to do good and to establish the Kingdom on earth with or without a conception of God, would be discarded following the challenge of different theological preconceptions and the events which led ultimately to the outbreak of war in 1939. The 1920s was a remarkably productive period, yet the end of the decade saw the first failures to co-operate in the production of theological work, and theological work which the liberal theologians had claimed for years to be vitally necessary for the renewal of society and for the advancement of religion. The point is that theological liberalism would no longer be promulgated to the same degree of vigour as it had previously been. Philosophical conceptions were being replaced, world events caused more concern than the more local social problem, the liberals were growing old and younger theologians held different opinions. But while a new theological conceptualization had been suggested, it was never associated with the same extent of constructive theological activity. Perhaps the failure to complete the Theological Dictionary and the Guild of Graduates trilogy was the result of an overall decline in interest in religious thought and activity. As has already been suggested, the liberals may have contributed to the decline. What is certain is that the dialectic theologians could do nothing to stem the tide.

Positively, this period is characterized by the interaction of theology with other disciplines which led to a valuable and rich theological debate. It was recognized more strongly than ever before that Christian faith needed to be lived in and through economic and political structures as well as in personal piety and human relationships. Nonconformist theologians had maintained that Christian life, in its individual and social applications, required a commitment to the highest ethical ideals. Unfortunately, these were often left as abstract conceptions in their thought. Insufficient guidance was given as to how the good, the true and the beautiful affected human life, and how men and women could apply such concepts concretely to their lives. Sadly, their call for a practical outworking of religion was accompanied by a tendency to be obscure and impractical in their theological pronouncements. That they overemphasized the role of the individual to the detriment of God's involvement in the salvific scheme is undeniable. So too is the fact that the Kingdom of God was for them exclusively an ethical concept with no apocalyptic element. But because they were seeking the transformation of the 'Kingdom of the world' into the 'Kingdom of the Lord' at a time when the problems of the former were recognized, rightly, to be immense, their contribution was a significant one in Welsh religious history, even if ultimately its success was limited by an absolute dependence on philosophical forms which were rapidly losing favour. More than anything, they were men of their age constrained by ideological exigency and social convention but ultimately attempting in their own, genuine, way to realize the promise of their Lord that in first seeking God's Kingdom a true and fulfilled life could be found for themselves and for all succeeding generations (Mt. 6.33).

Notes

Chapter 1   Discovering Jerusalem

[1] R. Tudur Jones, *Ffydd ac Argyfwng Cenedl I, Prysurdeb a Phryder* (Swansea, 1981), p. 15.

[2] John Davies, *Hanes Cymru* (London, 1990), pp. 411–12.

[3] For Kant, Hegel, Schleiermacher and Ritschl, see relevant articles in theological dictionaries such as J. Macquarrie and James Childress (eds.), *A New Dictionary of Christian Ethics* (London, 1986) and Alan Richardson and John Bowden (eds.), *A New Dictionary of Christian Theology* (London, 1983).

[4] For Kant, see Roger Scruton, *Kant* (Oxford, 1982).

[5] For Hegel, see Peter Singer, *Hegel* (Oxford, 1983).

[6] For Schleiermacher, see Stephen Sykes, *Friedrich Schleiermacher* (Woking, 1971); F. D. E. Schleiermacher, *On Religion: Speeches to its Cultured Despisers* (London, 1893); idem, *The Christian Faith* (Edinburgh, 1928).

[7] For Ritschl, see Alfred E. Garvie, *The Ritschlian Theology* (Edinburgh, 1899).

[8] See Otto, *The Idea of the Holy* (this edition London, 1980).

[9] D. Miall Edwards, 'Neges gymdeithasol yr Efengyl', in D. Miall Edwards (ed.), *Efengyl y Deyrnas* (Bala, 1927), p. 23.

[10] See Keith W. Clements, *Lovers of Discord: Twentieth Century Theological Controversies in England* (London, 1980), pp. 41–3; Charles Gore, *The New Theology and the Old Religion* (London, 1907).

[11] Hugh Jones, 'Y dduwinyddiaeth newydd', *Yr Eurgrawn Wesleaidd* (1908), 135, 178, 249.

[12] B. P. Jones, *The King's Champions 1863–1933* (Redhill, 1968), p. 46.

[13] D. Hugh Matthews, *Hanes Tŷ Cwrdd Castle Street* (Swansea, 1989), p. 29.

[14] *South Wales Daily News*, 21 July 1891.

[15] E. Griffith-Jones, 'Y dduwinyddiaeth newydd', *Y Geninen* (1907), 35.

[16] T. Rhondda Williams, *How I Found My Faith* (London, 1938), p. 92.

[17] David Adams, *Yr Hen a'r Newydd mewn Diwinyddiaeth* (Dolgellau, 1907), p. 26; Glyn Richards, *Datblygiad Rhyddfrydiaeth Ddiwinyddol ymhlith yr Annibynwyr* (Swansea, 1957), p. 12.

[18] W. Eifion Powell, 'Cyfraniad diwinyddol David Adams (1845–1923)', *Y Traethodydd* (1979), 166; David Adams, *Yr Hen a'r Newydd*, pp. 17, 117–18.

[19] Adams, *Yr Hen a'r Newydd*, pp. 115–16; David Adams, *Moeseg Cristionogol* (Dolgellau, 1901), p. 195.

[20] *Moeseg Cristionogol*, pp. 195–6.

[21] David Adams, *Yr Eglwys a Gwareiddiad Diweddar* (Merthyr Tydfil, 1914), p. 147.

[22] Ibid., p. 109.

[23] Ibid., p. 223.

[24] *Aberdare Leader*, 26 July 1902, p. 2.

[25] R. G. Owen, 'Y Prifathro John Morgan Jones M.A.', *Y Dysgedydd* (1939), 198–9.

[26] *Aberdare Leader*, 26 July 1902, p. 2.

[27] Cf. John Hick, *An Interpretation of Religion* (London, 1989), pp. 3–5.

[28] Herbert Morgan, 'The religious outlook in Wales', *Welsh Outlook* (1914), 13.

[29] E. Griffith-Jones, *The Ascent through Christ* (London, 1899), p. 393.

Chapter 2   Wales and the Social Gospel

[1] Edward Foulkes, 'Sosialaeth', *Y Geninen* (1908), 21–2.

[2] *Llais Llafur*, 6 May 1911, p. 5.

[3] Ibid., 25 March 1911, p. 1.

[4] D. L. Thomas and Herbert Morgan, *Housing Conditions in Wales* (London, 1912), pp. 2–6.

[5] See Robert Pope, *Building Jerusalem: Nonconformity, Labour and the Social Question in Wales 1906–1939* (Cardiff, 1998), pp. 130–47.

[6] William DeWitt Hyde, *Outlines of Social Theology* (London, 1895), introduction, p. vi.

[7] Ibid., pp. 147, 215; cf. Owen Jones, 'Perthynas dyn a chymdeithas', *Y Drysorfa* (1921), 406, 410.

[8] Charles A. Ellwood, *The Reconstruction of Religion* (New York, 1923), pp. 120–31.

[9] M. D. Johnson, *The Dissolution of Dissent 1850–1918* (New York, 1987), pp. 268–74; James Orr, *The Ritschlian Theology and the Evangelical Faith* (London, 1898), pp. 1–2.

[10] A. E. Garvie, *The Ritschlian Theology* (Edinburgh, 1899), p. 16.

[11] Ibid., p. 18.
[12] Ibid., p. 20; Orr, *The Ritschlian Theology and the Evangelical Faith*, pp. 7, 77.
[13] Alfred E. Garvie, *Memories and Meanings of My Life* (London, 1938), p. 116.
[14] For D. Miall Edwards, see R. T. Jenkins and E. D. Jones (eds.), *Y Bywgraffiadur Cymreig 1940–1950* (London, 1970), pp. 13–14; D. Arafnah Thomas, 'D. Miall Edwards', in W. T. Pennar Davies (ed.), *Athrawon ac Annibynwyr* (Swansea, 1971), pp. 42–5; W. Eifion Powell, 'Diwinyddiaeth D. Miall Edwards', in Pennar Davies (ed.), *Athrawon ac Annibynwyr*, pp. 46–51; T. Eirug Davies, 'David Miall Edwards 1873–1941', *Efrydiau Athronyddol* (1941), 3–7; 'A.J.', 'Y Parchedig Athro D. Miall Edwards M.A., Ph.D., D.D.', *Y Dysgedydd* (1941), 101–4; J. Morgan Jones, 'Miall Edwards', *Y Dysgedydd* (1955), 309–12; T. Robin Chapman, 'Argyfwng ffydd D. Miall Edwards 1916–1923', *Y Traethodydd* (1982), 188–92; *Y Tyst*, 18 January 1973, p. 5; 1 February 1973, p. 5.
[15] D. Miall Edwards, 'The present religious situation in Wales', *Welsh Outlook* (1920), 141.
[16] Ibid., 141–2.
[17] D. Miall Edwards, *Crefydd a Bywyd* (Dolgellau, 1915), pp. 303–4.
[18] Ibid., pp. 290–1.
[19] D. Miall Edwards, *Bannau'r Ffydd* (Wrexham, 1929), p. 211.
[20] D. Miall Edwards, 'The doctrine of the person of Christ', *Hibbert Journal* (1925), 454–67.
[21] D. Miall Edwards, 'The Christian philosophy of life in its relation to the social problem', in Gwilym Davies (ed.), *Social Problems in Wales* (Swansea, 1913), p. 44.
[22] Ibid., p. 45.
[23] D. Miall Edwards, 'Athrawiaeth y Drindod', *Y Traethodydd* (1932), 220.
[24] 'The Christian philosophy of life in its relation to the social problem', p. 46; *Crefydd a Bywyd*, pp. 300–1.
[25] 'The Christian philosophy of life in its relation to the social problem', pp. 46–7; *Crefydd a Bywyd*, p. 303.
[26] 'The Christian philosophy of life in its relation to the social problem', p. 47.
[27] *Bannau'r Ffydd*, pp. 39, 372.
[28] 'The doctrine of the person of Christ', p. 467.
[29] 'Address to Hereford Federation of Free Church Councils 29 March 1913', D. Miall Edwards Papers, Box 3, National Library of Wales, Aberystwyth (hereafter, NLW).
[30] D. Miall Edwards, *Crist a Gwareiddiad* (Dolgellau, 1921), p. 44.

[31] Ibid., p. 47.
[32] E.g. *Bannau'r Ffydd*, p. 257.
[33] D. Miall Edwards, *Llenyddiaeth a Diwinyddiaeth yr Efengylau* (Swansea, 1921), p. 54.
[34] *Bannau'r Ffydd*, p. 135.
[35] Ibid., p. 136.
[36] 'The Christian philosophy of life in its relation to the social problem', p. 49; cf. *Crefydd a Bywyd*, pp. 306, 309.
[37] D. Miall Edwards, *The Philosophy of Religion* (London, 1924), p. 73.
[38] *Crefydd a Bywyd*, pp. 306, 317; D. Miall Edwards, *Yr Antur Fawr* (Wrexham, 1932), p. 139; 'The Christian philosophy of life in its relation to the social problem', p. 53.
[39] D. Miall Edwards, 'The religion of the future', *Welsh Outlook* (1917), 224; 'Address to Hereford Federation of Free Church Councils'.
[40] *Crefydd a Bywyd*, p. 347; cf. *Crist a Gwareiddiad*, p. 79; 'Address to Hereford Federation of Free Church Councils'.
[41] D. Miall Edwards, 'Christianity and the social problem in industrial areas', *Welsh Outlook* (1921), 129.
[42] *Crefydd a Bywyd*, p. 342; *Yr Antur Fawr*, p. 170.
[43] *Crefydd a Bywyd*, pp. 308–9; cf. D. Miall Edwards, 'Theology and the present religious situation', *Congregational Quarterly* (1930), 425.
[44] 'The Christian philosophy of life and its relation to social problems', p. 55.
[45] *Crefydd a Bywyd*, p. 342; 'The Christian philosophy of life in its relation to the social problem', pp. 50–1.
[46] 'The present religious situation in Wales', 142.
[47] Ibid., 129–30.
[48] Ibid., 131.
[49] *Crist a Gwareiddiad*, pp. 67, 76, 410.
[50] 'The present religious situation in Wales', 143.
[51] D. Miall Edwards, 'The social gospel', *Welsh Outlook* (1922), 236, 237.
[52] 'The present religious situation in Wales', 164–5; *Crist a Gwareiddiad*, p. 404.
[53] 'The present religious situation in Wales', 166.
[54] *Crist a Gwareiddiad*, p. 311; D. Miall Edwards, 'Ysbrydolrwydd', *Y Dysgedydd* (1904), 269–70.
[55] *Crefydd a Bywyd*, p. 290.
[56] D. Miall Edwards and M. E. Davies, *Cyflwr Crefydd yng Nghymru*, Traethodau'r Deyrnas no. 1 (Wrexham, 1924), pp. 4–5.
[57] Ibid., p. 7.

[58] 'The present religious situation in Wales', 142–3.

[59] 'Christianity and the social problem in industrial areas', 129–30; cf. *Crist a Gwareiddiad*, p. 49.

[60] D. Miall Edwards, *Iaith a Diwylliant Cenedl* (Dolgellau, 1927).

[61] *Crist a Gwareiddiad*, p. 411.

[62] *Iaith a Diwylliant Cenedl*, p. 37.

[63] Ibid., p. 74.

[64] Ibid., p. 13.

[65] *Bannau'r Ffydd*, pp. 377–80.

[66] *Yr Antur Fawr*, p. 170.

[67] 'Christianity and the social problem in industrial areas', 129.

[68] D. Miall Edwards, *Religion in Wales*, Traethodau'r Deyrnas English Series no. 3 (Wrexham, 1926), pp. 5–6.

[69] 'Gweddi dros fyfyrwyr', *Yr Efrydydd* I/5 (February 1925), 133; 'Emynau cymdeithasol', *Y Dysgedydd* (1920), 99.

[70] (Lord God, hallowed be your name / On the earth where I live. / And sanctify me also / To the service of mankind; / Light in me the flame of your love / As a sacrificial heavenly fire, / That I can completely endeavour / To turn the world's wailing into a song.)

[71] (O God, my Saviour / Give your Spirit to me now / A spirit of service / Bound to your great love; / You the doctor of men's wounds / Help me to take up the cross / And completely consecrate my life / To ease human pain.)

[72] D. J. Williams, 'Hanes Coleg Bala-Bangor a'i athrawon a'i fyfyrwyr o'i ddechreuad hyd y flwyddyn 1942', unpublished essay, NLW, p. 140.

[73] For Thomas Rees, see 'Rhifyn Coffa Thomas Rees', *Y Dysgedydd* (July, 1926), 197–232; Miall Edwards, 'Dr Thomas Rees of Bangor', *Welsh Outlook* (1926), 182–5; T. Eirug Davies (ed.), *Y Prifathro Thomas Rees: Ei Fywyd a'i Waith* (Llandysul, 1939); J. E. Lloyd and R. T. Jenkins (eds.), *The Dictionary of Welsh Biography down to 1940* (London, 1953) (hereafter *DWB*), pp. 830–1.

[74] Miall Edwards, 'Dr Thomas Rees of Bangor', 182; *DWB*, pp. 830–1; R. T. Jenkins, *Edrych yn Ôl* (London, 1968), p. 205.

[75] 'The work of the ministry in the light of the social mission of the Church', Thomas Rees Papers, NLW.

[76] R. J. Jones, 'Prifathro Coleg Bala-Bangor', in Eirug Davies (ed.), *Y Prifathro Thomas Rees: Ei Fywyd a'i Waith*, p. 77.

[77] Ll. C. Huws, 'Y diwygiwr (parhad)', in Eirug Davies (ed.), *Y Prifathro Thomas Rees*, p. 114.

[78] Thomas Rees, 'The crisis of Welsh Nonconformity', *Welsh Outlook* (1920), 58; cf. Ll. C. Huws, 'Y diwygiwr', in Eirug Davies (ed.), *Y Prifathro Thomas Rees*, pp. 111–12.

NOTES

79 Thomas Rees, *Gwleidyddiaeth yng Nghymru*, Traethodau'r Deyrnas no. 7 (Wrexham, 1924), p. 7.
80 'The crisis of Welsh Nonconformity', 59.
81 Ibid., 60.
82 'The Kingdom of God', Thomas Rees Papers, NLW; cf. Thomas Rees, *Paham yr Wyf yn Brotestant, yn Ymneillduwr ac Annibynwr* (Swansea, 1911), p. 17.
83 'The work of the Ministry in the light of the social mission of the church'.
84 'Angen Cymru am ddiwygiad mewn cymdeithas a gwasanaeth', Thomas Rees Papers, NLW.
85 'Now the Lord is Spirit', Bala-Bangor Collection, Principal Thomas Rees Papers, University of Wales Bangor (hereafter, UWB).
86 'Pregethau'r Undeb', Union of Welsh Independents Reports, 1920, Ton a'r Pentre, p. 366.
87 'The Christian social conscience', Thomas Rees Papers, NLW.
88 *Gwleidyddiaeth yng Nghymru*, p. 12; cf. Thomas Rees, *Cenadwri'r Eglwys a Phroblemau'r Dydd* (Wrexham, 1923), p. 204.
89 *Cenadwri'r Eglwys a Phroblemau'r Dydd*, p. 67.
90 *Gwleidyddiaeth yng Nghymru*, p. 9.
91 Thomas Rees, 'Yr addoliad cyhoeddus', *Y Dysgedydd* (1915), 437.
92 *Gwleidyddiaeth yng Nghymru*, p. 12.
93 Thomas Rees, *Duw, Ei Fodolaeth a'i Natur* (Wrexham, 1910), p. 20.
94 Thomas Rees, 'Datblygiad yr athrawiaethau Cristnogol', *Y Dysgedydd* (1903), 85–90.
95 *Cenadwri'r Eglwys a Phroblemau'r Dydd*, pp. 191–2.
96 Ibid., p. 204.
97 Ibid., pp. 211–12.
98 Thomas Rees, *Dinasyddiaeth Bur* (address given during the Gwynedd Temperance Association meeting in Bangor, 18 October 1923) (Liverpool, 1923), p. 4.
99 Ibid., p. 15.
100 Ibid., p. 6.
101 Ibid., p. 10.
102 Ibid., p. 11.
103 Ibid., p. 13.
104 Ibid., p. 14.
105 Ibid., p. 15.
106 For John Morgan Jones, see *Y Bywgraffiadur Cymraeg 1940–1950*, pp. 30–1; R. G. Owen, 'Y Prifathro John Morgan Jones M.A.', *Y Dysgedydd* (1939), 197–201; E. Aman Jones, 'John Morgan Jones (1873–1946)', *Y Dysgedydd* (1946), 107–11; J. E. Lloyd, 'Y Diweddar Brifathro J. Morgan Jones', *Y Dysgedydd* (1946), 87–8;

NOTES

Mary Silyn Roberts, 'John Morgan Jones', *Lleufer* (1946), 40–1; Eluned Parry, 'Yr Arloeswyr 8: John Morgan Jones', *Lleufer* (1952), 173–6; E. Watkin Jones, 'Y Diweddar Brifathro J. Morgan Jones M.A.', *Y Drysorfa* (1947), 59–63; Trebor Lloyd Evans, 'John Morgan Jones', *Y Genhinen* (1961–62), 9–17; 'John Morgan Jones', *Yr Efrydydd* (Summer 1946), 3; R. T. Jenkins, *Cyfoedion* (London, 1974), pp. 83–8; Trebor Lloyd Evans, 'John Morgan Jones', in Pennar Davies (ed.), *Athrawon ac Annibynwyr*, pp. 69–78.

[107] For Josiah Towyn Jones 1858–1925, see *DWB*, p. 491.

[108] John Morgan Jones, 'Adolf von Harnack 1851–1930', *Yr Efrydydd*, VI/11 (August 1930), 285.

[109] Ibid.

[110] *Aberdare Leader*, 6 July 1940, p. 6.

[111] Letter: Keir Hardie to John Morgan Jones, 12 October 1913, Bala-Bangor Collection, Principal John Morgan Jones Papers, University of Wales, Bangor (hereafter, JMJ Papers).

[112] A. Mor-O'Brien (ed.), *The Autobiography of Edmund Stonelake* (Cardiff, 1981), p. 180.

[113] *Llais Llafur*, 30 March 1907, p. 1.

[114] *Y Tyst*, 11 April 1946, p. 6; Trebor Lloyd Evans, 'John Morgan Jones', p. 13.

[115] John Morgan Jones, *Paul of Tarsus: The Apostle and His Message* (York, 1915), pp. 3, 18.

[116] Ibid., p. 30; John Morgan Jones, 'Cymhwyso'r efengyl at yr angen: Gwersi'r Deyrnas 5', *Y Deyrnas* (February 1917), 11.

[117] John Morgan Jones, *Y Testament Newydd ei Hanes a'i Hamcan* (Cardiff, 1930), p. 169.

[118] John Morgan Jones, 'Beth yw diwinyddiaeth Gristionogol', *Yr Efrydydd*, IX/7 (April 1933), 183.

[119] 'Do we need a New Theology?', sermons, JMJ Papers.

[120] 'Why do we need a New Theology?', sermons, JMJ Papers.

[121] Ibid.; John Morgan Jones, 'The social element in the personality, work and message of Jesus Christ', *Pilgrim*, VI/3 (April 1926), 275–6.

[122] 'Crefydd a chredo', 18 January 1935, radio addresses, JMJ Papers.

[123] John Morgan Jones, *The New Testament in Modern Education* (London, 1922), pp. 98–9.

[124] (John Morgan Jones), 'Iesu Grist a gwaith y byd', *Yr Efrydydd*, VI/9 (June 1930), 226.

[125] John Morgan Jones, *Dysgeidiaeth Iesu Grist* (Cardiff, 1937), p. 128.

[126] Ibid., p. 2.

[127] 'The Christian mission in the modern world', addresses, JMJ Papers; cf. John Morgan Jones, 'Y genhadaeth Gristionogol', *Yr Efrydydd*, I/4 (June 1921), 80.

[128] (John Morgan Jones), 'Myfyrdodau'r mis', *Yr Efrydydd*, VII/4 (January 1931), 89.

[129] *Dysgeidiaeth Iesu Grist*, p. 33; John Morgan Jones, 'Apêl ymerodrol yr Efengyl', *Y Dysgedydd* (1916), 8.

[130] E.g. 'The social element in the personality, work and message of Jesus Christ', 273.

[131] Ibid., 266; cf. *The New Testament in Modern Education*, p. 101.

[132] 'The state and the individual', address, JMJ Papers.

[133] 'Myfyrdodau'r mis', *Yr Efrydydd* (January 1931), 88.

[134] 'Church and State', 1937, address, JMJ Papers.

[135] 'Evangelisation and social reform', address, JMJ Papers.

[136] John Morgan Jones, 'Neges gymdeithasol yr Iesu: Gwersi'r Deyrnas 3', *Y Deyrnas* (December 1916), 10; John Morgan Jones, 'Cymhwyso'r Efengyl at yr angen: Gwersi'r Deyrnas 5', *Y Deyrnas* (February 1917), 10.

[137] 'The social element in the personality, work and message of Jesus Christ', p. 279; cf. 'Iesu Grist a gwaith y byd', 225.

[138] John Morgan Jones, 'Ystyr a gwerth neges yr Iesu: Gwersi'r Deyrnas 4', *Y Deyrnas* (January 1917), 11; cf. 'Myfyrdodau'r mis', *Yr Efrydydd* (January 1931), 87; (John Morgan Jones), 'Iesu Grist a chyfundrefn masnach', *Yr Efrydydd*, VI/11 (August 1930), 297.

[139] John Morgan Jones, 'Iesu Grist a chyfundrefn masnach: Gwersi'r Deyrnas 9', *Y Deyrnas* (July 1917), 10.

[140] John Morgan Jones, 'A ellir byw'r Bregeth ar y Mynydd', *Y Deyrnas* (May 1918), 4.

[141] 'Myfyrdodau'r mis', *Yr Efrydydd*, (January 1931), 87.

[142] 'Church and labour' and 'Jesus Christ and the social question', lectures, JMJ Papers.

[143] 'Iesu Grist a chyfundrefn masnach', 295–6.

[144] 'The dedicated nation', address, JMJ Papers.

[145] 'Iesu Grist a chyfundrefn masnach', 297–8.

[146] E.g. 'A ellir byw'r Bregeth ar y Mynydd?', 5; 'Myfyrdodau'r mis', *Yr Efrydydd* (January 1931), 89.

[147] E.g. John Morgan Jones, 'Cymdeithas Addysg y Gweithwyr – Sgwrs', Bangor (radio broadcast, 13 December 1940), 8.

[148] Lloyd Evans, 'John Morgan Jones', 15.

[149] See J. E. Daniel's tribute in *Y Tyst*, 21 March 1946, p. 4.

[150] As one comic poet wrote of John Morgan Jones in metric verse, '*Crefu wnaf am* Craven A' (I crave for a Craven A); see Lloyd Evans, 'John Morgan Jones', p. 9.

[151] For Herbert Morgan, see *Y Bywgraffiadur Cymraeg 1941–1950*, p. 44; R. I. Aaron, 'Herbert Morgan 1875–1946', *Efrydiau Athronyddol* (1947), 6–8; *Herbert Morgan 1875–1946* (Carmarthen,

1946); Robert Pope, 'Lladmerydd y Deyrnas: Herbert Morgan 1875–1946', *Trafodion Cymdeithas Hanes y Bedyddwyr* (1994), 47–65.

[152] Herbert Morgan 'The religious outlook in Wales', *Welsh Outlook* (1914), 13.

[153] Herbert Morgan, *The Church and the Social Problem* (Carmarthen, 1911), p. 7.

[154] Ibid., p. 13; cf. Herbert Morgan, 'The church and citizenship', *Welsh Outlook* (1922), 21.

[155] *The Church and the Social Problem*, p. 9.

[156] Herbert Morgan, *The Social Task in Wales* (London, 1919), p. 35.

[157] *The Church and the Social Problem*, pp. 7, 10–11.

[158] 'The church and citizenship', 21.

[159] *The Church and the Social Problem*, p. 9.

[160] Herbert Morgan, 'The church and labour: a symposium', *Welsh Outlook* (1918), 127–8.

[161] Herbert Morgan, *Diwydiant yng Nghymru*, Traethodau'r Deyrnas no. 3 (Wrexham, 1924), p. 14.

[162] Ibid., p. 16; cf. *The Social Task in Wales*, p. 33.

[163] *Diwydiant yng Nghymru*, p. 15.

[164] *The Social Task in Wales*, p. 36.

[165] Ibid.; cf. Nathaniel Micklem and Herbert Morgan, *Christ or Caesar?* (London, 1921), p. 48.

[166] *Diwydiant yng Nghymru*, p. 14; *The Social Task in Wales*, p. 49.

[167] Herbert Morgan, *Rhyfel a'r Testament Newydd*: Pamffledi Heddychwyr Cymru no. 5 (Denbigh, 1941), p. 20.

[168] *Diwydiant yng Nghymru*, p. 10.

[169] *The Social Task in Wales*, p. 87.

[170] Adolf Harnack, *What is Christianity?* (London, 1901), p. 56.

[171] Nathaniel Micklem and Herbert Morgan, *Christ or Caesar?*, p. 80.

[172] Ibid., p. 196.

[173] *Diwydiant yng Nghymru*, pp. 12–13.

[174] *The Social Task in Wales*, p. 90.

[175] Ibid., pp. 82–6.

[176] *Seren Cymru*, 27 July 1945, p. 8.

[177] Ibid., 4 October 1946, p. 3.

[178] *Y Tyst*, 24 April 1924, p. 2.

[179] Nathaniel Micklem, *The Box and the Puppets* (London, 1957), p. 56.

[180] 'Christianity and the social problem in industrial areas', p. 129.

[181] Cf. Adolf Harnack and Wilhelm Herrmann, *Essays on the Social Gospel* (London, 1907), p. 13; Adolf Harnack, *What is Christianity?*, p. 101.

[182] *The New Testament in Modern Education*, pp. 99–100.

[183] John J. Vincent, 'Christian Discipleship and Politics', in Dan Cohn-Sherbok and David McLellan (eds.), *Religion in Public Life* (London, 1992), p. 38.

[184] See e.g. W. F. Phillips, 'Crist a chymdeithas', *Y Traethodydd* (1913), 26.

[185] See e.g. D. Miall Edwards, 'The doctrine of the person of Christ', p. 467.

[186] 'Now the Lord is Spirit', Bala-Bangor Collection, Principal Thomas Rees Papers, UWB; Pregethau'r Undeb, Union of Welsh Independents Reports, 1920, Ton a'r Pentre, p. 366; D. Miall Edwards, 'Athrawiaeth y Drindod', *Y Traethodydd* (1932), 213–22.

[187] Miall Edwards, 'Dr Thomas Rees of Bangor', p. 184.

[188] T. Rhondda Williams, *How I Found My Faith* (London, 1938), p. 99.

[189] For Herbert Dunnico (1876–1953), see *Who Was Who*, vol. V, *1951–1960* (London, 1961), pp. 329–30.

[190] *Llais Llafur*, 20 March 1909, p. 3; Leonard Smith, *Religion and the Rise of Labour* (Keele, 1993), pp. 15, 100, 102.

[191] *Merthyr Pioneer*, 17 May 1913, p. 6; cf. *Labour Leader*, 8 May 1913, p. 9.

[192] David Thomas, *Silyn* (Liverpool, 1956), p. 77.

[193] For D. D. Walters (1862–1934), see *Dyddiadur yr Annibynwyr am 1935*, 209; *Y Tyst*, 8 November 1934, p. 11; 15 November 1934, p. 9.

[194] For the wider theological context, see A. E. Garvie, *The Christian Ideal for Human Society* (London, 1930); idem, *Can Christ Save Society* (London, 1935); idem, *The Fatherly Rule of God* (London, 1935); Ebenezer Griffith-Jones, *The Challenge of Christianity to a World at War* (London, 1915); idem, *Providence Divine and Human*, I, *Some Problems of Divine Providence* (London, 1925); idem, *Providence Divine and Human*, II, *The Dominion of Man* (London, 1926); S. E. Keeble, *The Social Teaching of the Bible* (London, 1909); idem, *Towards the New Era: A Draft Scheme of Industrial Reconstruction* (London, 1917); idem, *Christian Responsibility for the Social Order* (London, 1922); Will Reason, *The Issues of Personal Faith in Social Service* (London, 1916); idem, *Christianity and Social Renewal* (London, 1919); T. Rhondda Williams, *The Church and the Labour Cause*, Christian Commonwealth Sermon Supplements (London, 1911); idem, *The Working Faith of a Liberal Theologian* (London, 1914); idem, *Making the Better World* (London, 1929); idem, *Faith without Fear* (London, 1933).

[195] For the social gospel in America see John Macquarrie, *Twentieth Century Religious Thought* (4th edition, London, 1989), pp. 162–6; Sydney E. Ahlstrom, *A Religious History of the American People*

(London, 1972), pp. 785–804; Robert Handy (ed.), *The Social Gospel in America 1870–1920* (New York, 1966); F. G. Peabody, *Jesus and the Social Question* (London, 1925).

196 Handy (ed.), *The Social Gospel in America*, p. 5.

197 For Walter Rauschenbusch (1861–1918), see Benson Y. Landis, *A Rauschenbusch Reader* (New York, 1957); Ernest E. Fricke, *Socialism and Christianity in Walter Rauschenbusch* (Berwyn, Ill., 1965).

198 Walter Rauschenbusch, *A Theology for the Social Gospel* (New York, 1918), preface.

199 Landis, *A Rauschenbusch Reader*, p. xiii.

200 Handy (ed.), *The Social Gospel in America*, pp. 260, 268.

201 Walter Rauschenbusch, *Christianity and the Social Crisis* (London, 1912), introduction, p. xiii; cf. *Christianizing the Social Order* (New York, 1919), pp. 6, 460, 465.

202 *Christianity and the Social Crisis*, p. 412.

203 *A Theology for the Social Gospel*, p. 5.

204 *Christianizing the Social Order*, introduction, p. viii.

205 *A Theology for the Social Gospel*, p. 43.

206 Ibid., p. 127.

207 Ibid., pp. 99, 100.

208 Ibid., p. 108.

209 Ibid., p. 95.

210 *Christianizing the Social Order*, p. 7.

211 Ibid., p. 122.

212 *A Theology for the Social Gospel*, p. 15.

213 Ibid., p. 140.

214 Ibid., p. 131.

215 'Notes for Christian witness questionnaire', D. Miall Edwards Papers, Box 4, NLW.

216 'Ateb cwestiynau: Cyfarfod Ordeinio Salem, Blaenau Ffestiniog, 11 October 1900', ibid., Box 3.

217 Herbert Morgan, *The Social Task in Wales*, p. 80.

218 D. Miall Edwards, 'Neges gymdeithasol yr Efengyl', in Miall Edwards (ed.), *Efengyl y Deyrnas*, p. 22.

Chapter 3   A Crisis for Faith

1 *Labour Voice*, 20 May 1933, p. 6.

2 J. H. Howard, *Jesus the Agitator* (Wrexham, 1934), pp. 2, 12, 89.

3 *Labour Voice*, 22 December 1933, p. 4.

4 J. D. Vernon Lewis, 'Diwinyddiaeth Karl Barth', *Yr Efrydydd*, III/10

(July 1927), 254–8; III/11 (August 1927), 281–7. For biographical details see E. Lewis Evans, 'John Daniel Vernon Lewis, 1879–1970', in W. T. Pennar Davies (ed.), *Athrawon ac Annibynwyr* (Swansea, 1971), pp. 79–88; E. D. Jones and B. F. Roberts (eds.), *Y Bywgraffiadur Cymreig 1951–1970* (London, 1997), pp. 126–7.

5 *Yr Efrydydd*, III/10, p. 254.

6 Ibid., 255.

7 Ibid., 256.

8 Ibid., III/11, p. 286.

9 Ibid., 287.

10 Ibid., III/10, p. 258.

11 Dewi Eirug Davies, 'Yr ymagwedd cynnar yng Nghymru i ddiwinyddiaeth Karl Barth', *Diwinyddiaeth*, XXXIV (1983), 52–76; rhan II, *Diwinyddiaeth*, XXXVII (1986), 53–85.

12 This is quoted from Douglas Horton's translation, *The Word of God and the Word of Man* (London, 1928), p. 120.

13 Karl Barth, *Church Dogmatics*, III/2 (ET Edinburgh, 1960), p. 399.

14 See D. Miall Edwards, 'Baron Friedrick von Hügel', *Yr Efrydydd*, V/10 (July 1929), 258ff.

15 *Y Tyst*, 24 September 1925, p. 6.

16 Morgan Watcyn-Williams, 'Jesus Christ and modern tendencies', *Treasury* (1938), 23–4.

17 *Herbert Morgan 1875–1946* (Carmarthen, 1946), pp. 11, 18.

18 For J. Gresham Machen, see N. B. Stonehouse, *J. Gresham Machen: A Biographical Memoir* (Edinburgh, 1987); W. Stanford Reid, 'J. Gresham Machen', in David F. Wells (ed.), *Reformed Theology in America: a History of its Modern Development* (Grand Rapids, 1985), pp. 102–18. The references to his book *Christianity and Liberalism* are to the (Grand Rapids, 1968) edition.

19 For Alfred E. Garvie see *Congregational Year Book* (1946), 440–1; and his autobiography *Memories and Meanings of My Life* (London, 1938).

20 A. E. Garvie, *The Ritschlian Theology* (Edinburgh, 1899), p. 20.

21 Ibid., p. 247.

22 G. Holland Williams, 'Diwinyddiaeth ac ysbryd yr oes', *Yr Efrydydd*, III/4 (January 1927), 99–100.

23 John Morgan Jones, 'Ymneilltuaeth yng Nghymru heddiw', *Yr Efrydydd*, IV/6 (March 1928), 158.

24 For D. Martyn Lloyd-Jones see Iain H. Murray, *David Martyn Lloyd-Jones: The First Forty Years 1899–1939* (Edinburgh, 1982).

25 For J. E. Daniel see R. Tudur Jones, 'J. E. Daniel', in Pennar Davies (ed.), *Athrawon ac Annibynwyr*, pp. 128–42; D. Densil Morgan (ed.), *Torri'r Seiliau Sicr* (Llandysul, 1993); Jones and Roberts (eds.),

Y Bywgraffiadur Cymreig 1951–1970, p. 21.

[26] For D. R. Davies see his autobiography *In Search of Myself* (London, 1961); also see his book *On to Orthodoxy* (London, 1939).

[27] *In Search of Myself*, pp. 64, 68f, 71.

[28] Ibid., p. 190.

[29] Ibid., pp. 192-3. See also Reinhold Niebuhr, *Moral Man and Immoral Society* (London, 1963).

[30] For Tom Nefyn Williams see his autobiography *Yr Ymchwil* (Denbigh, 1942); also W. Morris (ed.), *Tom Nefyn* (Caernarfon, 1962); Robert Pope, 'Corwynt gwyllt ynteu tyner awel? Helynt Tom Nefyn yn y Tymbl', *Y Traethodydd* (1997), 150–62.

[31] *Y Goleuad*, 18 April 1928, pp. 4, 6.

[32] John Morgan Jones, 'Crefydd a diwinyddiaeth Tom Nefyn', *Yr Efrydydd*, IV/7 (April 1928), 182.

[33] 'Cyffes ffydd yr efrydydd', *Yr Efrydydd*, V/1 (October 1928), 3.

[34] R. Tudur Jones (ed.), *Credu a Chofio: Ysgrifau Edwin Pryce Jones* (Swansea, 1991), p. 37.

[35] Ieuan Davies, *Lewis Tymbl* (Swansea, 1989), p. 96.

[36] For W. D. Davies (1897–1969), see John Thickens, 'Y Parch W. D. Davies MA, BD, Aberystwyth', *Y Drysorfa* (1928), 441–4; *Blwyddiadur y Methodistiaid Calfinaidd* (1970), p. 277; *Y Bywgraffiadur Cymreig 1951–1970* (London, 1997), p. 39.

[37] Thickens, 'Y Parch W. D. Davies MA BD', 444.

[38] John Morgan Jones, '"Beth yw diwinyddiaeth Gristionogol?"', *Yr Efrydydd*, IX/7 (April, 1933), 182

[39] Ibid., 183.

[40] Ibid., 183–4.

[41] It will be noted that John Thickens had recorded that Davies counted the Virgin Birth as dogmatically unimportant for faith. As a result, it could not be an essential *doctrine* even if it was substantially true.

[42] W. D. Davies, *Cristnogaeth a Meddwl yr Oes* (Caernarfon, 1932), p. 104.

[43] John Morgan Jones, '"Beth yw diwinyddiaeth Gristnogol?" Person Iesu Grist', *Yr Efrydydd*, IX/8 (May 1933), 212.

[44] Ibid., 213.

[45] W. D. Davies, '"Beth yw diwinyddiaeth Gristnogol?"', *Yr Efrydydd*, IX/10 (July 1933), 267.

[46] Ibid., 268.

[47] Trebor Lloyd Evans, 'John Morgan Jones', *Y Genhinen* (1961–2), 11.

[48] *Y Tyst*, 21 March 1946, p. 4.

[49] Joseph Warschauer, *The New Evangel: Studies in the 'New Theology'* (London, 1907).

[50] For the intended address see MS 204, 'Drafft o ysgrif ar Dr Miall

Edwards i'r BBC', JMJ Papers: for the address as broadcast see *Y Dysgedydd* (1955), 309–12. Broadcast 1944.

[51] With hindsight, Daniel's words are all the more potent because they were made in the very year in which his wife, Catherine, converted to Catholicism.

[52] Daniel's address 'Dyfodol crefydd Cymru', can be found in JMJ Papers. This final quotation makes use of a phrase from 1 Cor. 13.1.

[53] 'Anghenion crefyddol Cymru', *Y Dysgedydd* (1933), 292–3.

[54] Ibid., 293.

[55] Ibid., 294.

[56] Ibid., 295.

[57] Ibid., 296.

Chapter 4   The Question of Context

[1] D. Miall Edwards, 'Dr Thomas Rees of Bangor', *Welsh Outlook* (1926), 183–4.

[2] For an appreciation of the Dictionary see Gwilym H. Jones, *Geiriadura'r Gair* (Caernarfon, 1993), pp. 30–50.

[3] Cf. G. B. Caird, *Saint Luke*, Pelican New Testament Commentaries (Harmondsworth, 1963), p. 197.

[4] Jaroslav Pelikan, *Jesus Through the Centuries* (New York, 1987).

[5] D. Tracy, *Blessed Rage for Order* (2nd edition, Chicago, 1996), p. 213.

[6] Cf. Gwilym H. Jones, 'Cyfraniad Adran Ddiwinyddol Urdd y Graddedigion', *Diwinyddiaeth* XLV (1994), 27–8; D. Miall Edwards Papers, NLW, Box 1.

Sources and Bibliography

1. Personal Papers
2. Journals, Periodicals and Newspapers
3. Reports
4. Reference Works
5. Books, Pamphlets and Articles

1. Personal Papers

University of Wales, Bangor
Bala-Bangor Collection, Principal Thomas Rees Papers, Principal John Morgan Jones Papers

National Library of Wales
Professor D. Miall Edwards Papers
Principal Thomas Rees Papers

2. Journals, Periodicals and Newspapers

Y Beirniad
Y Deyrnas
Y Dysgedydd
Yr Efrydydd
Y Goleuad
Llais Llafur (including *Labour Voice* and *South Wales Voice*)
Y Llenor
Seren Cymru
Seren Gomer
Y Traethodydd
Treasury
Y Tyst
Welsh Outlook

3. Reports

Reports of the Annual Meetings of the Union of Welsh Independents, 1910–39.

Adroddiad Pwyllgor V, Comisiwn Ad-drefnu Cymdeithasfa Methodistiaid Calfinaidd Gogledd Cymru, Yr Eglwys a Chwestiynau Cymdeithasol, 1921.

South Wales Calvinistic Methodist Association Reconstruction Commission, the Report of the Fifth Committee on the Church and Social Questions, 1921.

Cenadwri Gymdeithasol yr Efengyl (Report of the sub-council of the Union of Welsh Independents), 1923.

4. Reference Works

J. E. Lloyd and R. T. Jenkins (eds.), *The Dictionary of Welsh Biography Down to 1940* (London, 1953).

R. T. Jenkins and E. D. Jones (eds.), *Y Bywgraffiadur Cymreig 1940–1950* (London, 1970).

E. D. Jones and B. F. Roberts (eds.), *Y Bywgraffiadur Cymreig 1951–1970* (London, 1997).

5. Books, Pamphlets and Articles

Anon., *The Tom Nefyn Controversy: An Account of the Crisis in Welsh Calvinistic Methodism* (Port Talbot, 1929).

Anon., *Herbert Morgan 1875–1946* (Carmarthen, 1946).

Adams, David, *Datblygiad yn ei Ddylanwad ar Foeseg a Duwinyddiaeth* (Wrexham, n.d.).

Idem, *Personoliaeth Dynol a'r Ymgnawdoliad* (Dolgellau, n.d.).

Idem, *Datblygiad yn ei Berthynas â'r Cwymp, yr Ymgnawdoliad a'r Adgyfodiad* (Caernarfon, 1893).

Idem, *Paul yng Ngoleuni'r Iesu* (Dolgellau, 1907).

Idem, *Moeseg Cristionogol* (Dolgellau, 1901).

Idem, *Yr Hen a'r Newydd mewn Duwinyddiaeth* (Dolgellau, 1907).

Idem, *Yr Eglwys a Gwareiddiad Diweddar* (Merthyr Tydfil, 1914).

Barth, Karl, *The Word of God and the Word of Man* (London, 1928).

Idem, *Church Dogmatics*, III/2 (Edinburgh, 1960).

Bodein, V. P., 'Walter Rauschenbusch', *Religion in Life*, VI (1937), 420–31.

Campbell, R. J., *The New Theology* (London, 1907).

Chapman, T. Robin, 'Argyfwng ffydd D. Miall Edwards 1916–1923', Y Traethodydd (1982), 188–92.

Cohn-Sherbok, Dan, and McLellan, D. (eds.), Religion in Public Life (London, 1992).

Daniel, J. E., et al., Cynllun a Sail (Llandysul, 1946).

Idem, Dysgeidiaeth yr Apostol Paul (Swansea, 1933).

Idem, Welsh Nationalism: What it Stands for (London, 1937).

Davies, Dewi Eirug, 'Yr ymagwedd cynnar yng Nghymru i ddiwinyddiaeth Karl Barth', Diwinyddiaeth XXIV (1983), 52–76.

Idem, 'Yr ymagwedd cynnar yng Nghymru i ddiwinyddiaeth Karl Barth rhan II', Diwinyddiaeth XXXVII (1986), 53–85.

Davies, D. R., On to Orthodoxy (London, 1939).

Idem, In Search of Myself (London, 1961).

Davies, Gwilym (ed.), Social Problems in Wales (Swansea, 1913).

Davies, Ieuan, Lewis, Tymbl (Swansea, 1989).

Davies, T. Eirug (ed.), Y Prifathro Thomas Rees: Ei Fywyd a'i Waith (Llandysul, 1939).

Davies, W. D., Cristnogaeth a Meddwl yr Oes (Caernarfon, 1932).

Idem, Datblygiad Duw: Efrydiau Diwinyddol (Caernarfon, 1934).

Davies, W. T. Pennar (ed.), Athrawon ac Annibynwyr (Swansea, 1971).

Edwards, D. Miall, Epistol Cyffredinol Iago (Aberdare, 1910).

Idem, Crefydd a Bywyd (Dolgellau, 1915).

Idem, Yr Ysgol Sul yng Nghymru (Cardiff, 1918).

Idem, Crist a Gwareiddiad (Dolgellau, 1921).

Idem, Llenyddiaeth a Diwinyddiaeth yr Efengylau (Swansea, 1921).

Idem, Epistol Cyffredinol Iago (2nd edition, Swansea, 1922).

Idem, Cristnogaeth a Chrefyddau Eraill (Dolgellau, 1923).

Idem (tr.), Traethawd ar Drefn Wyddonol, René Descartes, Cyfres y Werin 10 (Cardiff, 1923).

Idem, Yr Efengyl Gymdeithasol (published by the Welsh School of Social Service), n.d.

Idem, The Philosophy of Religion (London, 1924).

Idem, 'The doctrine of the person of Christ', Hibbert Journal (1925).

Idem, Religion in Wales, Traethodau'r Deyrnas, English Series 3 (Wrexham, 1926).

Idem (ed.), Efengyl y Deyrnas (Bala, 1927).

Idem, Iaith a Diwylliant Cenedl (Dolgellau, 1927).

Idem, Bannau'r Ffydd (Wrexham, 1929).

Idem, Christianity and Philosophy (Edinburgh, 1932).

Idem, Yr Antur Fawr: Pregethau (Wrexham, 1932).

Idem, Crefydd a Diwylliant (Wrexham, 1934).

Edwards, D. Miall, and Davies, M. E., Cyflwr Crefydd yng Nghymru, Traethodau'r Deyrnas 1 (Wrexham, 1924).

Edwards, D. Miall, and Rees, Thomas, *COPEC* (articles from *Y Tyst* published as a pamphlet by the Welsh School of Social Service, n.d.).

Edwards, G. A., and Jones, John Morgan, *Diwinyddiaeth yng Nghymru*, Traethodau'r Deyrnas 4 (Wrexham, 1924).

Ellwood, Charles A., *The Reconstruction of Religion* (New York, 1923).

Evans, David, *Labour Strife in the South Wales Coalfield 1910–1911* (Cardiff, 1911).

Evans, D. Emrys, *Crefydd a Chymdeithas*, Cyfres y Brifysgol a'r Werin 15 (Cardiff, 1933).

Evans, E. Keri, and Huws, W. Parri, *Cofiant y Parch. David Adams* (Liverpool, 1924).

Fricke, Ernest E., *Socialism and Christianity in Walter Rauschenbusch* (Berwyn, Ill., 1965).

Garvie, A. E., *The Ritschlian Theology* (Edinburgh, 1899).

Idem, *The Christian Ideal for Human Society* (London, 1930).

Idem, *Can Christ Save Society?* (London, 1935).

Idem, *The Fatherly Rule of God* (London, 1935).

Griffith-Jones, E., *The Ascent through Christ* (7th edition, London, 1901).

Idem, *The Challenge of Christianity to a World at War* (London, 1915).

Idem, *Providence Divine and Human*, I, *Some Problems of Divine Providence* (London, 1925).

Idem, *Providence Divine and Human*, II, *The Dominion of Man* (London, 1926).

Handy, Robert T. (ed.), *The Social Gospel in America 1870–1920* (New York, 1966).

Harnack, A., *What is Christianity?* (London, 1901).

Harnack, A., and Herrmann, W., *Essays on the Social Gospel* (London, 1907).

Howard, J. H., *Cristionogaeth a Chymdeithas* (Liverpool, 1914).

Idem, *Which Jesus? Young Britain's Choice* (Dolgellau, 1926).

Idem, *Jesus the Agitator* (Wrexham, 1934).

Idem, *Winding Lanes* (Caernarfon, 1938).

Howell, D., *Nicholas of Glais: The People's Champion* (Clydach, 1991).

Hyde, William DeWitte, *Outlines of Social Theology* (London, 1895).

Jenkins, R. T., *Edrych yn Ôl* (London, 1968).

Idem, *Cyfoedion* (London, 1974).

Johnson, M. D., *The Dissolution of Dissent 1850–1918* (New York, 1987).

Jones, Gwilym H., *Geiriadura'r Gair* (Caernarfon, 1993).

Idem, 'Cyfraniad Adran Ddiwinyddol Urdd y Graddedigion', *Diwinyddiaeth* XLV (1994), 4–41.

Jones, John Morgan, *Politics in Wales*, Free Lectures for the People (Aberdare, 1902).

Idem, *A Scheme and Syllabus of Moral and Biblical Instruction* (Aberdare, 1905).

Idem, *Paul of Tarsus: The Apostle and His Message*, Brother Richard's Bookshelf 8 (York, 1915).

Idem, *The New Testament in Modern Education* (London, 1922).

Idem, *Y Testament Newydd, Ei Hanes a'i Hamcan*, Cyfres y Brifysgol a'r Werin 2 (Cardiff, 1930).

Idem, *Dysgeidiaeth Iesu Grist*, Cyfres y Brifysgol a'r Werin 17 (Cardiff, 1937).

Idem, *Cymdeithas Addysg y Gweithwyr – Sgwrs*, Bangor (radio broadcast, 13 December 1940).

Jones, R. Tudur, *Congregationalism in England 1662–1962* (London, 1962).

Idem, *Hanes Annibynwyr Cymru* (Swansea, 1966).

Idem, *Diwinyddiaeth ym Mangor 1922–1972* (Cardiff, 1972).

Idem, *Yr Undeb* (Swansea, 1975).

Idem, *Ffydd ac Argyfwng Cenedl*, I, *Prysurdeb a Phryder* (Swansea, 1981).

Idem, *Ffydd ac Argyfwng Cenedl*, II, *Dryswch a Diwygiad* (Swansea, 1982).

Idem, *Credu a Chofio: Ysgrifau Edwin Pryce Jones* (Swansea, 1991).

Keeble, S. E. (ed.), *The Social Teaching of the Bible* (London, 1909).

Idem, *Towards the New Era: A Draft Scheme of Industrial Reconstruction* (London, 1917).

Idem, *Christian Responsibility for the Social Order* (London, 1922).

Landis, Benson Y., *A Rauschenbusch Reader: The Kingdom of God and the Social Gospel* (New York, 1957).

Lloyd-Jones, D. Martyn, *Evangelistic Sermons at Aberavon* (Edinburgh, 1983).

Machen, J. Gresham, *Christianity and Liberalism* (this edition Grand Rapids, 1968).

Macquarrie, John, *Twentieth Century Religious Thought* (4th edition, London, 1989).

Micklem, Nathaniel, *The Box and the Puppets* (London, 1957).

Micklem, Nathaniel, and Morgan, Herbert, *Christ and Caesar* (London, 1921).

Morgan, D. Densil (ed.), *Torri'r Seiliau Sicr: Detholiad o Ysgrifau J. E. Daniel* (Llandysul, 1993).

Morgan, Herbert, *The Church and the Social Problem* (Carmarthen, 1911).

Idem, *The Social Task in Wales* (London, 1919).

Idem, *Diwydiant yng Nghymru*, Traethodau'r Deyrnas 3 (Wrexham, 1924).

187

Idem, *Rhyfel a'r Testament Newydd*, Pamffledi Heddychwyr Cymru 5 (Denbigh, 1941).

Morgan, Kenneth O., *Wales in British Politics 1868–1922* (Oxford, 1963).

Idem, *Rebirth of a Nation: Wales 1880–1980* (Oxford, 1981).

Mor-O'Brien, A. (ed.), *An Autobiography of Edmund Stonelake* (Cardiff, 1981).

Morris, W. (ed.), *Tom Nefyn* (Caernarfon, 1961).

Murray, Iain H., *D. M. Lloyd-Jones: The First Forty Years* (Edinburgh, 1982).

Orr, James, *The Ritschlian Theology and the Evangelical Faith* (London, 1898).

Otto, Rudolf, *The Idea of the Holy* (this edition London, 1980).

Peabody, F. G., *Jesus and the Social Question* (London, 1925).

Pelikan, Jaroslav, *Jesus Through the Centuries* (New York, 1987).

Pope, Robert, 'Lladmerydd y Deyrnas: Herbert Morgan 1875–1946', *Trafodion Cymdeithas Hanes y Bedyddwyr* (1994), 47–65.

Idem, 'Corwynt gwyllt ynteu tyner awel? Helynt Tom Nefyn yn y Tymbl', *Y Traethodydd* (1997), 150–62.

Idem, *Building Jerusalem: Nonconformity, Labour and the Social Question in Wales 1906–1939* (Cardiff, 1998).

Powell, W. Eifion, *Bywyd a Gwaith Gwilym Bowyer* (Swansea, 1968).

Idem, 'Esboniadaeth Feiblaidd Ryddfrydol yng Nghymru', *Diwinyddiaeth* XXV (1974), 29–39.

Idem, 'Cyfraniad diwinyddol David Adams (1845–1923)', *Y Traethodydd* (1979), 162–70.

Rauschenbusch, W., *Christianity and the Social Crisis* (this edition London, 1912).

Idem, *Christianizing the Social Order* (this edition New York, 1919).

Idem, *The Social Principles of Jesus* (London, 1917).

Idem, *A Theology for the Social Gospel* (New York, 1918).

Reason, Will, *The Social Problem for Christian Citizens* (2nd edition, London, 1913).

Idem, *The Issues of Personal Faith in Social Service* (London, 1916).

Idem, *Christianity and Social Renewal* (London, 1919).

Rees, Thomas, *Duw: Ei Fodolaeth a'i Natur*, Llawlyfrau Diwinyddol i'r Werin 1 (Wrexham, 1910).

Idem, *Paham yr Wyf yn Brotestant, yn Ymneillduwr ac Annibynwr* (Swansea, 1911).

Idem, *The Holy Spirit in Thought and Experience* (London, 1915).

Idem, *Dinasyddiaeth Bur* (an address to the Gwynedd Temperance Assembly given at Bangor, 18 October 1923) (Liverpool, 1923).

Idem, *Cenadwri'r Eglwys a Phroblemau'r Dydd* (Wrexham, 1923).

Idem, *Gwleidyddiaeth yng Nghymru*, Traethodau'r Deyrnas 7 (Wrexham, 1924).

Richards, Glyn, *Datblygiad Rhyddfrydiaeth Ddiwinyddol ymhlith yr Annibynwyr* (Swansea, 1957).

Robbins, Keith, 'The Spiritual Pilgrimage of the Rev. R. J. Campbell', *The Journal of Ecclesiastical History*, XXX/2 (1979), 261–76.

Smith, Leonard, *Religion and the Rise of Labour* (Keele, 1993).

Thomas, D. L., and Morgan, Herbert, *Housing Conditions in Wales* (London, 1912).

Tracy, David, *Blessed Rage for Order* (2nd edition, Chicago, 1996).

Watcyn-Williams, M., *The Beatitudes in the Modern World* (London, 1935).

Idem, *When the Shoe Pinches* (London, 1936).

Idem, *From Khaki to Cloth* (Caernarfon, 1949).

Williams, Tom Nefyn, *Y Ffordd yr Edrychaf ar Bethau* (Dolgellau, 1928).

Idem, *Yr Ymchwil* (Denbigh, 1949).

Williams, T. Rhondda, *The Social Gospel* (London, 1902).

Idem, *The New Theology: An Exposition* (London, 1907).

Idem, *The Church and the Labour Cause*, Christian Commonwealth Sermon Supplements (London, 1911).

Idem, *The Working Faith of a Liberal Theologian* (London, 1914).

Idem, *Making the Better World* (London, 1929).

Idem, *Faith Without Fear* (London, 1933).

Idem, *How I Found My Faith* (London, 1938).

Index

190

INDEX

Daily Mail 11
Daniel, J. E. 82, 126, 127, 129,
141–9, 150, 151, 153, 165, 167
Darian, Y 53
Das Wesen des Christentums 68
Das Wort Gottes 113, 114
*Datblygiad Duw: Efrydiau
Diwinyddol* 140
Davies, Revd D. H. 107
Davies, D. R. 127, 128, 129, 151, 165
Davies, Dewi Eirug 113
Davies, Margaret Jane 133
Davies, Revd H. A. 24, 141
Davies, Revd Isaac 133
Davies, Revd W. D. 132, 133–41,
150, 151
Davies, S. O. 15
deism 13
Descartes, René 9, 113, 115
dialectic theology 107, 120, 122, 124,
128, 129, 130, 147, 150, 167
Discours de la méthode 113
disestablishment 56, 58
Dodd, C. H. 126, 167
Dostoevsky, Fyodor 108
Dunnico, Revd Herbert 97, 98, 99, 100
Dysgedydd, Y 12, 53, 145

education 66, 69, 77, 78, 79, 80, 148
reform 4
Education Act (1902) 65
Edwards, D. Miall 10, 28, 37, 38–55,
56, 62, 63, 64, 66, 67, 69, 80, 81,
85, 91, 94–5, 96, 99, 100, 104,
111–20, 122, 126, 138, 141, 142,
150, 155, 159, 163, 166, 167
Efrydydd, Yr 53, 110, 111, 131, 134
Eisteddfod, National 17, 20, 33, 82
Elim Four Square Pentecostal
Movement 2
Evans, Revd D. Silyn 24
Evans, Revd Trebor Lloyd 141
evolution 17, 21, 141

Fairbairn, Andrew Martin 36, 37
Fascism 90, 151
Fatherhood of God 5, 29, 36, 42, 43,
44, 52, 57, 63, 71, 72, 84, 87, 98,
101, 118, 119, 125, 158, 160
First World War *see* Great War
Foulkes, Edward 32, 34

Gandhi, Mahatma 148

Garnant 67
Garvie, Alfred E. 36, 37, 101, 124,
125
Geiriadur Beiblaidd, Y 67, 155, 166
Geiriadur Diwinyddol 166
Geninen, Y 32, 99
Glais 99
Gore, Charles 12
Great War (First World War) 26, 27,
28, 29, 56, 57, 61, 64, 73, 85, 91,
95, 97, 99, 106, 107, 108, 110,
123, 125, 134, 154, 161, 165,
166
Green, T. H. 8
Griffith-Jones, E. 16, 17, 19, 20, 30,
101
Griffiths, James 15
Griffiths, Revd J. 53
Griffiths, Revd Peter Hughes 131

Hardie, Keir 4, 15, 27, 28, 68, 69
Harnack, Adolf 10, 68, 82, 84, 87,
96, 104, 105, 108, 128
Hegel, Georg Wilhelm Friedrich 5, 6,
7, 8, 12, 16, 18, 20, 40, 50, 62,
94, 97, 108, 109, 112, 120, 141,
150
Herrmann, Wilhelm 10, 82, 108
Hitler, Adolf 121, 147
Hodge, Caspar Wister 123
Holy Spirit 42, 43, 58, 59, 67, 109
How I Found my Faith 120
Howard, Revd J. H. 106
Huxley, Julian 148

Idealism 7, 8, 16, 18, 20, 36, 40, 43,
48, 55, 56, 57, 66, 82, 94, 95, 96,
98, 100, 109, 114, 120, 126, 134,
140, 141, 150, 152, 155, 159,
164, 165
ILP (Independent Labour Party) 4, 5,
14, 27, 32, 69, 82, 95, 97, 98
immanence 7, 8, 9, 13, 15, 18, 40, 42,
49, 55, 62, 81, 90, 93, 103, 115,
116, 118, 119, 142, 150, 157,
159
immortality 41
incarnation 21, 42, 117, 130, 141
International Conference on Life and
Work (1925) 108, 109, 120

Jeffreys, George 2
Jenkins, John (Gwili) 27, 166

191

INDEX

INDEX

Biblical references

Psalm	8.5	118
	22.6	118
	136.6	119
Matthew	5–7	156
	6.24	156
	6.33	5, 168
	19.21	156
	22.37–9	11, 61, 110, 156
Mark	10.21	156
	12.30–1	11, 156
Luke	10.27	11
	10.36–7	156
	17.21	22, 157
	18.22	156
John	8.32	164
	10.10	64
	12.25	72
	13.34–5	61
	15.13	110
	16.8–11	58
Acts	2.44–5	32, 75, 158
	4.32	11, 32, 75, 158
	5.1–11	11
1 Corinthians	9.22	154
	12.8–10	2
	14.34–5	160
Galatians	3.28	157, 158, 159
Ephesians	4.25	158
Philippians	2.12	164
	3.20	3
Colossians	3.1–3	30
	3.20	3
1 Timothy	2.11–12	160
Titus	2.1	106
1 John	4.20	30
Revelation	21.10	1